MARTIN LUTHER KING, JR.
AND THE CIVIL RIGHTS MOVEMENT

Edited by David J. Garrow

A CARLSON PUBLISHING SERIES

Conscience of a Troubled South

THE SOUTHERN CONFERENCE EDUCATIONAL FUND, 1946-1966

Irwin Klibaner

CARLSON
Publishing Inc

BROOKLYN, NEW YORK, 1989

Library of Congress Cataloging-in Publication Data

Klibaner, Irwin, 1933-
  Conscience of a troubled South : the Southern Conference Educational Fund, 1946-1966 /
Irwin Klibaner
      p.   cm.—(Martin Luther King, Jr. and the Civil Rights Movement : 14)
  Revision of the author's thesis (Ph.D.)—University of Wisconsin, 1971; originally presented
under title: The Southern Conference Educational Fund.
  Bibliography: p.
  Includes index.
  1. Southern Conference Educational Fund—History. 2. Segregation in education—
Southern States—History. 3. School integration—Southern States—History. 4. Afro-
Americans—Education—Southern States—History. 5. Afro-Americans—Civil rights—Southern
States—History. I. Title. II. Series
LC212.522.S7K58 1989   370. 19'344'0975—dc19   89-894
ISBN 0-926019-08-2 (alk. paper)

Typographic design: Julian Waters

Typeface: Bitstream ITC Galliard

The index to this book was created using NL Cindex, a scholarly indexing program
from the Newberry Library.

For a complete listing of the volumes in this series, please see the back of this book.

Printed on acid-free, 250-year-life paper

Manufactured in the United States of America.

Table of Contents

List of Tables

Series Editor's Preface

Irwin Klibaner's *Conscience of a Troubled South: The Southern Conference Educational Fund, 1946-1966* is a detailed and extremely valuable study of one of the small and oftentimes unheralded organizations that made an important contribution to the southern civil rights struggle. SCEF (usually called "skeff") played a significant role in linking the earlier, pre-1954 traditions of fragmentary white dissent from the South's segregationist consensus to the post-1954 era when a modest number of white southerners joined with black activists in an aggressively determined struggle for racial justice and equality.

SCEF's roots lay in the Southern Conference for Human Welfare, a white liberal group that foundered amidst the political shoals of the immediate post-World War II years. Especially in the "quiet years" of the early 1950s, SCEF and its two initial leading figures, Aubrey Williams and James Dombrowski, played a crucial role in keeping alive the honorable tradition of white southern dissent from the region's racial norms and segregation statutes. By the late 1950s, when two white Kentucky activists, Carl and Anne Braden, became energetic full-time staff representatives for SCEF, the organization increasingly served as a stimulus and source of advice for younger black activists who were moving to the fore in greater and greater numbers.

Throughout the 1950s and into the mid-1960s as well, SCEF's contributions to the southern civil rights struggle were continually hampered by allegations of Communist affiliations and sympathies that a succession of state and federal legislators aimed at SCEF staff members and supporters. In some instances, as with the NAACP and the Southern Regional Council, civil rights proponents felt they could do better without SCEF's committed staffers at their sides; in other instances, such as with the Southern Christian Leadership Conference and especially the Student Nonviolent Coordinating Committee, black activists welcomed SCEF's contributions and learned from the tradition of hard-earned experience that SCEF's activists brought to their work.

Klibaner's important study tells a generally little-known story, one that is of considerable value both to the historiography of white southern liberalism on the issue of race and to the historiography of white support for the black freedom struggle of the 1950s and 1960s. From his tracing of SCEF's origins in the late 1940s to Chapter 12's valuable and unique depiction of the founding of the Southern Student Organizing Committee (SSOC) in the mid-1960s, Klibaner's history of SCEF makes a notable contribution to civil rights historiography. I am very pleased that its inclusion in Carlson Publishing's series of volumes on *Martin Luther King, Jr. and the Civil Rights Movement* will help bring both its scholarly insights as well as the story of SCEF itself to many students of civil rights who otherwise might remain ignorant of this important but little-publicized part of southern civil rights history.

David J. Garrow

Preface
1989

Reading one's own words written almost twenty years ago can be a cruelly unusual punishment. Dissertations, like Pandora's box, have the reputation of causing their authors to rue re-opening them. Thankfully, however, it has not been unpleasant in this case. Reacquainting myself with the people with whom I lived, if only in my imagination, so closely for a period of two years through the research and writing of this work has reinforced my belief that it was a task well worth doing. My regrets are only that I did not pursue publishing it in book form years ago. I am indebted to Ralph Carlson, my publisher, and through him to David J. Garrow, the editor of this series, for making it more accessible.

I believe the essential story of the Southern Conference Educational Fund (SCEF) remains as portrayed here. In fact, little has emerged in print over the years to alter the details of its history as presented. There have been a number of works by or about some of the persons active in SCEF, revealing more of their personal lives, emphasizing the enormous price paid for challenging the taboos of the white caste in the effort to bring the South abreast of the revolutionary post-World War II era. In her autobiography, *Outside the Magic Circle,* Virginia Foster Durr has given a sharply etched account of an upper-class white woman alive to the evils of segregation. By attempting to live according to her deepest convictions and to move others to share them, she suffered the fate of a pariah in Alabama in those bitter years. John A. Salmond has written a valuable biography of Aubrey Williams, *A Southern Rebel*, chronicling the life of that extraordinary man, the first president of SCEF. Salmond's work had the benefit of this dissertation and also additional sources unavailable to me, such as the personal recollections and papers of Anita Williams, Aubrey's widow, and the papers of Hugo Black. Unfortunately, no work on James Dombrowski, the first director of SCEF, has yet appeared, though rumors of one in preparation by Frank Adams, chronicler of the Highlander Folk School in Tennessee (of which

Dombrowski was an early member) have come to my attention. After the completion of this dissertation, I consulted the Dombrowski papers which he deposited at the Tuskegee Institute's Hollis Burke Frissell Library before his death. These materials were still not fully catalogued at the time, and included much duplication of the bulk of SCEF materials already in the Carl and Anne Braden Papers at the State Historical Society of Wisconsin. Some of the Dombrowski papers were useful to me when I wrote an article bringing the history of SCEF up to 1976, concluding its last decade of activity ("The Travail of Southern Radicals: The Southern Conference Educational Fund, 1946-1976", *The Journal of Southern History*, Vol. XLIX, No. 2, May 1983, pp. 180-202.).

Histories of the civil rights movement have become something of a boom industry since the appearance of this work. A number of them are relevant to SCEF, the most notable being David J. Garrow's *Bearing the Cross: Martin Luther King, Jr. and the Southern Christian Leadership Conference, 1955-1968*, and Clayborne Carson's *In Struggle: SNCC and the Black Awakening of the 1960s*. SCEF was close to both of these organizations and these books give a fuller picture of the interrelationships between the black movement and white liberals. Garrow's book, and his other work, *The FBI and Martin Luther King, Jr.*, throw a much-needed light on the activities of J. Edgar Hoover's FBI during the late fifties and sixties when it was more of an obstacle than a help to the civil rights movement.

There is valuable information yet to be unearthed in the FBI files and those of the various Congressional investigating committees on the surveillance and persecution of SCEF and its sympathizers. Certainly more will be gleaned from an examination of the career of Senator James O. Eastland of Mississippi, perennial antagonist of SCEF, when and if that (un)worthy's papers become available. A fuller picture of the effectiveness of SCEF in the South, and of the efforts of its opponents to undermine it, would most certainly emerge from studies of the origins of the civil rights movement in the separate southern states from the forties to the sixties. We have something of this in Aldon Morris's work on the black movement, *The Origins of the Civil Rights Movement: Black Communities Organizing for Change*, but very little on the white opponents of segregation, with the exception of a recent study of the very interesting career of Judge J. Waties Waring, Federal Judge from South Carolina, Tinsley E. Yarbrough's *A Passion for Justice: J. Waties Waring and Civil Rights*. Waring was instrumental in preparing the groundwork for the landmark *Brown* decision of 1954.

A thorough investigation of the papers of John F. Kennedy and members of his administration, particularly in relation to the Justice Department's handling of Carl Braden's 1961 contempt of Congress conviction and the subsequent effort to obtain a pardon for him would be useful. A source which was unavailable to me when researching the dissertation, but which may now be accessible is the files of the Leadership Conference on Civil Rights, the clearing house of movement organizations, which essentially boycotted SCEF in the late fifties and sixties, an effort which is detailed in this dissertation from the SCEF perspective. It would be interesting to see to what extent this perspective was valid and not simply the understandable reaction of SCEF officials whose nerves were rubbed raw from years of harassment from erstwhile friends as well as avowed enemies.

The last years of SCEF, when it supported the anti-Vietnam war movement and then was caught up in the disputes between black nationalists and guilt-tripping white radicals, have been discussed in my above-mentioned 1983 article. For these years insightful details about the Cointelpro operations of the Nixon administration from already available or obtainable materials, could give a more complete picture of the role of government repression in the demise of SCEF. I do not believe such details would change my conclusions. Government harassment was a factor hastening the process of decay already under way because of the unwillingness of blacks and the ineptitude of white radicals to continue an alliance which had lost its vitality. Newer concerns, such as the women's movement, captured the attention of radicals, while the problems of racism were less amenable to the tactics the movement adopted in the sixties. The struggle would be advanced by others. SCEF would be their heritage.

Preface
1971

The present study owes its inspiration to two out-standing events of the contemporary period: the civil rights movement of the 50's and early 60's and the black student agitation of the late 60's. As a participant in the earlier movement at a time when it lacked the wide support that it eventually received, especially at the 1963 March on Washington, the significance of the black freedom struggle made a deep and lasting impression on me. Since the frustrations of the earlier effort troubled me for an explanation, the present study has provided me the opportunity of finding or working out some parts of the puzzle. It is my hope that it will perform a service to others equally concerned. As a student at the University of Wisconsin during the black student strike of 1968-1969 I was profoundly moved by the new-found sense of pride and self-awareness of black youth. Their assertion of the significance of the culture and history of black people stimulated me to re-examine my own conceptions of the American past. It was vivid proof to me that history is a continuing confrontation between a past that endures and a present that must pay it heed.

I am indebted to Carl and Anne Braden in a special way. It was their willingness to allow me use of the papers of the Southern Conference Educational Fund that made this study possible. Also, Carl was particularly helpful and gracious in his written communications and personal interviews which filled in gaps and gave additional insights into the work of the Fund and the brave people who have continued its work, often under fire.

My intellectual debts are great and in many ways far too deep to articulate, to Professors William Appleman Williams and Hans Gerth of the University of Wisconsin whose seminars and personal discussions shaped my thinking and gave direction to my interest in history and social problems. Fellow graduate students performed a similar service, in particular, Fran and Lee Cary, Dick Commerford, Donald Murphy and the editorial staff of *Studies on the Left* with whom I spent several exciting years when it was a vital part of the intellectual scene in Madison. Professor Paul Glad supervised the completion of the dissertation, bore nobly with my shortcomings, and offered useful suggestions and criticisms. Professor Paul Conkin forced me to clarify terms and sharpen arguments, a task which was exasperating but which made this a clearer work than had I not had the benefit of his criticisms.

My debts are great to Miss Josephine Harper, director of the Manuscripts division, and Mrs. Barbara Kayser, director of the Social Action Collection, of the Wisconsin State Historical Society, and their staff for the valuable assistance their expertise afforded me. My typist, Mrs. Margery Borgrud, deserves thanks for her patience and precision. Finally, I owe so much to my wife, Helen, for her constant encouragement and support through the years, that she deserves to be considered co-author.

Introduction

Many Americans associate the civil rights movement with the personality of Martin Luther King, Jr., and with the movement that propelled him into public attention, the Montgomery bus boycott of 1956. As every social event or process furnishes its own symbols for posterity, it is only natural that King and the Montgomery boycott should cling to the memory and enlarge to take in the far broader phenomenon of which they were so seminal a part. The present study will not cast doubt upon the validity of the symbols, but will examine the contributions of an organization hitherto ignored in studies of this broad social movement.

The civil rights movement of the sixties had a number of forerunners in the earlier New Deal period. One of them was an interracial organization, the Southern Conference Educational Fund. It was an offshoot of the Southern Conference for Human Welfare whose accomplishments Thomas Krueger related in *And Promises to Keep*.[1] The present study is a history of the Fund based, in the main, upon its own records and publications and the correspondence of its officers.

Published accounts of the civil rights movement center upon the activities of Northern groups sympathetic to black aspirations, or upon those of Southern black organizations. This work deals with an organization which, while inter-racial, appealed mainly to Southern whites for support. Though a distinct minority in the civil rights movement, Southern whites participated in the revival of the contemporary battle for racial equality. Thus the conflict has been a national one with its focus first in the South and then moving to other areas, rather than a sectional controversy between North and South. Howard Zinn has effectively argued this thesis in *The Southern Mystique*,[2] concluding that the South is but a magnified mirror image of the nation. Regardless of whether one accepts all of Zinn's argument, the present study accepts his principal thesis.

The importance of the Cold War climate in which the Fund sought to desegregate the South cannot be exaggerated. The adoption of anti-Communism as a new political orthodoxy by most Americans after 1945 created conditions in which suspicion of dissenters and destruction of their personal reputations thrived. The anti-Communist fixation in American foreign and domestic policy disrupted many efforts for peaceful social change including a number of attempts to equalize black opportunities and rights. Consequently, the Supreme Court's historic decision of 1954 declaring segregation in public schools unconstitutional, a milestone on the road to black equality, found potential supporters too weak and disorganized and segregationists too strong for the decision to have much effect. As in the Reconstruction period after the Civil War, opponents of black equality maintained the initiative largely because of the default of its reputed sympathizers.

Diminished in numbers relative to those in the forties who supported the Southern Conference for Human Welfare and isolated in the fifties from many former allies, the Southern Conference Educational Fund persisted nevertheless and, after 1956, developed strong ties with new black organizations in the South. It worked closely with the Southern Christian Leadership Conference, many local branches of the NAACP, and the numerous black voter leagues. With its wealth of organizational experience, the Fund contributed to the post-1956 restoration of the voting rights of Southern blacks. The Fund looked upon black political power as a lever to pry open the tight white-supremacist control of Southern society. By ending that control, the Fund hoped, many Southern integrationists of both races would more freely be able to air their views and work for their acceptance.

When the sit-ins and freedom rides of 1960-1961 made civil rights the most important social issue facing the nation, the Fund contributed significantly to the revived movement. Its expertise in publicity and its numerous connections with local groups of integrationists throughout the region helped to coordinate efforts of various organizations which lacked its skills and knowledge of the South. As the object of a number of investigations by Congressional committees and their state counterparts, the Fund carried on an educational effort to enlighten others in the civil rights movement as to the importance of civil liberties. It thereby deepened the understanding among integrationists of the interrelationship between civil rights and other social and political issues.

The appearance of a new black nationalism in 1965 was a challenge to integrationists and the Fund was one of the few organizations with a largely white constituency that did not recoil from "black power," the rallying cry of the new trend among blacks. Instead, after blacks requested their white

2

associates to leave Southern black communities, the Fund found new reason for working among Southern whites. Forming part of the left wing of the civil rights movement, the Fund widened its perspective to include problems of peace, poverty and unemployment and cooperated with non-Southerners to initiate a national anti-Vietnam war movement in 1965.

In 1966, the civil rights movement effectively split and the Southern Conference Educational Fund became part of a national revival of the political left. With legal segregation no longer its central concern, the Fund entered upon a period of re-definition of its goals and program. Integration no longer constituted the *raison d'etre* of the Fund. In its present perspective, the mass of poor whites and blacks in the South share common economic and social needs which can only be met by developing their political power through grass-roots organization. The Fund has directed its efforts since 1966 toward developing such organization in the hopes of realizing in the process an alliance of poor and working-class whites and blacks. Resembling in its program similar efforts by Socialists and Communists in the thirties, the Fund, while it has no formal ties with these parties and lacks a clear doctrine, shares an affinity with them in desiring some form of socialism in the United States. It is thus one of the few surviving links between an older and a new left in America.

A NOTE ON TERMINOLOGY

It might be useful to clarify here how I use some of the frequently employed terms in this study. "Segregationists," at times also referred to as "conservatives" or "neo-Bourbons," supported the system of laws and customs known as segregation. They upheld the values of "white supremacy," a belief in the superiority of whites and their right to dominate black people. "Integrationists," also referred to as "liberals" and "reformers," opposed both segregation and white supremacy as contrary to basic human rights, constitutional liberties, and democratic practices. They sought to eliminate segregation and re-educate white Southerners about the basic validity and necessity of equality of rights and opportunities for all members of society. "Moderates," in parts of the South often a majority of the population, generally supported segregation up to 1954. After the Brown decision of that year declaring segregated public education unconstitutional, many moderates went along with the Court's ruling, though others demurred and sought alternatives which would preserve segregation. It was from the "moderates" that attempts originated to ameliorate the conditions of blacks while preserving segregation, both before and after 1954. Many moderates rejected white supremacy as an ideology, at least in its more fanatical expressions. Their attitudes and behavior toward blacks often reflected a paternalism traditional to upper-class and educated Southern whites. In the years covered by this work, a number of moderates joined with integrationists at times in common efforts to reform social conditions for both races in the South. In this context, the term "reformers" refers to both moderates and integrationists when they worked toward common ends. "Radicals," in distinction from "liberals," or "integrationists," while sharing their goals of racial equality, sought deeper transformations of all of American society. They were all critical of capitalism; though such criticisms ranged from a desire for some form of cooperative commonwealth to socialism; at least this was true of white radicals. Black radicals, as is clear in the context of the discussion, sought racial adjustments beyond, or other than either segregation or integration. Many black radicals also shared the wider social aims of their white counterparts.

ONE

New Deal Origins: The Southern Conference for Human Welfare

The depression of the 1930s provoked Americans to question some long-accepted social practices. Among the customs challenged as a result of that cataclysm, and yet stubbornly resistant to change were racial discrimination and segregation. The cracks in American society produced by the disruption of the economy provided blacks and sympathetic whites an opportunity to try to overcome the inequities facing black people. A number of reformers worked within President Franklin D. Roosevelt's New Deal to change the racial climate.

The New Deal itself did not make reversing the traditional role of black people in American life one of its priorities. As Frank Freidel has stated, however, "the white supremacy issue seems important in retrospect...in helping to explain the sweeping Southern constitutionalist attacks on the New Deal."[1] Some of the measures the Roosevelt administration took to combat the depression aroused the uneasiness of Southern ruling groups long accustomed to unrivalled dominance in their region. Sectional feeling, ever present in American politics, arose in response to some New Deal programs. The agricultural program of crop limitations antagonized cotton producers and distributors; industrial codes and labor standards annoyed employers; relief policies raised the issue of wage differentials based upon race. In one way or another, many programs impinged upon racial discrimination in their application and effects, threatening to upset existing relationships of power.

The Southern county-seat elites resented New Deal inroads on their power which rested on the control of property, labor, credit, and local government. Relief projects reduced dependency; labor standards raised wages (except for agricultural labor); government credit by-passed many bankers; new federal programs skirted the county commissioners and sometimes even state agencies. In party politics, after the overwhelming 1936 election triumph, the Democratic party seemed to move in a direction less amenable to Southern interests. In that year, also, the Democratic national convention eliminated the two-thirds rule for Presidential nominations, thereby removing the South's veto power within the party. To add insult to injury, the convention seated black delegates from key Northern industrial states.[2]

In the face of Southern disquiet, influential Administration officials helped to water down Federal policies and programs when applied to the South. This often occurred with President Roosevelt's concurrence, for he depended upon Southern support in Congress. Also, the President personally enjoyed close ties to the South. In the twenties, convalescing at Warm Springs, Georgia, Roosevelt formed warm friendships with Southern politicians as well as his rural neighbors. This paid off politically, earning him Southern support at the 1932 Democratic convention, where he was regarded as the candidate of the South and West. Attentive to Southern opinion, he adopted his own approach to Southern problems. To Roosevelt the greatest challenge facing the South was the alleviation of poverty, not the maintenance (or, for that matter, the elimination) of white supremacy."[3]

Despite his own indifference to blacks, Roosevelt's administration reversed by several degrees the course of the Federal government in regard to black problems. As a first step, cabinet officers and agency heads retained black advisers to help assure a more equitable share for black people in relief and recovery programs. Harold Ickes led the way by adding to his staff in the Interior Department a white Southerner from Georgia, Clark Foreman, who in turn opened the department's doors to capable black administrators in a variety of bureaus. Harry Hopkins, chief of the Federal Emergency Relief Administration, also enlisted a white Southerner sympathetic to the black cause, Alabama-born Aubrey Williams. As Hopkins' Deputy Administrator, first of the FERA and then of the Works Progress Administration Williams kept a sharp eye for any sign of discrimination or inequity in relief programs. Later, as head of the National Youth Administration, Williams appointed Mrs. Mary McLeod Bethune director of a newly-created Division of Negro Affairs. She was the first black woman to hold a top Federal administrative position. Ambrose Caliver, a black educator appointed to the U.S. Office of Education, helped to initiate an important study of the condition of Negro education, a study that had wide ramifications for the approach of the Federal government and private voluntary groups toward the improvement of educational opportunity for blacks. As never before, professional opportunities in the Federal government began to open up. No longer relegated solely to janitorial and kitchen duties, many blacks entered government service as lawyers, engineers, architects, economists, statisticians, librarians, office managers, and office clerks. The color bar, made rigid by another Democrat, Woodrow Wilson, broke down in many places.

The change in official Washington attitudes notwithstanding, Jim Crow remained strong on the state and local levels of government. Relief agencies in the South and elsewhere, despite the efforts of Aubrey Williams, distributed money in greater proportion to whites even where blacks were the more numerous in the ranks of the unemployed and destitute. A favorite target for black complaints was the National Recovery Administration. T. Arnold Hill, one of Ickes' black advisers, termed NRA "a complete failure" because of the policies of Hugh Johnson, its director. NRA officials countered that they had no jurisdiction over agricultural labor, domestics, the service trades, or most other unskilled work in which blacks were concentrated, and which had been exempted by statute from the codes. The NRA codes regulating hours, wages and working conditions deferred to regional standards in these matters, leaving blacks not much more than crumbs.

Other New Deal programs received their share of criticism. The Tennessee Valley Authority earned some notoriety by setting up an all-white town at Norris, Tennessee. White workers lived in substantial homes on TVA projects, while blacks had to settle for substandard temporary housing. Labor crews were segregated, and the skilled jobs went first to whites. Perhaps no other program was the focus of as much denunciation as the Agricultural Adjustment Administration. The crop reduction policy led to the eviction of thousands of sharecroppers and tenant farmers, forcing many of them into unemployment in the towns and cities of the South. White landlords deprived others of crop-reduction bonuses, and also resorted to violence when organizers attempted to form tenant unions. Since the majority of Southern blacks lived in rural areas, AAA policies hit them hardest and hastened their exodus from the region.

Of all the New Deal programs, the National Youth Administration was among the most equitable to blacks. Its director, Aubrey Williams, used his authority to upset color lines on NYA projects and within the agency bureaucracy itself. In addition to placing Mrs. Bethune at the head of the Division of Negro Affairs, Williams hired state supervisors of Negro affairs.

By 1940, there were twenty-seven such state supervisors who helped NYA to avoid the racial controversies plaguing such other agencies as the Civilian Conservation Corps, which permitted segregation in its camps. At the end of 1939, black secondary and college students all over the South had received more than their proportion of aid. Most importantly, the NYA did not tolerate regional racial differentials so that, in effect, blacks received substantially greater assistance in comparison to that received from other agencies.[4]

Williams' record as a white Southerner opposed to white supremacy made him anathema to Southern segregationists in Congress. They sniped at him at every opportunity, grilled him before Congressional committees, and denounced him on the floor of Congress. Their unceasing hostility dogged him the rest of his days in the Roosevelt administration. Eventually they succeeded in liquidating the National Youth Administration, and then kept Williams from returning to government service by rejecting his nomination, in 1945, as administrator of the Rural Electrification Administration.[5]

The economic crisis, nevertheless, compelled Southerners, black and white, to concern themselves with the problems of their region more than at any time since Reconstruction. Regionalism as a sociological concept became the focus of the work of Howard Odum and his students at the University of North Carolina. Apart from Odum's circle, a significant group of Southerners in the Federal bureaucracy and Congress met regularly in Washington, D.C. to ponder the relative backwardness of the South and the region's inability to capitalize fully on its vast resources. Among them were Lowell Mellet, a member of the President's National Emergency Council, U.S. Commissioner Louise O. Charlton, of Birmingham, and Clark Foreman, of Atlanta. Senators Lister Hill of Alabama and Claude Pepper of Florida joined house members Brooks Hays of Arkansas and Luther Patrick of Alabama, among others, in the group's discussions. A third group of concerned Southerners centered around Joseph Gelders, member of a well-known Birmingham Jewish family and a self-styled independent radical. While organizing unions in the Birmingham area in 1936, Gelders had been kidnapped, savagely beaten and left for dead on a deserted country road. This incident made him a determined foe of the "Southern way of life," and he helped spark a national campaign to abolish the poll tax, an important instrument of white supremacy.

The efforts of these groups found favor with Mrs. Roosevelt, who arranged a conference for Joseph Gelders with the President early in 1938.

At the time, the President was engaged in his ill-fated purge of the Democratic Party and he was eager to foster some home-grown opposition to his opponents among Southern Democrats. His encouragement provided the spur for the convening, on November 20, 1938, of the first meeting of the Southern Conference for Human Welfare in Birmingham.[6]

The convention attracted representatives of the newly-organized CIO unions in the South who were then active in the Birmingham region, particularly in the steel and coal industries. Conference leaders hoped to enlist broad support for their organization from the Southern middle-classes. Among those whose support they sought were editor Mark Ethridge and publisher Barry Bingham of the Louisville *Courier-Journal*, Frank P. Graham, president of the University of North Carolina, and youth groups stimulated by the New Deal youth programs, as well as black leaders who, for the first time, participated on an equal basis with whites in an interracial organization in the South. A landmark at the time, the convention attempted to desegregate its final convention. But the Birmingham police at the last minute forced adherence to city statutes demanding segregation of all public meetings. In an act of symbolic defiance, Mrs.Roosevelt had her chair placed in the aisle between the white and black delegates and there, throughout the sessions of the three-day gathering, she remained.

Administration support emboldened Conference participants and broadened their vision of regional welfare. They had, initially, come together in response to the Report of the President's National Emergency Council which spotlighted the South as the nation's "Number One economic problem." Their ability to gain Federal patronage and responsibility for implementing Federal programs enabled them to challenge local and state oligarchies.[7] From the outset, however, there were disparate, and potentially conflicting, interests within the Conference. Educators concentrated on turning it toward programs of federal aid to education; labor delegates sought a strong orientation in favor of unionization; businessmen lobbied for support of tariffs and other subsidies for regional industry; youth emphasized their problems; blacks urged an open break with Southern racial practices; and politicians dramatized themselves. It was a congeries of interest groups that often worked at cross-purposes. For the period of its greatest activity, the Conference was a vital influence in the South. "It was a great liberal upsurge--the only liberal upsurge, it might be noted, that thus far in this century in the South joined masses of whites and Negroes together in common effort," wrote one observer years later.[8]

9

Among its goals, anti-lynching and anti-poll tax legislation won it the support of the NAACP as well as other national organizations. The Conference undertook to enlighten the Southern white populace and to spur affirmative action by Congress and the Executive branch of government against that barbarity of Southern "justice", lynching. Besides the campaign for a Federal anti-lynching law, the anti-poll tax drive was a central part of the Conference's strategy to make accessible to blacks and poor whites greater participation in Southern politics. Though the Conference estimated that the poll tax had disenfranchised upwards of eleven million potential voters, it was probably closer to five million. This figure would have increased the Southern electorate from twenty-five to thirty-three percent of the national total, a substantial margin.[9]

The poll tax had been under attack for some time in the South, in fact, from its inception. In 1920, North Carolina had abolished it; in 1934, Huey Long backed its repeal to bolster his regime in Louisiana; in 1934, Claude Pepper's forces had accomplished the feat in Florida. Opposition to the tax in the forties brought together in common cause the Socialists and Communists in the South, the League of Women Voters, the Women's Division of the Democratic National Committee, organized labor and leading black organizations. It was a difficult battle. The anti-poll tax forces lost their first legal encounter before the U.S. Supreme Court. In 1939 the Court refused to reverse its ruling in *Breedlove v. Suttles* which held that the poll tax was not an infringement on voting qualifications. This setback was mainly due to the poor legal case and tactics employed by the anti-poll tax forces. Henceforth, they turned to in-depth studies of the deleterious effects of the tax, seeking to develop greater public pressure against it. In September, 1939, Joseph Gelders, the sparkplug of the movement, in the absence of support from Southern Congressmen, persuaded a California Representative, Lee Geyer, to introduce an anti-poll tax bill in the House. But Southerners blocked its passage.

The campaign received an infusion of new vigor in 1940 when John L. Lewis, in hopes of uniting the Southern Conference with his CIO Non-Partisan League, pumped funds into the campaign. William Mitch, of the United Mine Workers, joined the Civil Rights Committee of the Southern Conference and, subsequently, other organizations enlisted in the effort. The American Civil Liberties Union, the International Ladies Garment Workers Union, the National Lawyers Guild, the National Federation for Constitutional Liberties, the American Newspaper Guild, the American

Federation of Labor, and the CIO, all helped to give the Southern Conference nationwide scope. The broad nature of the movement made possible the creation of a separate agency, the National Committee for the Abolition of the Poll Tax, which took over the campaign for the next nine years. Until 1948, sympathetic Congressmen introduced legislation in both houses of Congress at every session. The twenty-fourth Amendment, which ultimately abolished the poll tax, was partly due to the Conference's efforts.[10]

Not long after its formation, the Southern Conference for Human Welfare began to develop its thinking about the place of the black man in American life. Aside from anti-poll tax and anti-lynching resolutions at the first convention in 1938, and demands for the freedom of the remaining Scottsboro "boys" still in prison, the organization did little to indicate that the welfare of black people was a central concern. It placed its emphasis upon "proper qualifications for voting," which might well have had the effect of excluding blacks and poor whites. It took a stand against the practice of wage differentials between racial groups," yet it did not oppose Jim Crow employment policies. Aside from favoring Federal aid to education, it urged that public disbursements be based upon "school populations," and it favored "adequate appropriations...for Negro graduate work in Southern state-supported Negro institutions." It also supported opportunities for "qualified Negro physicians...to render professional service to Negro patients in tax supported institutions" and called for the Federal government to build a playground and recreational facility for the black youth of Birmingham. While integrating its own meetings, the Southern Conference did not, for a number of years, attempt to integrate Southern schools, hospitals or playgrounds.

At its second convention in Chattanooga in 1940, the conference reiterated many of its earlier demands in the areas of labor relations, agriculture and civil liberties. It again spelled out its position with regard to blacks. The Conference declared that the

> special limitations of life imposed upon the Negro people through race discrimination, limited job opportunities, inadequate and unequal school and recreational facilities... require the Southern people to work toward the general equalization of opportunity in all spheres, and toward the development of the friendliest of relations between our two racial groups.[11]

In effect, the Conference, though more militant, remained within the Southern white moderate tradition, i.e., it favored genuine equality along with separation of the races; segregation per se was not a target.

World War II had a dramatic effect on American race relations and on the Southern Conference. Blacks broadened and intensified their attacks upon racial practices such as lynching, discrimination, educational inequities and political disfranchisement. By the war's end, the very basis of segregation lay open to challenge. "It was as if some universal message had come through to the great mass of Negroes," Howard Odum wrote in 1943, "urging them to dream new dreams and to protest against the old order."12

War tension, overcrowding, and persistent racial discrimination ignited riots in New York, Detroit, and Los Angeles. Racial discrimination soured blacks on the war effort, compelling NAACP official Roy Wilkins to protest that it sounds pretty foolish to be against park benches marked 'Jude' in Berlin, but to be for park benches marked 'Colored' in Tallahassee, Florida." He failed to see much difference between the Nazi ideology of Aryan supremacy and the American ideology of white supremacy.13 Statements such as Wilkins' elicited admonitions directed to the black press from Southerners. Virginius Dabney, editor of the Richmond Virginia *Times-Dispatch*, charged that "extremist" black newspapers and black leaders were "demanding an overnight revolution in race relations," and as a consequence they were "stirring up interracial hate." Dabney further warned that "it is a foregone conclusion that if an attempt is made forcibly to abolish segregation throughout the South, violence and bloodshed will result."14

Dabney's attitude was an expression of much wider and deeper resentment on the part of white Americans. An Office of War Information intelligence report in 1942 revealed that six out of ten white Americans felt that blacks were satisfied with the status quo, and that they received all the opportunities they deserved. More than half of all whites interviewed in the Northeast and West believed that the races should have separate schools, separate restaurants, and separate neighborhoods. Nationwide, a majority of whites thought blacks would not be treated any better after the war than in 1942, and that the black man's lesser role in society derived from his own shortcomings rather than from anything whites had done.15 Indifferent toward black grievances, state and Federal governments proved reluctant to carry out fundamental reform that would mollify blacks.

The second World War had diverse consequences for black people. It revived a stagnant economy by stimulating the nation's industries, not least in the South. The great demand for labor, especially since the military was drying up the pool of younger men, created new opportunities for blacks in the industries of North and South. Migration of Southern rural blacks and whites to urban areas quickened, enlarging cities in the South and giving them a new vitality. At the same time the pressures of population growth upon older economic and social institutions increased friction between the races. The inherited patterns of Southern social behavior, however, underwent remarkably few changes. White Southerners, as did most Americans, thought that external enemies, not their compatriots, had committed the sins that made the war imperative. Germany and Japan were the objects of this bloody crusade which they believed could be won without affecting segregation. This assumption proved to be substantially correct, since World War II caused no fundamental alteration in the segregated patterns of Southern life. Southerners resisted any interference with their customary racial standards, a Southern white historian, Francis Butler Simkins, wrote. "They opposed successfully all attempts of the Negro to assume political power and prevented the destruction of race distinctions both in the armed forces and war industries."[16]

Integrationists did, nevertheless, attempt to undermine entrenched values and the practices that embodied them. They compelled the Roosevelt administration to adopt a Fair Employment Practices Commission; sought unsuccessfully to end discrimination in the armed forces; and tried to open up the channels of opportunity in education, employment, housing, and politics. A continuation of the attempts of the late thirties to raise the South from "the nation's number one economic problem," these efforts broadened into an assault upon some of the basic features of the entire American social and political economy. As blacks used the emergency to press for full equality, the Southern Conference joined them and for the first time, publicly opposed Jim Crow in employment. The Conference supported FEPC in 1941 and censured the officials of Mobile, Alabama, for importing rural whites to work in the city's booming shipyards instead of hiring Mobile's black workers. The Conference also called for an end to discrimination in labor unions, and it increased the tempo of the movement to obtain qualitative improvements in black education and health on a basis of parity with whites.[17]

The year 1943 was pivotal for the Conference. Its informal alliance with the Administration assumed greater significance because of the Conference's decision to engage formally in electoral politics. The Roosevelt administration's election reversals of 1942 enabled a Republican Southern Democratic coalition to take command of Congress. In response, the Southern Conference implemented an earlier proposal to form state committees in order to more effectively engage in politics. By 1944, there were eleven state committees, the strongest in North Carolina, Georgia and Alabama, where the main thrust was on voter registration. The new stance of the organization was primarily the work of Clark Foreman. He took up the chairmanship of the Conference in 1942 after the failure of efforts to attract Frank Graham, or more illustrious personages, for the position. Foreman was a member of an old Atlanta family; his grandfather had been an editor of the Atlanta *Constitution*. He viewed the South's problems as economic at root, and the solution he envisioned was Northern-style industrialization tempered by New Deal social reforms. He focused on electing to office liberals who would enact legislation to raise Southern mass purchasing power, and he confidently expected this to trigger Southern economic development. An aggressive administrator, Foreman labored to shape the Conference in his own image, which increased the susceptibility of the organization to internal feuds. For the next few years, however, it continued to he a significant factor in Southern politics.

Indicative of its new orientation, the Conference entered into an alliance with the newly-formed CIO Political Action Committee, set up and directed by Sidney Hillman, president of the Amalgamated Clothing Workers and a CIO vice-president. Hillman wanted to unite labor unions and non-labor reformers in a coalition to undo the anti-New Deal election victory of 1942, and work for the re-election of Franklin Roosevelt in 1944. He toured industrial centers to gather support. In January, 1944, at a CIO-PAC-sponsored meeting in New York, the coalition adopted a program calling for full employment to avoid a post-war depression and for the elimination of American dependence upon foreign markets by means of increased domestic purchasing power. The program's fulfillment depended upon the re-election of Roosevelt in 1944 to direct it through the Congress. In the summer of 1944, Hillman announced the formation of a National Citizens Political Action Committee as the coalition's instrument to help accomplish these goals. Several Southern Conference leaders, including Foreman and James Dombrowski, its executive secretary, joined the new group and became active in the campaign. Their aim was two-fold: to help re-elect Roosevelt, and to get CIO backing for the Southern Conference.

After the 1944 election, Foreman and Dombrowski continued to enlighten Hillman and other CIO leaders about the problems of the South and the Conference's work in the region. The Southern Conference leaders emphasized the South's potential as the most progressive area of the nation. CIO aid to the Conference, its officers hoped, would help stimulate the political and economic changes vital for the future of the labor movement and of all reform forces in the South. The Conference relied upon the support of organized labor to aid in efforts to end the poll tax, defeat anti-labor Congressmen, and undermine the oil and lumber interests thwarting Southern unionization. Voting statistics helped to bolster their arguments. Though there were two million union members in the South, and a potential of several million more, the actual election figures revealed an almost total absence of labor influence in the political life of the South. In 1944, in Alabama, only one-fourth of the total number of industrial workers had vote; in Georgia, one-third; in Virginia, one-half. The need for a vigorous mass registration campaign was obvious, and the Conference saw itself as the ideal agent to undertake the task because it was Southern and could not be labelled a group of "outside agitators." It required funds, however, to broaden its activity and permit its state committees to become more effective.

The Conference's appeal was successful. In November, 1944, the CIO Executive Board endorsed the Southern Conference, and urged its constituent unions to contribute funds to the Southern group. The CIO also decided against organizing National Citizens Political Action Committee branches in states where the Southern Conference already had functioning state committees. With firm labor backing, the Southern Conference was on the threshold of its most prosperous and influential period of activity. The U.S. Supreme Court provided additional, unexpected aid. In 1941, the Court had declared that state primaries intimately bound up with Federal elections were subject to Federal regulation; in 1944 it followed this with a decision making the Texas Democratic party "white" primaries unconstitutional under the terms of the Fifteenth Amendment. These decisions offset the Court's rulings favoring the poll tax and were an indirect sanction of the Conference's criticism of Southern voting restrictions. The decisions gave a green light to the Conference to activate greater black and labor participation in Southern politics.

In its campaign to renovate the South, the Conference adopted a number of tactics. There were petition drives opposing both the poll tax and the Southern Democratic Senate filibuster against a permanent FEPC. The

15

Conference also worked to keep the race question out of the 1944 Alabama Senatorial contest between Lister Hill and Jim Simpson. The Committee of Writers and Editors of the South, formed by the Conference in 1944, called for abolition of the poll tax and the "white" primary. The Committee afforded Ellis Arnall, moderate governor of Georgia, the opportunity to maneuver the Georgia legislature into abolishing the poll tax in 1945, thereby relieving Arnall of the need to issue an executive order outlawing it.

A favorite Conference device was the use of public opinion polls to sample Southern white opinion on the views expressed by pro-segregation Senators. When Senator Eastland of Mississippi, on the floor of the U.S. Senate, declared that the black soldier "was an utter and dismal failure" who "will not fight" and "will not work," the Conference polled Southern newspapers. More than eighty percent of the two hundred-fifty that replied asserted that Eastland's remark hindered the war effort, while seventy-five percent held that his remark did not represent true Southern opinion on the matter. These actions earned the Conference the special hatred of Eastland and his Mississippi colleague, Senator Theodore Bilbo, who termed the Conference the South's "number one enemy."

The Conference journal, the *Southern Patriot*, had a circulation in 1945 of 17,000, and it played an effective role in communicating the organization's program to the Southern public. Every issue spotlighted the activities of anti-labor groups and personalities, particularly white supremacy groups such as the Christian American Association, which utilized business support to pressure for state right-to-work laws. The *Patriot* ran features on Southern education, health, industry and agriculture, and also published pamphlets condemning white supremacy and upholding interracial toleration.

The most vocal and active of the state branches was the Committee for Washington, D.C. Its success was due to the large contingent of Southerners of both races in the Executive departments and in Congress. Its chairman was Alabama born Virginia Durr, wife of Clifford J. Durr, a member of the Federal Communications Commission. Mrs. Durr also headed the National Committee Against the Poll Tax. Other members of the Washington group were Helen Fuller, an editor of the *New Republic*, Will Alexander, former head of the Farm Security Administration, Frank Graham, Mary McLeod Bethune, Arthur F. Raper, sociologist and author of *The Crime of Lynching*, and John P. Davis, formerly executive secretary of the National Negro Congress. The Washington Committee, and the Committee for New York, regularly held public interracial dinners, and also went beyond the

Conference program by calling for an end to discrimination in travel accommodations, housing and recreation. By the end of 1945 the Washington Committee had 288 members.[18]

As the Conference's reputation spread, other groups such as the NAACP urged their members to contribute funds to it. In 1946, Mrs. Bethune went on a national tour for the Conference, and her efforts led to the addition of six thousand new members. The Conference's income from foundations, unions and individuals reached an all-time high of $82,583 in 1945. Its success led to a structural change in the organization. As a full-fledged political action group, it faced the loss of the tax-exempt status for which it had qualified as an educational organization. In May, 1945, the Southern Conference for Human Welfare created a committee on reorganization and, in January, 1946, at Durham, North Carolina, adopted a new organizational structure. To direct its educational activities and, most importantly, to accept tax-exempt donations, it established the Southern Conference Educational Fund. The parent group, the Southern Conference for Human Welfare became solely a political action organization in the form of the various state committees.

Through 1946, the enthusiasm of SCHW members grew. They actively worked for a permanent FEPC, and secured a petition signed by 4,000 Southerners opposing another Senate filibuster by segregationist Southern Democrats against the measure. Voter registration projects were in full swing, pushing the number registered from 15,000 to 60,000 in Savannah, Georgia, alone and increasing black registration there from 900 to 19,000. Even its setbacks attested to the vigor of the organization. When the Conference attempted to defeat the Boswell amendment to the Alabama state constitution, an amendment that lodged registration authority in local boards as a way of maintaining white control, the Conference prevailed upon organized labor in the state to oppose it. The Catholic Bishop of Mobile also urged its defeat. Though approved by a fifty-three percent margin, the amendment was voided three years later by a Federal district court. In addition, the SCHW, probably exaggerating its strength, took credit for the election of neo-populist "Big Jim" Folsom to the Alabama governorship in 1946.

Eight-hundred-fifty strong and buoyed by the Conference's work elsewhere, the Washington Committee sponsored a public meeting in 1946 to call for an end to compulsory segregation in the District of Columbia. The Committee sought to maintain war-time rent ceilings and supported a strike of government cafeteria workers; it also bolstered the National Negro Congress in its effort to force the hiring of blacks by the Capitol Transit Company. Along with the NAACP, the Southern Conference for Human Welfare took a leading role in defense of blacks who were the objects of police and white mob attack in Columbia, Tennessee, in 1946. Their efforts saved twenty-five black men from probable conviction and long prison sentences. Employing its influence with the Administration, the Conference made a determined effort to prevent similar outbreaks elsewhere, thus forestalling a repetition of the post-World War I race riots.

Abruptly in the midst of this upswing of activity, however, the Southern Conference became the object of a damaging attack from its chief ally and financial supporter, the CIO. In 1946, the CIO had announced the opening of a Southern organizing drive, "Operation Dixie," budgeting one million dollars for it and establishing the Southern Organizing Committee as its spearhead. Early in the year, some New York sympathizers called a rally in support of "Operation Dixie," in Harlem. But on April 18, Southern Organizing Committee director Van Bittner bitterly denounced the rally, disavowing aid from its participants and other "outsiders." "That goes for the Southern Conference for Human Welfare and any other organization living off the CIO," he asserted.[19]

A letter from black SCHW field representative Osceola McKaine to CIO Vice-President Allan S. Haywood had prompted this outburst. McKaine praised the CIO drive, but he also complained about "the attitudes of a certain number of white CIO organizers in this region...[who] could be readily mistaken for AFL or Railway Brotherhood organizers if one judged them by their racial attitudes and approaches. They should be told," McKaine advised, "that the CIO expects them ...whenever and where it is possible to practice what the CIO professes." He offered to be more specific if Haywood so desired. Angrily, but evasively, Haywood replied:

> There isn't a movement in America doing as much to overcome the unjust and discriminatory practices against not only the colored but other groups, than the CIO is, and the men on our staff in the South in the main deal with the problems they have in a realistic way, having one objective in mind, that is, the elimination of these conditions referred to and establishing for all our people the things... which must he established...in order to maintain and perpetuate our democracy.[20]

Both Bittner's and Haywood's remarks were symptomatic of developments within the CIO in the post-war period. Their hands tied during the war because of the no-strike pledge given the Administration, the CIO, and to a lesser extent the AFL, looked upon electoral politics at the time primarily as a way of protecting labor's interests. When the war ended, the labor federations renewed pre-war efforts to utilize their economic power in behalf of their members. Labor's political action then became auxiliary to militant economic demands and aggressive tactics at the factory gate and on the shop floor. Hence, organized labor considered groups like the Southern Conference for Human Welfare, which had little or no economic clout, dispensable. There was another reason for the shift in labor's attitude. Sensing a change in the political climate upon Roosevelt's death and the breakup of the wartime alliance with Russia, the CIO, in its anxiety to preserve influence with the Truman administration, began to view left-wing allies as a liability. One of the first casualties of this new outlook was the CIO tie to the Southern Conference for Human Welfare, which included a number of active Communists in its ranks. Soon, Operation Dixie ground to a halt and the South remained for decades an anti-union stronghold. Bittner's public irritation with the Southern Conference thus reflected a developing opposition to leftists and communists in the CIO.

Though leaders of both organizations attempted to patch up the quarrel, the damage was done, mainly to the Southern Conference. The CIO formally dropped its support early in 1947 and its member unions cut back their financial contributions to the SCHW. Toward the end of 1946, the organization's income dropped by one half. In early 1947, the SCHW no longer appeared on the list of organizations approved by CIO departments and commissions, and other defections followed that of the CIO. After Franklin Roosevelt's death, the Administration ended its unofficial support of the Conference. Mrs. Roosevelt, who had regarded the Conference as her protege, failed to attend its 1946 New Orleans convention, preferring instead to wire a message of support, as did other prominent supporters such as Henry Wallace, Walter Reuther, Philip Murray, James G. Patton of the National Farmers Union, and A. F. Whitney, head of the Railway Brotherhoods. While politicians, labor unions, and many white professionals withdrew, the black contingent remained as the major source of the Conference's popular support.[21]

The commencement of the Cold War in 1945-46 deepened the division among New Dealers between supporters and opponents of continued

19

cooperation with the Soviet Union as a basis of American foreign policy and increasingly commanded their energies and attention, often at the expense of other interests. The Southern Conference for Human Welfare suffered further splits and new attacks for its refusal to take sides in the Cold War. Contributing to its difficulties was an internal feud between Clark Foreman, the organization's president, and James Dombrowski, its executive secretary. The quarrel concerned a shuffle in positions, and had little to do with the Conference's overall ideology or strategy. It thus served merely to embitter the participants, making the cooperation between them fragile.

Foreman had decided to revamp the administrative leadership of the SCHW in late 1946 by replacing Dombrowski and moving him to the Fund to serve as its Director. Foreman selected Miss Branson Price, head of the New York Committee, to assume a new position as Administrator in Conference headquarters in New Orleans in December, 1946. Foreman decided to make policy decisions himself, leaving in her hands only administrative and financial chores; Dombrowski, in effect, was muscled into a lesser position. Taken without prior notice or consultation, Foreman's move disturbed the usually easy going Dombrowski, and he undertook to fight his removal before the full Board of the Conference. Several of the most active members, among them Lucy Randolph Mason and Virginia Durr, supported him, and they attempted to get Foreman to reconsider. Foreman was determined, however, and while impressing upon Dombrowski the potential importance of the Fund, he prevented an open break only by convincing the Board of the difficult position facing the Conference and the need for more vigorous leadership.[22]

Aubrey Williams, who was a close friend of Dombrowski and a Board member, urged him to accept his new position and to "stop all of this internal conflict."[23] Another Board member and a CIO-PAC officer, Palmer Weber, prevailed upon Dombrowski to overcome personal affronts. It seemed to Weber that "the problem is how the various parts can be made to function so that we get the job done....Either we get the funds or March will find us dead." Weber insisted that "we have a fighting group now in the South." He assured Dombrowski that he was essential to the organization and "as responsible to hold it and make it grow as anyone else."[24]

By June 1947, Dombrowski had overcome his misgivings and decided to take the Fund position. The decision was a fortunate one for the Southern Conference Educational Fund, providing it with the patient, dogged leadership that few but Dombrowski could supply. He assumed the new post, however, on condition that there be no public announcement of his transfer to the Fund. Furthermore, he insisted on taking the post of editor of the *Southern Patriot*. As part of a general move to cut expenses, Foreman was to go onto a non-paying basis as joint president of the Conference and the Fund. At the time, the Fund had a grand total of $6,455 in assets, far below its needs for an extensive educational program for the South.[25]

In contrast to the leadership controversy, there was a consensus among the Board members on a program for the Fund. In a memo to the Board, Foreman formulated his concept of its task. "The general object," he stated, "would be to awaken those parts of the southern population which we cannot reach through a political action group to the understanding of the fundamental principles involved in our work." He considered it wise to place emphasis upon one facet of the program to the exclusion of others. Noting Dombrowski's suggestion that the Fund concern itself with the voting issue, Foreman felt that "we might do better to take advantage now of the general interest in education and teachers' salaries, so as to build a broader understanding of education itself, which could be translated into action by the Southern Conference for Human Welfare...."[26]

The Southern Conference Educational Fund thus initiated its program of re-educating the South to reform its institutions and reconstruct its values. Shortly thereafter the Fund also began to part ways with the Conference. Through the pages of the *Southern Patriot* the Fund began to create an identity for itself. The idea of formally separating the two agencies became a matter for private discussion in mid-1947. Before accepting his position as Director of the Fund, Dombrowski urged the Board members to ponder matters of structure, as well as budget and program. In place of a single president for both the Conference and the Fund, he thought it would be consonant with previous decisions to withdraw the political from the educational functions, replacing the Conference with two distinct agencies. Such a division of labor, Dombrowski believed, "would strengthen the possibilities of getting funds if the president of the Educational Fund were not at the same time the president of a political action agency." Its own president would give added emphasis to the distinctly educational character of the SCEF," and also permit more time for fund raising than would be available to a single president of both groups. Because of Clark Foreman's strenuous objection, however, the Board decided to straddle the issue. It appointed a committee to consider the question of form, making its consideration secondary to devising a budget and a program for the Fund.[27]

The internal structure and the future direction of both the Conference and the Fund continued to engage the attention of others besides Dombrowski. In a letter to him, Virginia Durr reflected on the alternatives before them. She saw three courses of action: for one, the Conference could link up with the Progressive Citizens of America, an organization of leftist former New Dealers, and thus "be strengthened by being part of a national organization." This would, however, cost the Southern Conference the support of those who balked at affiliation with the Progressive Citizens of America. The other courses were to revert to being a small educational group and letting the state committees of the Conference fend for themselves, or "keep on the way we are going at present and end up nowhere."[28]

Lucy Randolph Mason offered the clearest ideas concerning the future course of the Southern Conference and the Fund. An active and esteemed member of the Conference, she had an impressive family tree; one of her ancestors, George Mason, had signed the original Virginia Bill of Rights. She also rated high among New Dealers as a CIO organizer in the South, and her opinions carried weight with other Conference members. Miss Mason submitted a memo in April, 1947, in the form of a proposal for the future structure and program of the Conference. In her eyes, the situation was "desperate," and while she hoped the Conference would survive and make further contributions to the development of a progressive South, she advised taking a fresh look at its situation. The Conference was "an icebreaker, a spear-head, a standard bearer" with a "frontier program," she noted. As such, it could not be a mass political organization, since the Southern masses were not ready to follow it. Its record and its image among the mass of Southerners were ineluctable and it had little choice, this side of extinction, but to accomplish its goals by different means. The chief weakness of the Conference, and the cause of its present difficulties, she believed, was a failure to understand clearly its position in Southern history and society. The Southern Conference had, unwittingly, misled people into believing that it could produce far more than circumstances justified. Specifically, since the adoption of the expanded program two years before, she declared

> the highest membership has been about 5,000 from all the southern states combined....If the Conference's entire southern membership was concentrated in one state it would not constitute a mass political movement in that state.... Yet I fear that donors too often get the impression that the Conference, of itself, can produce mass political pressure. The fact that it cannot do this is becoming more generally known and is leading to loss of prestige.

A relatively small organization, the Conference had set itself a program demanding a mass political movement for its accomplishment. In order to fulfill its stated aims, the Conference had entered into many unsound financial arrangements, anticipating income that had not materialized. The debts had piled up to a point where the organization could no longer proceed without redeeming them. More importantly, where the Conference should have been building a strong grass roots organization on the local level, it spent too much time, thought, and indeed too much money, in trying to meet the expectation it had created in the public mind. "As a result," she declared, "there is no denying that we have built a top-heavy operation, with the Conference itself dying at the grass roots in southern states."

By revising its self-image in consonance with its function as a catalyst influencing other organizations, pressuring and guiding politicians, and working aggressively on a limited number of issues, Miss Mason argued, the Conference could continue to act as a leaven in the South. Working quietly outside the public glare, and often foregoing credit for a great many of its accomplishments, the Conference would in time have a considerable effect upon Southern thinking. It was, however, imperative that the organization continue to be indigenous to the South; all of its officers had to reside in the region. The Conference's policy and program, she felt, must also be determined by residents of the South and its work directed by Southerners. The entire operation, in effect, so as to offset charges of outside influence, must be controlled within the region.

For the Conference to attain healthy, rather than hothouse growth, she emphasized the need for sound financial management. By limiting itself to a few basic issues, the Conference would be more effective than if it dissipated its energies upon a wide range of problems. She suggested establishing a reserve fund as part of a sound financial structure, insisting that the Conference live within its income rather than upon anticipated funds. Since only a small portion of the funds could be raised in the South, the Conference would have to continue to seek aid from outside the region, but it was necessary to develop fund-raising techniques that would not damage the program in the South. The expense of raising funds had to be kept to a minimum, avoiding the error common to affairs in New York City, where funds purportedly gathered for the South often went to defray local expenses.

In addition to cutting down overhead, she recommended that a single person be selected to act as a full-time fund raiser. He would concentrate on seeking individual donations, arranging interviews and small group affairs, as well as appeals to other sympathetic organizations. Entertainment, a costly overhead, had to be eliminated or cut to the bone. The fund raiser, Miss Mason advised, should work primarily in the wealthy, larger cities such as New York, Boston, Chicago and Los Angeles. He should be a person in complete sympathy with the purposes of the Conference, and most essentially, "be in tune with the problems of the South and understand them thoroughly." The central Conference staff must also be reduced to conform with the more limited nature of its program, and, in the immediate future, ought to devote its energies to eliminating the debt.[29] In sum, Lucy Mason had sketched a working model which the Southern Conference Educational Fund alone would follow in a period less amenable to social reform.

What ultimately set the Fund upon an independent course, however, was the 1948 campaign of Henry A. Wallace, Presidential nominee of the Progressive party. The Wallace candidacy unintentionally delivered the *coup de grace* to the Southern Conference for Human Welfare. The Conference shared Wallace's commitment to the expansion of the domestic social reforms of the New Deal, as well as a fundamental attachment to cooperation with the Soviet Union internationally as the foundation of a peaceful world order. The marked shift in the policies of the Truman administration away from continuation of the wartime alliance with Russia, symbolized by its increasing hostility toward Russian policies in Eastern Europe, and the Administration's denial of credits to assist Soviet post-war reconstruction, compelled Wallace to take a critical attitude to the Administration. His public disagreement with the direction of American foreign policy had led to Wallace's dismissal from the post of Secretary of Commerce in September, 1946. Many intellectuals, who had rallied to the New Deal in the thirties and particularly during the second World War, followed Wallace out of the Administration.[30]

The Southern Conference for Human Welfare publicly expressed its agreement with Wallace's views in a report released in April, 1947. The report decried the disparity between the New Deal promises to create an Economic Bill of Rights in the post-war period and what it considered the "mutilation of the Wage and Hour Act, the threatened destruction of the entire Southern labor movement, and the increasing encroachment of absentee monopoly control of Southern business." It deplored "the crippling of many federal agencies whose services are most acutely needed in the

South, and the neglect of social legislation to meet the most severe housing, education, health, child welfare and social security needs." In place of federal and state legislation to abolish the poll tax and outlaw lynching, the report lamented, there were "white primary bills," a series of post-war lynchings, and renewed organized "hate" campaigns. The growing anxiety about "internal security" had resulted in a "federal executive order and proposed legislation which enemies of the Southern people can use to intimidate all individual and organized democratic expression and action." And, overshadowing all, was "the fear of atomic energy as a means of universal destruction and the threat of World War III." Faced with these ominous trends the Conference was convinced that "the greatest political need of the Southern people" was to give urgent consideration, through their churches, labor unions, and associations of all kinds, to the best way of reversing them. Prompt, effective action would "lay the basis for a political decision in 1948" which would both enable the South to realize her own magnificent possibilities," contributing to "the national and international good," and, simultaneously, frustrate "reactionary programs of either traditional party."[31]

From this perspective, the Conference enthusiastically agreed to sponsor a tour by Henry Wallace in June, 1947. The trip to Texas, Louisiana, Alabama, Georgia, North Carolina, and Virginia carried his message of dissent to the Southern people.[32] While the Southern Conference for Human Welfare endorsed Wallace's views, his decision to form a new party as the political base of his Presidential race in 1948 forced many in the organization to have second thoughts. Quite willing to approve Wallace's criticisms of American foreign policy and the domestic shortcomings of the Truman administration, many Conference members were not ready to break with the Democratic party and the hope that with it lay the best promise for future reforms.

Labor union officials, such as William Mitch of the United Mine Workers, felt particularly the pressures from their organizations. They had to reject not only the Progressive Party, but also the Southern Conference since it was, in the public mind, so closely associated with the Wallace camp. Union leaders also disliked the prominent role Communists assumed in the Wallace movement, and their suspicions also fell on the Southern Conference. Writing to Dombrowski Mitch refused to reconsider his resignation from the Conference. He claimed that "it was partly because of the Southern Conference outliving its usefulness in the South." It was, also, "because of the infiltration of Communists into the group in Alabama." He referred to

Alabama member Sam Hall who allegedly let the press know that he was the head of the Communist Party in Alabama. "Certainly," Mitch insisted, "there were people in the Southern Conference in Alabama who brought him into the meeting and promoted him to Chairmanship of the Southern Conference some time ago and knew his standing as a Communist at that time." Though these and other incidents necessitated his decision, Mitch expressed his regrets, "because I know there are so many people working in the Southern Conference who try to do something in the South...."[33]

There were others whose predicament was more complex. Luther P. Jackson's was a case in point. A well-known black educator from the Virginia State College at Petersburg, he had been an active member of the Committee for Virginia, and one of its best fund-raisers. For years Jackson had raised money for Carter G. Woodson and his Negro history movement, the Virginia Voters League, and a number of other groups in Virginia. He had also been active in behalf of the Southern Conference for Human Welfare. On three different occasions, he had raised a total of $700 for the Conference, mainly from small contributors who "are the type to stick provided I stick with them," he informed Virginia Durr. Though he and some of his associates were Wallace supporters, they did not permit this sentiment to dominate their own Committee activities. The actions of some members, however, in releasing to the press the pro-Wallace proceedings and endorsement by the Virginia Committee had the effect of driving the most dependable members further away from the organization. "I deem it regrettable," he concluded, "that our organization is one which has had so many schisms and resignations...I am wondering just what shall my position be now in as much as I find myself all dressed up with no place to go."[34]

Virginia Durr, also a member of the Virginia Committee, had proposed that all who could not go along actively for Wallace should attach themselves to the Southern Conference Educational Fund at New Orleans. But Jackson was hesitant. He was "not certain whether my friends will be willing to go along with me," though he had planned to conduct a membership drive in the state in June. "Now I do not know what to do," he confessed.[35]

Unlike the Southern Conference for Human Welfare, the Educational Fund remained aloof from the Wallace campaign. Elected president of the Fund in January, 1948, Aubrey Williams, while sympathetic to Wallace and sharing many of his views, remained loyal to the Democratic Party, particularly after its adoption of an outspoken civil rights plank at its convention in the summer of 1948. In the face of these divergent views, and because of his prominent role in the Wallace movement, Clark Foreman resigned from the presidency of the SCHW in May, 1948. He believed the Wallace-Glenn Taylor candidacy to be "the most important movement in the country," and one that "offers the South the greatest chance it has ever had to escape from the feudalism that has been such a curse to its people and to the rest of the country." Yet because others on the Board did not share his outlook, he stepped aside to give them the opportunity of selecting a president who could "give more time and thought to their problems in the months ahead."[36]

The resignation of Foreman, and the diversion of the energies of others into the Progressive Party, created a crisis for the Southern Conference for Human Welfare. On behalf of the Educational Fund, Aubrey Williams wrote George Googe, AFL leader in the South, on November 12, 1948: "We have completely severed all connections with the Southern Conference for Human Welfare." Meeting at the Phyllis Wheatley Y.W.C.A. in Richmond, on November 21, the Board of the Southern Conference wound up its affairs. In a final resolution, the members paid homage to the Conference for making "a major contribution to a southwide awakening" since its inception "at a time when political activity in the South was generally limited to one all-white party." The 1948 election had produced "unmistakable evidence of the increased effect of the Negro vote, the recognition of civil rights as a major political issue, and the beginning of new political alignments and independent political action--in large degree the logical result of the ten years of work by the Conference," the statement asserted. It nevertheless saw "new political forces" such as the Progressive Party superceding the Southern Conference for Human Welfare and absorbing its political energies. This made continuation of the Conference "unnecessary and a duplication of effort. "The intensive educational work" of the Conference henceforth would be carried on by the Southern Conference Educational Fund.[37]

TWO

The Cost of Segregation: Search for a Program, 1947-1948

The failure of electoral politics in the forties to uproot segregation compelled Southern reformers to rethink their strategy. Their expectations of victory through elections had shriveled. It was evident that the segregationist white power-holders were too strong within the major parties to be shaken loose solely by electoral campaigns. Underlying the strength of the segregationists was the deeply-rooted sense of racial superiority of the Southern white population. Patterns of culture so ingrained required other, more imaginative approaches for their reconstruction. As a way of dealing with mass popular attitudes, the Southern Conference Educational Fund worked to break down white supremacist beliefs, as well as segregation practices, in the South.

Compared to previous reform efforts in Southern history, the Fund made a significant departure in program. Those who had decided, in the face of many disappointments, to sustain the Fund had concluded that with the elimination of segregation, they could more easily resolve every other problem. The leaders of the Fund thus perceived a critical need for a militant interracial group dedicated to this one objective. For the Fund, "the fixed star in its heaven" was to be the proposition that "segregation must he completely eliminated--now, immediately, not at some future time--and this must be done by Negro and white Southerners working together."[1]

Prior to the formation of Southern Conference Educational Fund, white Southern groups concerned with interracial relations had adopted a policy of paternalism rather than fraternal cooperation between the races. The Populists briefly attempted a *political* alliance with black farmers in the nineties, but they never accorded social equality to their black allies. When that alliance seemed to threaten the power structure of the white South compelling it, in self-interest, to retaliate by means of terror, chicanery and the inflammation of latent racial passions, the Populists wavered. One of their leaders, Tom Watson of Georgia, henceforth became a symbol of savage anti-black prejudices, and consequently a power in the South until his death in 1920.

It was not until 1912 with the appearance of the Southern Sociological Congress that other interracial endeavors appeared in the region. James Hardy Dillard, a member of the Sociological Congress and director of the Jeanes and Slater Funds for Negro education, initiated the University Commission on Southern Race Questions which met annually to encourage college-educated white Southerners to become more sophisticated in their understanding of race problems. Utilizing grants from the Phelps-Stokes Foundation, the Commission sponsored courses in Southern universities and publications on race relations. Similar in approach was the work of Willis D. Weatherford, student director of the YMCA, and Mrs. L. H. Hammond, wife of the white president of Payne College for Negroes in Augusta, Georgia. Both authored books on black problems in the South and were active in church affairs. Common to the outlook of these groups and individuals was a combination of paternalism and the urge for social justice characteristic of many progressives of the early twentieth century. They sought black advancement safely within the framework of segregation, encouraging only "discreet contacts across the veil of separation."[2]

These stirrings of concern for the black man culminated in the founding of the Commission on Interracial Cooperation, which took shape following the fearful race riots of 1919 in Atlanta, Chicago, and other cities in the South and Midwest. Will W. Alexander, a former minister active in YMCA work in the U.S. Army during World War I, was the guiding spirit of the Commission. During the twenties and thirties the Interracial Commission formed numerous state, local and municipal committees all over the South, and claimed to have averted numerous lynchings by keeping contacts open between white and black leaders in crisis situations. The innumerable conferences sponsored by the organization won support for it from Southern governors and other political leaders. This support was possible, however, only because the Commission avoided the segregation issue. The Interracial Commission never adopted an interracial creed as a condition for membership. One of its spokesmen conceded that "unless those forms of separation which are meant to safeguard the purity of the races are present, the majority of the white people flatly refuse to cooperate with Negroes."[3]

The Commission, nevertheless, set precedents later followed by the Southern Conference for Human Welfare and the Southern Conference Educational Fund. Its leaders, particularly Alexander, were convinced that action in behalf of racial harmony and cooperation merely treated symptoms rather than the disease; prejudiced attitudes had to be undermined by a program of education. In 1922 the organization set up an education department under the direction of Robert B. Eleazer, Jr. , and after 1926, under Arthur F. Raper, both noted sociologists. Studies and pamphlets, conferences, and other publicity devices soon inundated the South. College interracial forums, another popular device, appeared in Southern cities frequently after 1923. A press service also provided information about racial matters to both white and black newspapers. An important aspect of this work was the college interracial movement promoted by the Fellowship of Reconciliation through its Southern Interracial Secretary, Howard Kester, of Vanderbilt University.[4]

Admirable and important though all of this activity was, it reached, at best, an elite minority. The interracial meetings themselves were painfully formal affairs. As one Memphis black put it

> the whites are hell-bent upon being broadminded. The Negroes affect to take it all as a matter of course. But nobody present ever dares to speak the blunt truth. They drift on clouds of sentimentality. They pass meaningless resolutions.[5]

Despite this, Gunnar Myrdal was accurate when he concluded that it was a monumental accomplishment merely "to have rendered interracial work socially respectable in the conservative South."[6]

The Interracial Commission continued into the thirties and forties, an era of rising black militancy, as well as race riots and rumors of race riots, though it was practically defunct; Will Alexander interred it in 1943. His assistant, University of Tennessee sociologist, William E. Cole, in a final report called it "static, colorless...not charged with social action...'Uncle Tomish' in nature." The Commission's demise was but prelude to its rebirth in another, less ambitious form: the Southern Regional Council. The new organization was inspired by sociologist Howard W. Odum, who since the early thirties had worked for the formation of a Council on Southern regional development. Invited to participate in the founding of the Southern Conference for Human Welfare, Odum refused to join for fear he would not be in command and his ideas would be pushed aside in favor of more socially radical or politically opportune programs.[7]

Odum was among a number of white moderates who, in association with like-minded black notables, arranged several conferences in 1942-43. At the first meeting in October, 1942, at Durham, North Carolina, a group of leading black academics met and called upon Southern whites to take a stand in behalf of black people. They called upon the South to provide access to the ballot, full civil rights, greater employment opportunity, and equal access to public services. In reply, over one hundred whites met in Atlanta in April, 1943, and proposed a joint conference to be held in Richmond. The latter meeting, on February 16, 1944, formed the Southern Regional Council with Odum as president and Guy B. Johnson a black educator as executive secretary. The Southern Regional Council set itself a broad agenda of activity in support of economic development, better race relations, and social welfare, but its lack of militancy provoked criticism from other Southern reformers. Prominent white writer, Lillian Smith pointedly asked, "Are we merely trying to avoid...more 'tensions', which embarrass white folks, or are we trying to secure for the Negro his full human rights?"[8] Odum fumed, complaining privately to Birmingham columnist John Temple Graves. "If we could just stop talking about social equality and segregation and go to work, it would be a day for us, wouldn't it?"[9]

With the Southern Conference for Human Welfare setting the pace for reform-minded White Southerners, the Southern Regional Council could, at its first meeting in December, 1944, do no less than endorse a program for equal employment opportunity, the hiring of black police and firemen, equalization of education and access to public transportation, black voting rights, and increased public financing for medical care. During 1945 it revived interracial committees in ten states, surveyed bus segregation in Atlanta, established a veterans service to promote equal treatment for returned servicemen, and began the periodical New South.

But the Southern Regional Council did not arouse much support from either blacks or whites. "It seems foolish," Odum wrote Johnson early in 1945, "...to talk about getting the South back of the movement when there is no indication anywhere of leadership or of business and professional people following," not even "that brilliant coterie of liberals we counted on." As for the Southern Conference for Human Welfare, it went out of its way to avoid criticism or attacks upon the new group. Clark Foreman used his influence to keep the Southern Patriot from sniping at the Council. He also urged its editor, James Dombrowski, to reject a critical article by Lillian Smith, who had refused to join the Southern Regional Council because it stopped short of openly opposing segregation. "I don't want to attack the SRC in the *Patriot*. There is room enough for both organizations and if Lillian wants to work only with us, that's fine," stated Foreman. But since there were others who would work only with the Council Foreman declared, "let's have both and no time wasted in attacking each other."[10]

In contrast to the Southern Regional Council, the more militant Southern Conference Educational Fund entered the post-war period hopeful of its ability to improve race relations. Early in 1947 Foreman urged its Board members to think seriously about the economic situation and the ominous forecasts being made about another depression. He thought it would be helpful if the Fund issued a clear statement on the economic issues confronting the South. With the 1938 report to the President on Southern conditions in mind, he urged that the data be brought up to date to "provide us with a charter for future action."[11]

The fear of a new depression as a basis for a program, however, had less relevance than a new critique of the South. The Fund challenged the South to look within for the ills that kept it backward and poverty-stricken. Commenting on two court decisions, one by the United States Supreme Court striking down discriminatory freight rates, and the other by Federal District Judge J. Waties Waring of Charleston, South Carolina, forbidding discrimination against blacks in the South Carolina Democratic primaries, the *Southern Patriot* contrasted the two problems. In the former case, the South had won a long-fought battle to break down its position of colonial dependency vis-a-vis the industrial-banking interests of the Northeast. "But the South that fights righteously from without," it stated, "has been slow to end or even to see discrimination that is self-imposed. Antiquated prejudices molded in a dead past stand today like a brick wall blocking the road to progress in the South." A modern industrializing economy needed well-paid workers to provide the skilled labor force and the important consumer market for the products of its mills, factories and farms. By maintaining a racial caste system, the South condemned ten million of its citizens, a fourth of the total Southern population, to the economic backwaters of unskilled labor and domestic service with a commensurately low income. In its brief against discriminatory freight rates, the *Patriot* asserted, the South was correct in its argument that the welfare of the nation was one with that of the South. By the same logic, however, the South could not prosper if it

33

persisted in keeping a fourth of its own population outside the mainstream of economic and political life. "For its own sake, if for no higher reason, the *Patriot* declared, "the white South must aid the black South in its fight for emancipation, for only in this way can we rid the South of its illiteracy, pellagra, and generally low living standards for all." Judge Waring's decision, the paper thought, provided the means for dealing with segregation and poverty. By eliminating discrimination at the ballot box, Waring went to the tapwaters of the problem, "for it is an axiom of history that an exploited group must achieve political freedom before it can gain economic equality."[12]

The interrelations of segregation and political disfranchisement were at the center of the Fund's strategy to undermine and transform the white South. Fund leaders Dombrowski and Foreman saw a great opportunity in October, 1947, with the public release of the Report of President Truman's Commission on Civil Rights, "To Secure These Rights." Having the apparent blessing of the President of the United States, the Report was a victory for those working in behalf of civil rights throughout the nation. After a lengthy description of the state of individual rights and deprivations, particularly in the South, the Report urged Congress to pass legislation outlawing the poll tax; providing severe punishment for the crime of lynching; increasing protection for the right to vote; and creating a Joint Standing Committee on Civil Rights in Congress, as well as a permanent Civil Rights Commission in the Executive Branch and a greater role for the Civil Rights Section of the Justice Department. It also called for a permanent Fair Employment Practices Commission, Presidential orders ending discrimination in Federal agencies and in public employment, with adequate enforcement; more vigorous moves against restrictive housing covenants; and legislation prohibiting discrimination and segregation in public housing and interstate commerce.[13]

While the Northern and black press acclaimed the Report, it faced a different reception in the South. Some newspapers took a moderate approach. The Richmond *Times Dispatch* declared that "it is impossible for any sincere American to disagree with many of the general principles laid down in the Report." The Birmingham *News* was even more complimentary. While disagreeing with a number of recommendations of the committee it commented, "we not only approve strongly many of its proposals but admire the unquestionable courage and devotion with which it has carried out its...assignment. It has performed a notable service."[14] Most of the Southern press, however, bristled with hostility. The Nashville *Banner* felt that the report "originated in the left wing of imported politics." The Charlotte *News* viewed it as a "bombastic demand for upheaval." And the Anderson, South Carolina *Independent* declared that "if the report's proposals were made law they will need an army to enforce them."[15] Southern politicians overwhelmingly opposed the Report, and readied themselves for battle against the President's expected legislative proposals to implement it.

Fund director Dombrowski saw the Report as "of the first importance," and on a par with 1938 *Report on Economic Conditions of the South*. He also proudly noted that two members of the President's commission, Dr. Frank P. Graham and Dr. Channing Tobias, were members of the Fund's Board of Advisors. Accordingly, Dombrowski sought the views of his organization on the desirability of initiating a Southwide conference on human rights to discuss the Report's implications for the region and to build support for its recommendations. He advised that a distinguished committee of about one hundred Southerners, broadly representative of the region, sponsor the conference with the Fund coordinating details. Dombrowski also cautioned the Fund to expect a hostile reaction from the Southern press "on the traditional ground that Northerners do not understand the South and its problems, with the implied assumption that democracy and ethics have regional limitations." It was obvious, he thought, that support coming from Southerners "will be of the utmost importance if anything of a practical nature is to come from this report." He suggested the conference take place in mid-December, 1947.[16] Clark Foreman endorsed Dombrowski's suggestion, though wondering about the organization's ability to finance it. He suggested the conference meet in Atlanta, with Richmond as a second choice and he urged Dombrowski to attend the annual meeting of the Southern Regional Council in Atlanta, on November 11-12, in order to win its cooperation.[17]

Because of a drastic change in the political climate of the South following President Truman's special message to Congress on civil rights in January, 1948, the conference could not be held. Attempting to prevent the critical black vote in the North from bolting to Henry Wallace's Progressive Party in the 1948 election, Truman delivered a report to Congress urging adoption of his Commission's recommendations, none of which struck at segregation itself but whose thrust and tone augured ill for the future of the South's "peculiar system" of segregation. Southern Democrats snapped at Truman that "it is a mighty poor way for him to evince his gratitude" for Southern support in the 1944 Democratic convention that made him the heir to Franklin D. Roosevelt.[18] So intense was their opposition that the Omnibus Civil Rights Bill embodying Truman's proposals failed even to get the support of Alben Barkley, the Democratic minority leader in the Senate. When Truman persisted in his support for the bill, Southern Democrats openly rebelled, forming the Dixiecrat movement which took control of the party in the South. The turn for the worse in interracial politics discouraged the Fund from attempting to hold a public conference of liberal Southerners in support of the President's recommendations.

Its political efforts thwarted, and with the parent Southern Conference for Human Welfare becoming more involved in the presidential and congressional campaigns of 1948, the Fund turned its attention to education. Undoubtedly, the Fund's greatest asset in its educational work was the *Southern Patriot*, a newspaper with a Southwide circulation of about 15,000. As editor of the paper, James Dombrowski, had livened up its pages with his own perceptive commentary and had given more coverage to specifically Southern problem in the years after World War II. The war, and the Southern Conference for Human Welfare's intensely patriotic stance, had diluted much of the paper's regional character and interest. Now that the Fund was on a firmer basis, and because of Dombrowski's insistence that the Fund make the *Patriot* its own organ, the journal became the distinctive voice of militant Southern reformers. With segregation as the focus, Dombrowski made plans to publish several issues of the *Patriot* dealing with segregation's ill effects in various fields. Early in 1947, the *Patriot* had great success with a special issue on voting in the South, encouraging Dombrowski to plan an issue on segregation in education.[19]

Timed to coincide with release of the Presidential Commission's Report, the October, 1947, issue of the *Southern Patriot* was, according to Dombrowski, "the best thing by far...we have ever done and about the most timely."[20] Well-documented and put into superb charts "by one of the South's best artists," the issue turned a spotlight on the condition of schools, pupils, teachers and education generally in the District of Columbia and those states which maintained separate schools by law. Glaring disparities between white and black education--in length of school year, value of school property per pupil enrolled, the amount of money spent per pupil in elementary schools, and provision of bus transportation--stood out in graphic detail. Moreover, the differentials had not decreased appreciably between 1930 and 1945, the years covered in the survey.[21] In only one instance had some real closing of the gap occurred. Largely because of legal action undertaken by the NAACP in the forties, average salaries for elementary school teachers had narrowed from a difference of 65 per cent higher salaries for white teachers in 1930 to 40 per cent higher in 1945. Most startling were the differences discovered in graduate and professional education, as indicated in Table 1.

TABLE 1

Graduate and Professional Education in 1945 in Seventeen States and the District of Columbia where Segregation is Legal

Graduate Education	Total Number of Degree-Granting Schools	
	White	Black
Master's Degree (MA) state-school in	(A t l e a s t 1	supported
	each of 17 states)	
	17+	8
Doctor's Degree (PhD)	12	None (public or private)
Professional Education		
Dentistry	4	None
Law	16	4
Medicine	15	None
Pharmacy	14	None
Social Work	9	None
Library Science	11	1

In 1930, the expenditure per person in state-supported higher professional institutions in the South was $1.39 for whites and 33¢ for blacks; while in 1945, the comparison stood at $2.43 for whites and 56¢ for blacks. The differential in favor of whites had increased by 13 per cent during the period. Moreover, these disparities had an effect on social and medical services available to the two races. (see Table 2).

In thirteen Southern states, there was not a single school supported by public funds to educate black physicians or dentists. In Louisiana, there was but one black physician for every 8,000 blacks in the population, while the ratio for whites was one to every 800. Because of inadequate medical care, blacks suffered generally from poorer health and mortality rates were 30 to 40 per cent greater for blacks than for whites. The average life expectancy for blacks was ten to twelve years less than that for whites. The entire population, black and white, suffered, the *Patriot* asserted, for disease "observe(s) no color line."

Putting in bold relief the euphemistic character of the "separate but equal" rubric were the differences in sums spent on elementary education in various parts of the South. As of December, 1941, the city of Atlanta, reputedly the most progressive of Southern cities, invested $6 in school land and buildings for every white child and $1 for every black. Of the 65 public school buildings in the city, only 13, or 20 per cent, were for blacks, compared to 52, or 80 per cent, for whites, though the school population was 37.4 per cent black. In Louisiana, blacks received 17.6 per cent of the total public education funds, though comprising 36 per cent of the population. While blacks had no public trade schools, there were ten for whites at a cost of over one-half million dollars. In Mississippi, certainly the most dismal in this respect as in others, in 1944-45, there were 2,015 one-room, one-teacher black schools, in contrast to ten such schools for whites. The black schools were housed in churches, tenant houses and other inadequate structures. Whites received an annual $45.79 per pupil, while blacks received $10.10. White schools had a school term of eight months, while black schools ran for six months. White teachers, in 1946-47, received an average salary of $900; blacks $465.

Again, in Atlanta, 120 of the 155 black teachers in the elementary schools taught in double sessions, while none of the 612 white teachers did. As a result of this double session, black children received only 3 1/2 hours or less of daily instruction, representing a loss of 2 1/2 school years during the

TABLE 2
Professional Services Distributed by Race in
1945 in Seventeen States and District of Columbia
Where Segregation is Legal

	Ratio to Population by Race		Ratio in Favor of Whites	Selected Range of distribution in Favor of Whites
Profession	White	Black		
Physicians	1 to every 843	1 to every 4,409	5:1	Twice as many in Mo. to 22 times as many in Miss.
Dentists	1 to every 2,795	1 to every 12,101	4:1	Twice as many in D. of C. to 13 times as many in many in Miss.
Pharmacists	1 to every 1,714	1 to every 22,815	13:1	Twice as many in Delaware to 5 times as many in Miss.
Lawyers	1 to every 702	1 to every 24,997	35:1	5 times as many in W.Va. to 420 times as many in Miss.
Social Workers	1 to every 2,654	1 to every 11,537	4:1	1.28 times more blacks in Mo. to 40 times as many whites in Miss. (The only instance where blacks outnumber whites.
Engineers	1 to every 644	1 to every 130,700	202:1	42 times as many in Okla. to almost 900 times as many in S. Car. No black engineers reported at all from Delaware to Florida

child's first six years in school. Despite the double session system, black schools were overcrowded with an average of forty students to a class, eleven more students than in comparable white elementary school classes. There were 1.4 books per pupil in the black high school libraries as compared to 6.5 books per white pupil. The city provided a dental correction clinic in the City Hall for needy white children, but made no provision for black children.

It was a convincing demonstration of the bankruptcy of the concept of "separate but equal." Moreover, the *Patriot* argued, even if physical equality was achieved, equality would still not exist, for the value of a degree rested in part upon the value it had in the eyes of the community. "And the community does not regard a degree from a small separate black school as highly as it does the same degree from a large state university with a long...tradition and thousands of distinguished alumni...." Segregated schools, moreover, while good enough to perpetuate narrow, traditional patterns of thought and behavior, were totally inadequate for a new world in which the aim was "to substitute scientific attitudes for prejudice." If the aim of education was to help in the creation of one world, segregation was out of place, for segregated schools "cannot educate for an integrated world." As for the concept of establishing regional professional schools for blacks to make up for present inadequacies, the *Patriot* regarded it as a backward step. Regional schools, it asserted, "are not advocated in the first place by educators to solve an educational problem in a reasonable and ethical manner but by politicians as an escape from an embarrassing dilemma created by the *Gaines* decision." It urged the immediate opening of all professional schools to qualified students irrespective of race, religion, or ancestry.[22] The Fund pressed for the widest circulation of this issue of the *Patriot* throughout the South. Within six months, the Fund distributed over 70,000 copies to schools, churches, labor unions and other institutions, and gave similar promotion to a companion study on segregation in health conditions and facilities in March, 1948.[23]

Once set upon challenging segregation directly, the Fund faced the problem of devising a strategy and tactics suitable to its own resources. A number of proposals suggested encouragement of interracial businesses in the South. Pointing to several relatively successful interracial enterprises such as the radio station WQQW, in Washington, D.C., which contributed to interracial understanding in that area, some saw the feasibility of encouraging such radio stations in every Southern city with a population of more than 150,000. These stations, they believed, would provide a stimulus to other business enterprises and demonstrate the desirability of admitting black business capital to overall Southern development. They would also aid in undoing practices which discouraged the accumulation and investment of capital by blacks in areas such as Miami, Florida. In that city, no bank permitted a black person to open a checking or savings account; while in other areas of the South, particularly in small towns, bankers and merchants refused loans to black tenants seeking to purchase their own land. Interracial enterprises would encourage other banks and businesses to challenge such practices.

A most important area for interracial business was that of housing. In Washington, D.C., the chairman of the District Committee of the Southern Conference for Human Welfare owned an apartment building and made it a model of interracial occupancy, providing the stimulus for other jointly-owned buildings in the District. "The quiet business development of such projects," its proponents believed, "and the history of such projects in Southern communities will immeasurably assist in destroying certain Southern social myths which are today employed to support the segregation pattern." To encourage such developments, there were to be annual interracial meetings of businessmen in medium and large Southern cities, discussing and exploring areas of joint enterprise. Initial endeavors, they suggested, were to be in the fields of radio, banking and real estate.[24]

Considering the aims of the Fund, a more realistic project was the establishment of a weekly news service to provide every Southern newspaper accurate facts and figures on all aspects of Southern race relations. Since the press, next to the churches, had the most influence upon community thinking, Southern editors and writers were a critical force for good or evil. The South could boast a goodly number of courageous, intelligent journalists with considerable influence--men such as Josephus and Jonathan Daniels, Ralph McGill, Jennings Perry, Hodding Carter, Roscoe Dunjee, and Mark Ethridge. Though most wrote for city papers, the *Patriot* claimed "that for every one of these men there are twenty-five to fifty editors of country and weekly papers who in their own smaller communities represent the same courage and integrity." Moreover, though there were about 2,000 weekly and daily papers in the South, most suffered from poverty of material and a lack of financial resources. An interracial press service would make up for this, as well as fill a desperate need for communication and information between whites and blacks.

Basic informational features on the role of black people in the war effort had rarely, if at all, found a place in the southern press. The Columbia, Tennessee, race riot of 1946 had been inadequately covered because no wire service would furnish the information and weekly papers had no way of obtaining accurate news of the event. Interracial activity in labor and religion received little or no attention. Most importantly, many editors in the South had been active in attempts to prevent violence and lynchings, and there was need for their reactions to this aspect of Southern society to be systematically organized and disseminated by means of a sustained flow of feature articles. Materials of all kinds on black social and economic life, on interracial efforts to alter the pattern of segregation, on the struggle for black citizenship rights, on equal pay for teachers and on black cultural achievements would be an essential output of such a service. There was optimism "that the proper handling of Negro news and local Negro social and economic life will be advantageous to them in both circulation and subsequently in advertising." Jennings Perry, of the Nashville *Tennessean*, had agreed to serve as chairman of a Southwide committee of sponsoring editors for the project, as well as to assist in setting up state conferences of editors concerned with the entire field of race relations.[25]

To assist in the formulation of a program, the Fund sought the advice of authorities in the fields of education and public relations, among them Dr. Robert Hutchins, Chancellor of the University of Chicago, and Edward L. Bernays, a leading New York public relations expert. Bernays advised carrying out a preliminary research survey as a guide to the actual setting up of a program and campaign.[26] He advised the Fund to decide upon a field of action it wished to emphasize, and determine in advance the geographical location for the survey and the later campaign. The Fund was also to select a specific object for its attention among social patterns in education, housing, recreation, health, or segregation laws. After completing the preliminary work, Bernays suggested, it would then be necessary to select contacts among the group of leaders or opinion molders of both races. Finally, the Fund should devise the pattern of interviewing and either train interviewers or hire professionals. After conducting the survey, it could make a careful analysis of the existing patterns of "maladjustment, accommodation and non-accommodation" within the area and between different social and economic groups. From this pattern of action and interaction, the Fund could then chart its own course.[27]

The premises of the program were clear; the Fund did not believe that tampering with traditional patterns of segregation in the South would be met by undivided, bitter opposition, or violence. Its own experience, values and knowledge of the South led the Fund to view the region's population as quite diverse in its attitudes. In 1947, a bi-racial group toured the South to test the attitudes of Southern whites toward segregation in transportation. The group discovered that passengers exhibited little concern when blacks and whites sat together. Trouble came from the bus drivers, who were "aggressively hostile." In addition, the Fund's own poll of student opinion in three Southern universities in Texas, Louisiana, and North Carolina, indicated that a large proportion, though not a majority, of white students favored the admission of black students. Providing data too limited for any conclusive opinions, the poll yet cast, in the Fund's view, reasonable doubt upon the validity of the prevailing concept concerning the reception by Southern whites of changes in the pattern of segregation. The Fund was eager to discover precisely what support segregation enjoyed among the population in given areas, and particularly to what degree segregation depended upon the duress of laws and ordinances, as distinct from race prejudice. The Fund was already convinced that the most outspoken champions of white supremacy and rigid segregation were Southern politicians who, it believed, were a generation behind the attitudes of their own constituents. It was important to the organization, therefore, that an accurate sounding of public opinion be made before proceeding on the basis of its own pre-conceptions.[28]

In the spring of 1948, the Fund conducted a series of opinion polls of Southern college and university faculties and administrators concerning their attitudes toward desegregation. Following the *Sipuel* decision of the U.S. Supreme Court, ordering the admission of blacks to the University of Oklahoma, four distinct approaches emerged to deal with the crisis facing Southern higher education. The *Patriot* asked members of the Southern Sociological Society to choose among them. Plan A presented the policy of the University of Delaware which had opened its graduate schools, without segregation, to blacks when desired courses were not offered by a state-supported Negro college. Plan B of the University of Arkansas Law School, would admit blacks but with segregation. Plan C resulted from a decision of the University of Oklahoma to establish a new three-teacher school of law for blacks only, which had until then not attracted a single student. Plan D was a proposal of the Southern Governors Conference to set up regional graduate schools, but including a few schools for blacks alone, thus perpetuating segregation The returns encouraged the Fund to continue with this method of sounding Southern public opinion. Of the 240 ballots mailed, it received 73 replies, a 30 per cent return. Fifty-two replies (71%) favored Plan A, the one most approximating desegregation; 18 (25%) favored Plan D, for regional schools; three replies (4%) found all plans unsatisfactory. For the most part respondents favored Plan A because it was "more democratic," or secondarily, "more economical," and "more efficient, practical or expedient."[29]

Another poll, on similar lines but with clearer choices, followed. The second poll, of the faculties of Southern state universities, also offered four choices: Plan A to drop segregation in existing professional and graduate schools and admit blacks; Plan B, to admit blacks while segregating them; Plan C, to set up new graduate schools for blacks; and Plan D, to establish regional graduate schools with segregation. Again, the number of respondents was far less than hoped for; only 371 returned ballots. Of these, 255 (69%) voted for Plan A, dropping segregation; 105 (28%) favored Plan D, segregated regional schools; and 11 (3%) favored Plans B and C. The percentage favoring segregated regional schools was highest in Alabama, Mississippi, Georgia and South Carolina. However, the indication that approximately 70 per cent voted to drop segregation, while only 28 per cent voted for the regional school plan, appeared to justify optimism about the degree of latent integrationist sentiment in the South. Together with the previous poll, it also provided the Southern Conference Educational Fund with new contacts among liberal whites in Southern universities.[30]

The polls encouraged the Fund to revive the idea of calling a Southwide conference on civil rights. A regional gathering, the group thought, would give a needed boost in morale to the many Southern integrationists who, fearing isolation or worse, hesitated to make their convictions known. It would also help inspire others to face "the most pressing moral issue confronting the South today." The Fund hoped that the conference would help build a core of public opinion in support of a favorable decision from the United States Supreme Court on the constitutionality of segregation, "a decision which sooner or later must come."[31]

NOTE

The editor of the Richmond *News-Leader* disputed the contention that a majority of faculty in polled universities favored elimination of segregation, declaring that "fewer than 400 replies were received from a potential of more than 4,000." Dombrowski, in reply, noted that the Fund had consulted

a leading social scientist of the South who told us that the number of persons participating in our poll compared to the total group under consideration probably compared favorably with the average poll. However, we have no quarrel with you on this point, for we remember what happened to the pollsters in the recent election. It probably is true that the scientific accuracy of all polls as index of the opinion of those not participating in the poll is open to doubt.

Nevertheless, Dombrowski contended that the *News-Leader* editorial questioning the Fund's evaluation failed to point out

the most significant fact about this survey, that a substantial group of college teachers, 265 in number, from 11 Southern States, have advocated under certain conditions the admission of Negroes to graduate and professional schools.... If faculty members of our Southern State universities had the authority the results of this poll give some reason to believe that such a change would be made now, rather than waiting until the United States Supreme Court ruled, as it surely will in time, that segregation *per se* is unconstitutional....[32]

Dombrowski, obviously irked by the editor's questioning of the Fund's data, wrote again to him on July 22, 1948, providing additional data. "...In this collection," he wrote

your readers may be interested in the results of a recent poll taken at the University of Louisville. Of the 119 teachers polled, 79 replies were received. Eighty-two per cent or eight out of 10 of the replies favored admitting Negroes to existing graduate and professional schools, if desired courses were not offered by state-supported institutions for Negroes. 72 per cent of the faculty members voted in favor of admitting Negroes without segregation to all undergraduate schools of the University of Louisville. 73 per cent were opposed to the Day Law, the Kentucky law requiring separate schools for whites and colored. 15 per cent said they favored the law, and 12 per cent did not reply to this question. The 82 per cent of the faculty members of the University of Louisville voting to accept negroes without segregation at the graduate level may be compared with the figure of 69 per cent of the 371 replies received to our poll among the Faculty members of the 11 state universities.[33]

THREE

Separate But Equal: A Southern Myth

Timed as a reply to the reappearance of the Ku Klux Klan, and to the challenge of the Dixiecrats and other throwbacks, the Declaratory Conference on Civil Rights attracted a good number of white and black Southern integrationists. It was difficult in 1948 for all but the most outspoken to take a public stand for civil rights in the South. Long-time supporters of the Fund and the Southern Conference for Human Welfare proved reluctant to attend such a conference fearing it would further heighten sectional passions and isolate them from their more timid followers.[1]

Despite these fears, 200 Southerners, including ministers, educators, students, lawyers, and writers, assembled in Richmond, Virginia, on November 20, 1948, to formulate a statement of principles, recommend action, and affix their signatures to a "Declaration of Civil Rights." Aubrey Williams, president of the Fund, in a gesture symbolic of the liberal South's historic roots, led forty of the group to Thomas Jefferson's mountain-top home at Monticello to announce adoption of the statement. Prefacing the declaration, Williams called it "a great beginning." He detected "a growing feeling, even among the 'die-hards,' of the inevitability of the end of racial discrimination," and concluded that President Truman's victory "in spite of his civil rights proposals has changed the climate of the South. We must grasp this opportunity." He urged Southerners, and other Americans, not to develop a feeling that time alone would solve the race problem, and he called for standing against segregation "fearlessly, without shading or compromise."[2]

The "Declaration of Civil Rights" noted that many Americans, particularly in the South, were "unashamedly advocating ideas of racism and white supremacy contrary to American democracy." In opposition to the premise that "truth and justice are not bounded or divided by parallels of latitude," the statement proclaimed "this is one country and one people, governed under one constitution." A distinct liability in a world in which the United

States was claiming leadership, ideas of racial antagonism were also an anachronism in a period of great change which demanded new conceptions of equality and freedom. Calling for freedom of expression, the right to vote, and equality of treatment in public institutions, services, and employment, the Declaration saw no cause for self-congratulation in the limited advances made in these areas. Rather it looked upon such steps "as an incentive to greater progress and not as an excuse for our failure to meet present obligations." It also pointed to the ill-effects of discrimination and segregation in "lower living standards for those who discriminate as well as for those who are victims of discrimination," stressing the fact that the average income in the South was 40 per cent lower than that elsewhere in the nation.

The Declaration emphasized the importance of voluntary action by individuals and groups in the South to bring about more rapid, peaceful change. As a way of combatting prejudice, it urged individuals to speak out in specific instances of discrimination, and "to cultivate the habit of thinking of all persons as individuals, rather than as members of a group." Voluntary associations, such as churches, professional, fraternal and educational groups, in addition to enlightening their members about present inequities and injustices, should "secure their consent and approval of changes in constitutions, by-laws and practices needed to establish these rights." As a necessary aid to such efforts, the Declaration called for repeal of existing segregation statutes and passage of Federal, state, and local legislation ' to serve as a shield to the civil rights of the citizens."[3]

The Conference and the Declaration had a symbolic importance, demonstrating the Fund's ability to draw together an interracial group of Southerners to take a public stand against long established institutions. They also stimulated the Fund to further challenge the system of segregation. What the Fund demonstrated in the pages of the *Southern Patriot* and in its activities was that segregation provided something more than just a means of maintaining social *distance* between white and black. Segregation was a system of social *domination* by white people, or at least some of them, over blacks. "Separate but equal" was not only a misnomer, but an ideological mask for real oppression. So deeply was the fiction of "separate but equal" imbedded in the Southern white mind that recognition of the contrast between concept and reality was an inescapable necessity for establishing an integrated society. The *Patriot* continued to detail the meaning of "separate but equal" by throwing its light on the appalling facts of health in the South.[4]

As in education, income, and general living standards, the South lagged behind the rest of the nation in its health facilities and health conditions. The Second World War revealed this clearly when, in the period February to August, 1943, the proportion of draftees rejected for service from the South came to 49.6 per cent, compared to a total of 35.6 per cent for non-Southerners. The Army rejection totals reflected the disparity between the South and the rest of the nation in terms of availability of physician and hospital care, which also manifested itself in the greater infant death rate in the South.

TABLE 3

Differences in Health Facilities and Effects Between
South and non-South, 1940

	South	Non-South
Physicians per 10,000 people	9.4	14.9
General Hospital beds per 1,000 people	2.2	3.9
Infant mortality rate per 1,000 births	48.6	40.6

Moreover, the comparisons between the South and other parts of the country were less dramatic than those within the region itself where there were stark contrasts between black and white health conditions.

Southern whites, in comparison to blacks, would expect to live longer and give birth to children with greater assurance that they would see the light of day and enjoy the privileges of their parents.(see Table 4)

TABLE 4

Some Health Statistic Comparisons Between
Races in the South, 1940

	Black (years)	White (years)	Black Percentage Compared to White
Life expectancy	53.8	64.9	21% lower
Infant deaths per 1,000 live births	72.9	43.2	69% higher
Maternal deaths per 1,000 live births	7.8	3.2	143% higher
Still births per 1,000 live births	58.1	27.6	100% higher

TABLE 5

Annual Income in Racial Percentage
Nationwide, 1947

	Below $1,000	$1,000-3,500	$3,500+
Whites	22%	51%	27%
Blacks	75%	21%	4%

Common disease rates revealed a similar contrast. The black death rate was fourteen times higher than the white from pellagra, eight times from syphilis, and three and one-half times from pneumonia and tuberculosis. These differentials were due not merely to greater poverty and consequent undernourishment, but to actual medical neglect and the absence of proper medical treatment and care for blacks in the South, as well as a woeful lack of training and practice for blacks in the medical field.

There was a serious shortage of hospital beds for the black population. In the fifteen states where segregation was mandatory, only Maryland and Missouri provided as many as two beds per thousand black population, less than half the accepted standard for whites. Many states provided less than one-third, and in wide-spread areas less than one tenth, the necessary beds. Claiming the necessity of two beds for every death from tuberculosis, the American Public Health Association estimated between 20-25,000 beds were needed for blacks, who were dying at a rate of 10-11,000 annually from the disease; less than 6,000 beds were available. Where hospital facilities were available, they were often of inferior quality; a private room was virtually unobtainable.[5]

The general poverty of black people largely accounted for their inability to purchase the proper health care. In 1947 the Bureau of Labor Statistics estimated $3500 as the required annual income for a decent living for a family of four. According to a survey in *Fortune* magazine in December, 1947, only four per cent of the black families in the nation, in comparison to 27 per cent of the white families were able to reach or surpass such a level.(See table 5)

Ninety-six per cent of America's black families, with substandard income, were not able to afford healthful diets, or housing conducive to good health, and could not afford to call a physician when sick. The lack of income was in large part attributable to both historic and current discrimination and segregation in employment and education. In 1940, 70 per cent of the black wage earners in the nation were unskilled; 24 per cent were skilled workers; and only six per cent were nonmanual workers. Medical training and practice for blacks explained much about the general health condition of the black population. Discrimination in the nation's medical schools was the rule. Of seventy-seven medical schools in the United States only two unqualifiedly admitted black applicants, and both were all-black institutions; Howard University Medical School in Washington, D.C., and Meharry Medical School

51

in Nashville, Tennessee. In 1948 only 85 black students were enrolled in 20 other Northern and Western schools, whose total enrollment was 20,000 students. The picture was similar for black nurses; less than three per cent of registered nurses were blacks, and of 1300 nursing schools, over 1200 were for "whites only." An investigation by the New York City Council revealed that between 1920 and 1945, a mere fifty blacks had graduated from the city's medical colleges, and during that period, never more than three were enrolled in any one school. There were no black medical students at Cornell, for example, from 1920 to 1942.

These figures contrasted with the demand for medical education by blacks. Howard University had 1,341 applications for admission in 1947, but had places for only 74; and at Meharry, where 800 candidates had applied, there was room for only 65. Even those admitted had to work to support families in desperate need, adding to the burdens. Withal, 140 blacks graduated each year. Upon leaving school their problem was to find a hospital in which to intern. There were only fourteen black hospitals approved for internship. Residencies were almost impossible to find, thus forcing the black physician to become a general practitioner rather than enter a field such as surgery where his talents could be better used. Moreover, once in practice, black physicians soon discovered that, in most of the South, there were no modern hospitals whose facilities they might use to treat their patients. Nor were blacks seriously, if at all, considered for hospital staff appointments. Failing access to hospitals, black physicians lost patients to white physicians, thus complicating their economic problem. The low income level of black patients intensified the economic burden, forcing many black physicians to leave the South, further depleting the medical resources available to their people.

A serious obstacle to improvement of the health of black people was the American Medical Association. Its Southern affiliates barred blacks from membership, creating special difficulties for black physicians attempting to keep up to date on medical developments. The *Patriot* reported that the Atlanta Medical Society refused to admit black physicians to hear discussions of current medical problems. Blacks were not on the policy-making boards of public health services which affected the entire black population. In voluntary health agencies, there were usually special Negro divisions handling black programs instead of an integrated approach to the health problems of the whole community. This resulted in the "second-hand approach," the feeling that blacks could get along with less than whites, and could use to advantage what had been found inadequate for the white community. Clinics for black patients often treated them with condescension, lack of sympathy, and with little respect or dignity. Here too, lack of professional opportunity combined with wage discrimination to keep blacks from full participation in the use and operation of health facilities. Civic groups applied a common solution to these pressing needs by putting their energies and finances into the effort to establish new separate hospitals for blacks. Such hospitals rarely met with easy success, and never provided the equipment and facilities equivalent to the already existing public institutions for whites. One such arrangement was the plan of Dr. Amos H. Carnegie, president of a black association, the National Hospital Foundation. Dr. Carnegie had announced his intention to raise funds for a 200-bed black hospital in Washington, D.C., raising two million dollars from private foundations to be matched by another two million dollars gathered by black churches. Explaining the reasoning behind his program, Dr. Carnegie expressed doubts about integration:

> Until the Negro race, fifteen million strong, has something to offer to this partnership, the idea of integration is merely empty talk. If one side does all the giving and the other side does all the receiving, it is not reciprocity. The one that does the giving will feel a sense of superiority and the other that does the receiving will feel a sense of inferiority.[6]

The *Patriot* took issue with Dr. Carnegie's statement, as well as his program. Holding segregation and equal treatment to be mutually incompatible, it wondered where Carnegie was to find the medical staffs comparable to those of existing white hospitals. "What is more important," stated the journal, "he denies the dignity and birthright of the people whose case he is pleading by urging them to secede from a social development in which they--his negatory remarks notwithstanding--have participated." Rather than "jerry-build 'separate but equal' hutches which besmirch the dignity of the builder and tenant alike, the *Patriot* preferred to call for integration and an end to Jim Crow in hospitals and professional schools and in all public health facilities. It supported a national health program to distribute the costs of health on a more equitable, long-term basis, as proposed in the Murray-Wagner-Dingell bill then pending in Congress. That bill sought to broaden social security benefits to include complete medical care.[7] The *Patriot* also endorsed a proposal of the National Congress of Parents and Teachers to establish a federally-supported program of local public health centers for basic services in the fields of disease-control, maternal-child health clinics, and preventive medicine.

Coincident with its criticism of segregated professional schools and public health facilities, the Fund lent its support to institutions breaking down color bars. When the University of Arkansas Medical School accepted a twenty-year old black student from Hot Springs as a member of its 1948-49 freshman class, the *Southern Patriot* hailed the move as a "democratic, forward-looking step."[8] Contrasting it with the dilatory tactics of the University of Oklahoma, the *Patriot* congratulated the University of Arkansas for voluntarily relaxing the color bar. Noting that financial difficulties had forced this change in policy, and the inability of Arkansas adequately to support one medical school, much less separate racial institutions, editor Dombrowski commented that, nevertheless, "in this confused world, to follow the course of reason, often is the mark of a courageous, as well as a reasonable man." He also wrote Dr. H. Clay Chenault, vice-president in charge of medical education of the University of Arkansas, inquiring if Chenault had applied to the Rockefeller Foundation for a grant. Dombrowski offered to make inquiries among other Southern educators, as well as Fund contacts in the North, on behalf of the University Medical School.[9] Among those he contacted was the Chicago philanthropist Marshall Field. Dombrowski asked Field's advice about enlisting the aid of both the Rockefeller and Carnegie Foundations to eliminate segregation in Southern graduate and professional schools. Both foundations were leading financial supporters of such institutions at the time. Dombrowski suggested two methods: either restricting grants to institutions which did not discriminate against, or segregate, its black students, or making "especially generous grants to institutions now moving in a more democratic direction." Referring to favorable responses of ten Southern educators to his idea of aiding the University of Arkansas Medical School, Dombrowski emphasized that this was "an indication of a liberal trend in Southern education which should be encouraged."[10]

The Fund's concern for improved health treatment for blacks intensified after an incident involving a young black college student injured in an auto accident in North Carolina. On December 1, 1950, Maltheus R. Avery entered Alamance General Hospital in critical condition with multiple fractures of the skull, face, arms and legs. The hospital shunted him off to Duke University Hospital in Durham. There, after some deliberation and despite the confirmed seriousness of Avery's condition, the doctors ordered

54

his removal, without treatment, to Lincoln Hospital, a black institution. Within an hour of his arrival there, Avery died. Shocked at this denial of elementary human treatment the Fund began a campaign to highlight this and other incidents resulting from segregated medical practices. In an editorial, the *Patriot* admitted that, while it had often heard of such incidents previously, it had tended to dismiss them upon hearing denials from medical authorities. Avery's case outraged it, however, and forced the paper to think of the incident's relation to routine Southern hospital and medical practices. Since decent provision for black patients had proved to be inadequate, and the complex machinery of a great medical center was geared to exclude blacks even in routine matters, how could "any human attention be given in time of emergency? No," the *Patriot* irately commented

> the deaths of the Matthew Averys, however shocking, should not be surprising.... They represent the blind, inhuman extreme of 'normal' segregation practices that are, beneath the surface, as blind and inhuman.[11]

For the next several years, the *Patriot* publicized similar incidents and encouraged as a remedy grass-roots action such as the Interracial Hospital Movement in Kentucky. In 1951 the group garnered over 10,000 signatures to a petition demanding equal hospital facilities for all. The Fund also sought to publicize the practice of segregated medicine by printing and distributing over 25,000 copies of a pamphlet, "The Untouchables," graced with the tense, evocative sketches of artist Ben Shahn. It also polled over 2,000 hospital administrators and 46,000 members of the American Medical Association in 19 Southern and border states and the District of Columbia to ascertain their attitudes on admitting black patients to hospitals and extending hospital courtesies to black physicians.[12]

The Fund requested administrators to choose from among three plans for hospital treatment of blacks and whites: to admit all without segregation; to admit all to the same hospital with segregation; or to maintain separate black and white hospitals. Also, it asked their opinion on the question of admitting blacks to county medical societies, and granting hospital privileges to black physicians. The returns showed an overwhelming preponderance, over sixty-five per cent, in favor of admitting black and white patients to the same hospitals, but with segregation. Seventeen per cent favored integration, eleven per cent wanted separate hospitals, and the rest a combination of plans.

The *Patriot* saw some hope in these replies. It held that those voting for common hospitals with segregation were approving a move away from "separate but equal" facilities, particularly in Mississippi and South Carolina where such separate institutions prevailed. Also, the replies on admission of black physicians to county medical societies and hospitals provided hope.[13] Seventy-one per cent favored admission of black physicians to county medical societies and another three per cent gave qualified approval, while sixty-three per cent favored granting hospital privileges, and another fourteen per cent lent qualified backing.

These results, stated the *Patriot*, ran counter to the general practice of the medical societies in the states involved. Florida alone of the Deep South states made full membership available to black physicians. Georgia had created a limited membership affording them only the privilege of attending scientific meetings. In Oklahoma, only one black physician was a member of the state medical society, while the New Mexico State Medical Society, according to its secretary, did not accept blacks. The North Carolina society had petitioned the AMA to recognize the Old North State Medical Society, a black group, as a separate unit, and Kentucky was working on a similar arrangement.[14]

While far less cheerful in its picture of Southern racial attitudes than the previous survey of educators' views, the hospital survey, in the view of the *Patriot*, was merely an "opening gun" in a long campaign to alter practices of segregation in Southern hospitals, providing a spring-board for further studies. James Dombrowski felt that the poll, and a later survey taken of hospital facilities available to blacks, established the Fund's reputation for "objective presentation of findings," and that "subsequent releases would not be subject to question on the ground of their accuracy."[15] In order to facilitate this work, and to guard against faulty data, the Fund set up a Medical Advisory Committee to guide and evaluate its efforts in the project. The committee included physicians and medical school faculty from most of the Southern states.[16]

It was obvious, as the *Patriot's* data indicated, that significant advances in the state of health among black people would only ensue from greater numbers of blacks entering the medical field as doctors, nurses, technicians and aides. These professionals could then serve their own communities since it was manifest that whites would not meet the needs of black people without a great change in white social values and economic interests. Failing radical social upheavals altering this picture in the foreseeable future, more blacks had to become medically skilled and employed. But only through a marked strengthening of the preparation of black students at the elementary, secondary, and college level, and the application of uniform standards of admission and performance for white and black in the public schools would improvements occur. The public school was the fulcrum both for better health conditions and improved education in the South and public education, declared the *Patriot*, "for moral and financial reasons, cannot advance without racial integration."[17]

NOTE

A survey of eighteen Southern states, including New Mexico, West Virginia, and District of Columbia, revealed that blacks had access to 32.4 per cent of existing bed space in 676 medical institutions. Administrators of 2,414 hospitals listed in the region were polled by the Fund. Of a total of 102,969 beds, blacks were admitted to 33,451. Eighty-two per cent of the institutions accepted black patients, but only 31 per cent permitted black doctors staff courtesies. Aubrey Williams reported these results to the Board of the Fund, but demurred from its seemingly brighter picture than previous Fund polls revealed. "While the number of beds allotted Negroes may seem to be in proportion to census figures," he cautioned

> it should be remembered that prejudice, not actual need, often determines this number. Too many times a deserving patient is turned away because the bed space available is not in the ward designated for his color. Furthermore, in several states, a single large hospital offers almost half the number of beds listed as available to Negroes. The inconvenience and health dangers to people in distant areas can be imagined.

A segregated quota basis for black admissions was followed by 406 institutions, and 125, with 23,062 beds, did not accept black patients at all. Nearly six per cent of the hospitals practiced segregation, but placed no limit on black patients. An unsegregated, unlimited policy prevailed at 68 institutions (10.5%). Federal establishments were not covered in the poll. Asked what racial policy best met the needs of patients, hospital administrators replied as follows: of 711 polled, 479 favored segregation; 127 favored admission without segregation; 76 favored separate Negro hospitals and 69 either did not answer or offered other proposals.[18]

FOUR

Regional Education:
A Broken Pillar of
Segregation

As a critical institutional support for segregation, the Southern educational system became a focus of the Fund's attention in 1949. Contrary to the Fund's desires, the predominant white Southern sentiment, as expressed in court decisions, actions of Southern power holders, and the views of the Southern press, continued to insist upon segregated education as a part of the "Southern way of life." Indeed, even the United States Supreme Court appeared less than enthusiastic about upsetting the segregated pattern of Southern life. In the *Gaines* decision in 1938, upholding the right of black student Lloyd L. Gaines to attend the University of Missouri Law School, Chief Justice Charles Evans Hughes asserted for the majority of the court that the

> admissibility of laws separating the races in the enjoyment of privileges afforded by the State rests wholly upon the equality of the privileges which the laws give to the separated groups within the State.

Remaining within the limits of the *Plessy v. Ferguson* "separate but equal" doctrine as applied to education, the *Gaines* decision did not question its logic and social out-look. Similarly, succeeding decisions, such as the *Sipuel v. Board of Regents of the University of Oklahoma* (1948), *McLaurin v. University of Oklahoma* (1950), and even the *Sweatt v. University of Texas* (1950) ruling, all of which had enlarged the *Gaines* ruling in application, did not unambiguously reveal the underlying intentions of the U.S. Supreme Court. In none of these decisions did the Court rule upon segregation *per se*.[1] Rather, the Court, while declaring racial discrimination unconstitutional, seemed to regard it as, at best, incidental rather than inherent to segregation.

59

Thus it implicitly accepted the Southern argument favoring segregation as a legitimate social institution not in conflict with constitutional equality. The reluctance of the Supreme Court to declare itself unequivocally about segregation encouraged advocates of segregation to formulate and implement policies further extending the practice in Southern life. One attempt, which eventually embroiled the Southern Conference Educational Fund, was in the field of higher education.

As early as 1939, following the *Gaines* decision, Southern educators were aware of an impending crisis. Before the Southern University Conference, President Harmon W. Caldwell of the University of Georgia outlined the options facing Southerners: desegregation, separate graduate schools, separate classes within state universities,or state support to private Negro colleges. He went on, however, to express a preference for yet another option, regional institutions supported by the states, though he doubted that the courts would accept them as substitutes for equal opportunity within the states.[2]

Two currents joined to revive and bring to fruition the regional concept in education: the pressure of war upon educational needs and resources, and the post-war racial crisis. By hastening the industrialization of the South the second World War stimulated education as a necessity for professional and technological progress. Southern colleges and universities, as well as other Southern institutions, proved inadequate for their tasks. The Southern states were too poor to meet their needs. The rise in population together with federal subsidies for veterans' education, and the consequent intensification of demand, revived the idea of pooling regional resources.

Precedents for regional institutions existed as early as 1929 and the formation of the Atlanta University System in 1929. Atlanta University henceforth assumed responsibility for graduate and professional work, while Spelman and Morehouse Colleges became undergraduate centers for black women and men, respectively. Similarly, in 1938, the University Center in Georgia, also in Atlanta, comprised the University of Georgia, Columbia Theological Seminary, Emory University, the Georgia Institute of Technology, Georgia State College, and Agnes Scott College. These institutions cooperated in several ventures, shared visiting lecturers and research grants, and developed a union library catalogue. Similar arrangements appeared in the forties in Virginia, with the Richmond Area University; the Duke University of North Carolina joint libraries and course arrangements; and in Nashville, where Vanderbilt University, George Peabody College for Teachers, and Scarritt College agreed to exchange course credits, forego duplication of courses, and enter into joint financial and library arrangements. In 1944 the Tennessee Valley Authority and the Universities of Alabama, Tennessee and Georgia, and later Kentucky, arranged for the cooperative training of students in public administration. In 1943 the American Council on Education formed the Committee of Southern Regional Studies and Education which emphasized interstate cooperation to promote resource-use education and the application of research results. The Committee also sponsored or assisted other agencies, states, and institutions in organizing regional conferences. The University of Kentucky, George Peabody College, the University of North Carolina, and the TVA contributed staff time to the Committee's work, as did the Universities of Virginia, Texas, and Arkansas, the Florida Department of Education, Alabama Polytechnic Institute, Southern University, Tuskegee Institute and the Columbia, South Carolina, school system. The Committee soon became a regional agency, and its executive secretary, John E. Ivey, Jr., a student of Howard W. Odum and a professor of sociology, emerged as a leader in further regional educational developments.[3]

In 1943 another cooperative agreement involved the University of West Virginia and the University of Virginia Medical College. Through state legislation, the two institutions contracted for the admission of West Virginia students to the Virginia Medical College, with expenses and tuition in excess of those of Virginia students to be paid by West Virginia. Thus, West Virginia avoided the expense of establishing her own four-year medical school, and Virginia gained additional funds and a greater choice of students. Prior to this contract, West Virginia had only a two-year medical school, and its students then had to transfer to other schools at their own expense.

This became the model for a program in veterinary medicine at the Alabama Polytechnic Institute, the only professional school of its kind in the southeastern region. Because of mounting demands for admission after World War II, the college restricted its admissions to Alabama residents, thus losing applicants from surrounding states. Also, because the state could not meet rising costs, the institute faced loss of accreditation. Other schools throughout the country faced similar situations and, at a conference in Chicago on July 29, 1946, veterinary school administrators suggested the use of interstate compacts as a remedy for states lacking schools. Dr. Redding S. Sugg, dean of the Alabama School of Veterinary Medicine, made such contracts with other Southern states in September, 1946, and during the next two years interest in the project grew elsewhere in the South. In 1948, this interest resulted in the conclusion of a contract on the West Virginia-Virginia model for veterinary medical education in the whole Southeast.[4]

Paralleling the educators' interest in regional contracts were the concerns of Southern politicians, especially the governors. Again, the *Gaines* decision declaring out-of-state study for blacks unequal to in-state study for whites, provided the stimulus, or rather, the irritant. The politicians' search for a device to meet professional and constitutional standards of quality and equal, though separate, black higher education was the subject of intense discussion at the Southern Governors Conference in the years after 1945.[5] At the 1945 conference, Governor Chauncey Sparks of Alabama suggested a "treaty arrangement between the states." In 1946, Sparks and Governor R. Gregg Cherry of North Carolina again raised the question, and noted that their states sent black medical students to Meharry Medical College in Nashville, with Alabama paying $300 a year per student. Florida Governor Millard Caldwell urged the states to follow the Alabama Polytechnic Institute model and select one institution or establish new schools with joint state support. They were to provide free access for specialization for their residents and guarantee "the best in educational facilities in the South at a minimum cost."[6]

A breakthrough occurred in 1947. Before the session of the Governors conference that year, Meharry Medical College faced the prospect of closing its doors over lack of funds. Private philanthropic grants and investments from the Rockefeller and Kellogg Foundations no longer provided enough to continue its operations. It was a golden opportunity, both for professionals seeking to further the cause of regional education and for politicians anxious to preserve segregation. Their common problems came squarely into focus. Preservation of an established medical school was obviously valuable to the South as a whole and this school, in particular, afforded segregationists the opportunity to maintain a "separate but equal" facility.

Meharry's crisis soon reached the ear of Governor James Nance McCord of Tennessee who, in addition to being a staunch segregationist, was also an admirer of Howard Odum's work on regionalism. Prepared by the discussions at previous governors' conferences, McCord proposed, in an address to the governors on October 20, 1947,[7] that Meharry be the first object of interstate support of higher education. Following McCord, Governor Caldwell presented Doak S.Campbell, president of Florida State University, for the purpose of putting before the conference an analysis and a proposal formalizing the regional concept in education. The discussion pivoted on whether a state ought "to provide or purchase those educational services that are necessary for the education of sufficient number of its citizens to maintain the agencies and services essential to the public welfare." The key phrase was "provide or purchase." It established the criterion for the public welfare according to which a state could either provide its own facilities and educational services or purchase them elsewhere and make them available to state citizens. Campbell pointed to several fields where cooperation might be possible, and he gave special notice to the deficiencies in higher education for blacks. The 'how' of such a program of cooperation he left to statecraft. Special legislation, involving in some instances changes in state constitutions, would be necessary and he advised that above all, "citizens of our several states will need to be made aware of the possible benefits to be derived."[8]

Governor Caldwell put Campbell's proposition in the form of a motion to accept the provision, either within or outside the states, of adequate facilities for higher education for both whites and blacks and urged the formation of a committee to study the question. Governors William Preston Lane of Maryland, Fielding Wright of Mississippi, and Strom Thurmond of South Carolina, seconded, and the conference adopted the motion. Caldwell then moved McCord's special application of the proposal to Meharry, a motion the governors also adopted. Thus, the desire to maintain segregation in higher education provided the impetus that solely educational demands had not in effecting a compact for regional educational services.[9]

On January 17 and 18, 1948, a committee of governors visited Meharry to inspect its facilities and investigate its financial condition. One observer of the visit noted that the governors were also "incidentally...catching a glimpse of the larger possibilities of regional cooperation in higher education." He reported that "the atmosphere during the latter part of the visit came near to that of 'a religious experience.'"[10] Though Meharry authorities offered to place its operation in the collective hands of the Southern states, the governors' committee avoided commitments. At the same time, the committee firmly denied that its intent was to evade recent Supreme Court decisions; rather its aim, a spokesman declared, was to "obtain the best possible educational facilities for white and Negro students."[11]

A special meeting of the Southern Governors Conference assembled at Wakulla Springs, near Tallahassee, Florida, on February 7, 1948, to consider the committee report and to take action. Despite some initial opposition, a drafting committee comprised of Governor Caldwell, Cecil Sims, well-known Nashville attorney and adviser to Governor McCord, and Eugene Cook, attorney-general of Georgia, drew up a compact and submitted it to the governors the next day. The compact was to take effect when the legislatures of six states had ratified it; the nine governors at the conference signed it and sent it on its way.

According to the terms of the compact, the participating states agreed to constitute themselves

> a geographical district or region... for regional education supported by public funds derived from taxation by the constituent States and derived from other sources for the establishment, acquisition, operation and maintenance of regional educational schools and institutions for the benefit of citizens of the respective States.

Although the original intention of the governors, manifested in their desire to support Meharry Medical College for the use of the region's black medical students, was to have the new Southern Regional Education Board own and operate its own institutions, the Regional Board did not do so in the first year of its existence. It preferred instead to rely upon "educational services" of a joint nature. The governors were to appoint themselves, *ex officio*, and three other citizens of their respective states, including one educator, to the Board.[12]

The Southern Regional Education Board had the power to set up a finance committee and an executive committee to submit plans and recommendations to the legislatures regarding maintenance, establishment, operation and acquisition of educational institutions, and also to take title to them in the name of the Regional Board. On March 4, 1948, an Interim Council began to hire a staff, solicit foundation funds, and make a survey of higher education in the region. The Council had Governor Caldwell as chairman, North Carolina State Superintendent of Public Instruction Dr. Clyde Erwin as vice chairman, and University of Maryland President Harry C. Byrd as secretary-treasurer. It also recommended that the governors appoint black representatives to the Council, and eventually it became a practice to appoint the president of the state Negro college to the Board.

Soon after the establishment of the Regional Board, state legislatures met to ratify the compact. On April 3, South Carolina did so; Mississippi followed on April 13, and Louisiana on July 6, 1948. Most state legislatures were not to meet until 1949 and the compact had to wait until then for its full ratification. Two states, Kentucky and West Virginia, expressing fear that the proposed Board might be "a tool to perpetuate racial segregation in institutions of higher learning," delayed action.[13] This sentiment, which was not limited to those two states, prompted the governors to bid for Congressional approval of the compact, a move designed to secure national endorsement of their efforts to preserve segregation.

Representative Sam Hobbs of Alabama introduced a resolution in the House of Representatives and, on February 16, 1948, House Joint Resolution 334 giving Congressional consent to the compact was hastily reported favorably by the House Committee on the Judiciary, without benefit of public hearings. The House adopted it by a vote of 236 to 45. On February 25, 1948, twenty-seven Southern senators introduced a parallel Senate Joint Resolution 191. By the time of the scheduled Senate hearings on March 12-13, however, opposition had begun to form. Appearing in support of the resolutions were a number of Congressmen, governors and educators, while the sole black person testifying in favor was an official of Meharry. Voicing opposition was an array of black organizations--the National Association of Colored Graduate Nurses, the National Medical Association, the NAACP, the National Dental Association, the National Negro Insurance Association, the Negro Newspaper Publishers' Association, the American Teachers Association, the National Alliance of Postal Employees, the Washington Bureau National Fraternal Council of Negro Churches of America, the Conference of Negro Land Grant Colleges--as well as the Civil Rights Division of the CIO, and the National Lawyers Guild.[14]

A leading Southern newspaper, the Richmond *Times-Dispatch*, editorialized against the regional compact. It regarded the Southern Governors Conference as primarily aiming to preserve Meharry as "a sort of Siberia of medical education to which Negroes applying to white medical schools might be sent," and of hoping that like arrangements would he made in other fields.[15] The alumni of Meharry, likewise, opposed Southern state support and ownership, and urged the use of other funds to aid the college, while the Pittsburgh *Courier*, a leading black newspaper, protested Meharry's use "as a cat's paw" to "aid damnable Southern desires to evade the law and the high court of our land."[16]

Despite Florida Senator Spessard B. Holland's adroit managing of the resolution through the Judiciary Committee with the aid of Senator Alexander Wiley of Wisconsin, the resolution met strong resistance. Senator Wayne Morse of Oregon led a vigorous opposition to it on the floor. On the first day of Senate deliberation John Sherman Cooper of Kentucky withdrew as a sponsor of the resolution, and on the final vote to recommit both Kentucky senators voted against the compact. On May 13, by a margin of one vote, 38-37, the Senate sent the resolution back to committee and killed it.[17]

Congressional approval of the compact was not essential to its operation. In the absence of express Congressional disapproval, the states by tradition held the power to make interstate compacts. Senator Morse stated as much in his argument against approving the Regional compact. He wondered, however, why the compact had been submitted to Congress at all, if not to secure Congress's endorsement of efforts to preserve segregation. The opponents of the resolution never argued that the compact itself was invalid, holding only that any steps which the agency took to preserve segregation would be unconstitutional.[18]

In the pages of the *Patriot*, the Southern Conference Educational Fund had alerted others to the implications of the regional scheme. Continuing their opposition, Fund officers unsuccessfully challenged Regional Board spokesmen to public debate.[19] James Dombrowski urged the widely-heard radio symposium, "Town Meeting of the Air," to schedule a program on the subject of regional schools "since Supreme Court decisions have made it front page news for over a year," and especially because of the unsuccessful efforts to get Congressional approval.[20] When an aide to President Truman, John R. Steelman, attended a meeting of the Southern Regional Education Board, Aubrey Williams, Fund president, protested. Williams informed Steelman that the regional school business was

> a shameless attempt to beat down the effort all people of good will are trying to advance, namely an end to discrimination in education and an immediate end to segregation in institutions at the college and graduate level.

While expressing his belief in Truman's sincerity, Williams felt that Steelman was associating himself with those who were foremost in attempting to defeat the President's own civil rights program. "The trouble is, John," he wrote, "you being as close to Truman as you are, it puts what practically amounts to an official White House approval on the whole business.. .."[21]

Williams also stirred up controversy with officials of the Southern Regional Education Board by delivering speeches attacking the concept of "gradualism" in Southern race relations and charging that the regional program of the Board was an obvious segregationist ploy. John E. Ivey, Jr., director of the

Board of Control of the Southern Regional Education Board, hotly denied Williams' contention and attempted to get him to agree "that building more hate among Negro leadership is not the antitoxin for hate among white leadership."[22] Williams refused to do so, proclaiming his disgust at "the milk and water stuff" of those who too timidly accepted the status quo and "are able to stomach the fight at half humane stages." He could not "stomach it." Nor could he bring himself to sit in on meetings and participate in statements about the need to respect "Southern Attitudes," and "Southern Traditions." "I just can't do it when I know that these 'Attitudes' and these 'Traditions' when translated into social and economic acts mean acts of denials, and positive insults in every relationship of life," he declared. Rebuffing Ivey's contention that he and the Fund were "under a cloud" as to the true nature of the Regional Board, Williams replied that, to the contrary, it was Ivey and his group who were in that position. For they had "the task of explaining to the Negro people of the South, and to all Southern people who abhor this sickness of a segregated society, how this proposal of yours is going to aid in curing it." Williams believed that Ivey's new board appears rather to set up a new and formerly non-existent barrier which will make the breaking down of the barrier of segregation at the State level more difficult." And, most seriously, this new obstruction was taking shape just at the time the efforts of black youth and their backers were beginning to break down older bars in graduate schools at the state level. The Southern Conference Educational Fund, he informed Ivey, was convinced that "segregation is wrong--period, Wrong--anywhere and anytime."

Williams found it difficult to believe that men such as Millard Caldwell, Herman Talmadge, Fielding Wright and Strom Thurmond, whose "attitudes...on the question of segregation are too well-known to leave the slightest doubt as to what they think," were working to abolish segregation now or at any future time. Rather, he thought, they were aiming at nullifying the decisions of the Supreme Court. Williams urged Ivey to consider that he, Ivey, was either working at cross purposes to his sponsors, and "thus engaging in a conscious deception," or, as Williams was quite willing to concede, Ivey was committed against segregation. If the latter was the case, Ivey's position was untenable, since he was in reality furthering efforts to maintain segregation through his work with the Regional Board.[23]

Ivey remained unconvinced, emphasizing that his Board was attempting to develop quality education "regardless of whether or not states have laws providing for segregation or non-segregation." He offered as evidence of its success the recent approval of the compact by the Kentucky legislature one year after it had abolished segregation at the University of Kentucky.[24] Ivey also rejected Williams' argument that faculty and administrators in Southern colleges were working either for or against segregation, that there could be no neutral or impartial position. He thought Williams' letter "reflects the purest type of stereotyped thinking. The Southern mind has so many stereotypes of the past that the people of the region are frequently unable to move to new levels of accomplishment." This defect in Williams' thought, Ivey concluded, demonstrated the existence of a communications gap which, if shared by others, was potentially dangerous to democracy because it was "based on complete distrust of one another or lack of interest in the facts about the situations under discussion...."[25]

To throw more public light upon the regional plan, the Southern Conference Educational Fund made arrangements for a Conference on Discrimination in Higher Education at Atlanta University in April, 1950. The feature of the conference was a panel on the regional plan with both supporters and opponents presenting their views. Among the participants were E. Franklin Frazier, noted black sociologist and a Fund member, President Benjamin E. Mays of Morehouse College, a vice-president of the Fund Fr. James M. Nabrit Jr., professor of law and secretary of Howard University, President A. D. Beitel of Talladega College, President F. D. Patterson of Tuskegee Institute, Aubrey Williams, and interested faculty, administrators and students of Southern colleges.[26]

The conference immediately aroused opposition both from segregationist sources and from an unexpected quarter, the voice of Southern "moderation," the Atlanta *Constitution*. In an editorial on February 26, 1950, the paper delivered a red-baiting attack upon the Fund, linking it to the Southern Conference for Human Welfare as an organization "taken over by the commies" soon after its auspicious beginnings. The *Constitution* claimed that the Southern Conference for Human Welfare, and by association, James Dombrowski and the Fund

> seemed to many to exist merely for the purpose of dividing and confusing Southerners who were trying to be progressive.... The meeting in Atlanta can have but one purpose--although the announced purpose will be that of democracy and human rights. The real purpose, we believe, is to stir up trouble, to agitate the race question, and to 'bait' the South.... A meeting on the subject announced needs to be held and discrimination must be removed.

It will, in our opinion, be removed more slowly because of the Dombrowski organization.[27]

Aubrey Williams wanted to sue the journal, and he was particularly upset by its attack upon Dombrowski. Writing to a number of Fund supporters, including Lucy Mason, Dr. Glen Rainey of Georgia Institute of Technology, and President A. D. Beitel of Talladego College, he viewed the attack as serious, forcing many who would otherwise join their efforts to back away and refrain from doing what they would like to--and feel it their duty to do." Williams further argued that we must fight this sort of thing."[28]

As planned, however, the conference opened in Atlanta, on April 8, 1950, with E. Franklin Frazier as keynoter. He made a sweeping attack not only upon discrimination, but also upon Negro education itself as a barrier to the intellectual development of black people. Frazier noted that Negro education "has never been taken seriously as a form of intellectual discipline or as a part of the stream of intellectual life of the country," and contrasted the atmosphere of Negro institutions to the "free and unrestricted intellectual atmosphere of northern universities." Throughout the world, he asserted, scholarship and learning have broken down the barriers of race and class, and even the European colonial powers made no such distinctions where the question of science and scholarship was concerned. "Neither England nor France ever instituted anything resembling what has come to be known as Negro education," Frazier asserted. "A Negro was a doctor or engineer or what have you, but never a Negro doctor or a Negro engineer. These are the peculiar products of that American invention known as 'Negro education.' Furthermore, he asserted, the United Negro College Fund, the single greatest source of funds for the more than thirty Negro colleges, offered no solution to the problems of higher education for blacks. "The sudden interest of certain white people in this futile gesture," Frazier declared, "should convince anyone that their support is based upon pure sentimentality or, at worst, a calculated design to maintain segregated education." Pointing to the Fund's poll of educators revealing that 70 per cent of those replying favored immediate admission of black students to colleges and universities without segregation, Frazier concluded that

evidently the so-called liberals who pretend to speak for the South (but who are unwilling to attack segregated education), do not express the growing liberal opinion; they are more likely endeavoring to forge public opinion according to their own prejudice concerning what they regard as the Negro's proper place in the South.[29]

Frazier's views, however, did not meet with unanimous approval. Presidents F. D. Patterson of Tuskegee Institute and Hollis Price of LeMoyne College spoke in favor of the regional plan. They praised its concept of concentrating limited resources in designated institutions, and the attempt to gather "superior faculty talent at a few points rather than competition and dilution of effort on a state by state basis." As college administrators facing a difficult financial situation, their support for the plan was understandable. Other speakers, including black educators and white supporters such as Aubrey Williams, strongly rebutted the Negro college presidents' position. They pointed to the inequity of compelling a black student, "solely because of his color, to travel outside of his home state to receive educational services which are available to a white student within the borders of his own state." Again they insisted that segregation, *per se*, could not possibly serve the purposes of education in a democratic society.[30]

Despite the totally divergent viewpoints, the continuing criticism of the regional compact helped to alter its character. In the fall of 1949, when the first regional education contracts went into effect, a black woman, Miss Esther McCready, applied for admission to the School of Nursing at the University of Maryland. Upon her rejection, she sued the University in Baltimore City Court. In its defense, the University presented the provision for nursing education in the regional contract providing state support for black students to attend Meharry Medical College. The court upheld the University, and Miss McCready took her case to the Maryland Court of Appeals. On April 14, 1950, at Annapolis, the Court of Appeals issued a writ of mandamus compelling Maryland to admit Miss McCready to the University School of Nursing. Judge Charles Markell, while declaring that the "terms and details of these agreements [the regional contracts] are not now material," rejected the University's plea on grounds that "no compact or contract can extend the territorial boundaries on the State of Maryland to Nashville."[31]

Prior to Miss McCready's appeal, the officials of the Southern Regional Education Board, fearing adverse judicial reaction to its operations, remonstrated with the governor of Maryland and other state officials. The Board officers urged them to withdraw the University's use of the regional contract in the courts on grounds that "the use of regional arrangements in this manner would endanger the future activities of the Board and throw it into racial politics."[32] When the Maryland authorities rejected the appeal, the Regional Board Executive Committee authorized its chairman and director to put the Board's position before the public and the court and, if necessary, to intervene in the suit.[33] After the full Board upheld this position, its lawyers entered the suit with an *amicus* brief declaring "it is not the purpose of the Board that the regional compact and the contracts for educational services thereunder shall serve any state as a legal defense for avoiding responsibilities established under the existing State and Federal laws and Court decisions."[34] Forced to disavow segregation as its primary purpose, the Southern Regional Education Board thereby assured its future as an instrument to upgrade regional education, but lost its effectiveness as an instrument for perpetuating segregation.[35]

Despite such partial victories for integration, the mood of a greater part of Southern white leadership and public opinion in the early fifties had little taste for basic changes in the prevailing pattern of white supremacy.[36] Indeed, it appeared that while some states moved to eliminate the poll tax and the "white" primary, more rigid barriers developed in social and economic fields, intensifying segregation. As historian Francis B. Simkins commented

> the manifold nature of the State--its flexibility in one direction matched and even undone by rigidity in others bolstered the exclusion of the Negro from citizenship and served to nail him ever tighter to his condition of second-class servitude.[37]

Unheedful of the cost of maintaining two school systems, both consequently inadequate, Southern state authorities attempted to breathe some life into their "separate but equal" rational by undertaking school building programs for blacks. A white Alabama educator, writing to the *Southern Patriot* about his travels to schools in the Black Belt and cities such as Mobile, found school principals "drowning in paper work and routine decisions." Asked why they did not request assistants, the principals told him sadly, "All the money's going to Negro schools." They apologized to him for paper strewn about the lawns, explaining that their maintenance crews had all been drafted for repair work at Negro schools. Confirming this, the correspondent noted that "new and rehabilitated Negro schools are popping up like mushrooms--in outlandish places. There won't be even chickens around to roost in them once the Supreme Court ruling takes effect." While it pained him to see the state "betting so much money on a dead horse," he considered it even more tragic that

> while nearly all the supervisory school officials see that integration is inevitable nobody has the guts to prepare the teachers for the change. None of the state teachers colleges offers a course in racial relations. The teachers' association ignores the problem. They're all in a dream world....[38]

The unrealistic nature of segregationist actions strengthened the belief of Fund members in the essential correctness of their own outlook. They remained convinced that "the South is a generation ahead of its leadership," and that a substantial group of Southern whites, and certainly a majority of blacks, held segregation to be wrong on moral, religious and economic grounds. The Fund did not ignore the "almost complete silence on the part of the white South on this basic issue," however. Rather, it denied that the silence contradicted its own basic premise, and held that "it merely reflects the presence of wide-spread fear and intimidation." Accordingly, the Fund's strategy was to bolster the courage of the isolated Southern integrationist by affording him the knowledge that he was not alone. It sought to accustom white Southerners to seeing prominent whites, as well as blacks, take a public stand against segregation, and to provide the less fearful with opportunities for group action so as to "reduce the possibility of reprisals." In this way, the Fund hoped that more white citizens of the South would speak and act on their basically decent convictions.[39]

In working out an approach to the perennial problems involved in black-white relations, the Fund had broken decisively with the mythology of the white South, the fervent and profoundly illusory belief that harmony, equity and justice characterized the relations between the races in the region.[40] Accordingly, the leaders of the Fund looked forward to the future, and to the year 1954, "the Year of the Child...and of Hope."[41]

FIVE

The Battle of
New Orleans:
'Red Menace'
in Dixie

On March 5, 1954, Aubrey Williams was at his farm in Mulberry, Alabama, punching holes in fire ant heaps and pouring in a killing portion of gasoline when an automobile bearing a United States marshal drove up. The marshal presented him with a subpoena from the U.S. Senate Internal Security Subcommittee requesting him to appear on March 19 at the Federal building in New Orleans. "Well, you could not have come with it at a more appropriate time," Williams remarked. "I'm spending the afternoon killing one of the worst pests to be found in the South—fire ants. This subpoena has to do with some other pests in the South that some of us have been trying to eliminate from Southern life . . . and this is their way of fighting back."

His Scotch-Irish temper aroused, Williams also felt a sense of relief at being touched by the witchhunt then sweeping the country. He thought the hearing would at least provide him the satisfaction of getting in some blows in his own behalf.[1] When he returned to Montgomery and the office of his close friend, Clifford Durr, Williams found that subpoenas had also been served on Durr's wife, Virginia, James Dombrowski, Myles Horton and a number of others who had been active in the Southern Conference for Human Welfare. The New Orleans hearing was one in a long string of investigations that characterized the "loyalty-security" mania of the forties and fifties. This was a tormented time for many American reformers and radicals. A new "red scare" known as McCarthyism bedeviled critics of the American social order. To be exact, the sensational antics of Wisconsin Senator Joseph D. McCarthy were an extension in scale of the loyalty program inaugurated by the Truman Administration. In true partisan spirit, however, McCarthy had turned the politics of "loyalty" and "security against the Democrats, and he had succeeded in identifying the Democratic party to many Americans as the "party of treason."McCarthy's revelations of "communism" in the Federal government intensified the fears of many already defensive white Southerners. To them the entire movement against segregation was irrefutable proof of "communist subversion" in the national capitol. A vague uneasiness, soon to take a more virulent form, swept over the South. This paranoiac disquiet found expression in the person of another Senator, James O. Eastland of Mississippi.

In 1941, Mississippi Governor Paul B. Johnson, Sr., had hoped to elevate Woods Eastland, a wealthy Delta planter and a power in state politics, to the Senate seat vacated on the death of "Pat" Harrison, but the elder Eastland was uninterested, and he passed the prize on to his son. Having left the state legislature in the early thirties, James Eastland, until his appointment, appeared to be at the end of his political career after serving as a pliant tool of then Governor, Theodore Bilbo. A nonentity in Washington in his first term, James Eastland was simply another Southern vote for low tariffs and the Administration's foreign policy, and against labor unions and many social reforms. One of his Senate colleagues, describing the impression Eastland made, recalled that "to make Jim believable, I had to keep reminding myself that his grandfather actually rode with General Bedford Forrest." James Eastland did not impress as a politician; in fact, "if you looked at him very long, he would begin to disappear, like the Cheshire cat."[2]

In the early fifties as a member of the Senate Internal Security Subcommittee, Eastland hobnobbed with his fellow committeeman, Joseph McCarthy, and, picking up some pointers, grabbed newspaper headlines by attacking the U.S. Supreme Court. The two saw a common danger in the Court's decisions in civil liberties and civil rights cases, professing to believe that incompetence or "some communist influence is working within the court."[3] And by Eastland's standards the least loyal member was Justice Hugo L. Black, a fellow Southerner.[4]

By 1954, McCarthy, though not at the peak of his influence, was still powerful. In March of that year he launched his investigations into the United States Army, an affair which saw him accuse the Army of being riddled with Communists up to the highest ranks. Many on capitol hill thought that McCarthy undermined the authority of the Executive, and brought the Congress dangerously close to open conflict with the President.

Though he made the Republican establishment uneasy, McCarthy gained the hearty approval of James Eastland, who adopted a similar approach toward the Supreme Court and toward those who supported the Court's civil rights decisions. Eastland's opportunity to strike at both came through an investigation of Aubrey Williams, James Dombrowski and other Southern liberals once associated with the New Deal. Among them, Clifford and Virginia Durr were ideal targets for Justice Hugo Black's wife was Mrs. Durr's sister.[5]

Eastland's New Orleans expedition had the advantage of prior support from Herman Talmadge, Georgia's arch-segregationist governor. Along with Governor James F. Byrnes of South Carolina in the early fifties, Talmadge had been foremost in the leadership of the white supremacist campaign to preserve the segregated structure of Southern life. Early in 1954, after the U.S. Supreme Court's first hearing of arguments on five cases dealing with public school segregation, Williams engaged Talmadge in a radio debate on the subject and in arguing against segregation incurred the Governor's wrath.

According to Williams, Talmadge persuaded Republican Senator William E. Jenner, chairman of the full Senate Internal Security Subcommittee, to conduct hearings of alleged subversives in the South, with Williams and the Southern Conference Educational Fund as prime objects.[6] When Jenner announced to the press, on January 31, his intention of investigating the alleged "communist activities" of the Fund, Williams sent him an angry telegram. Charging that the thinly disguised routine investigation was "as dishonest as it is contemptible," Williams stated that Jenner was well aware that "in the prevalent state of fear and hysteria the words you use stand for subversion and disloyalty to the United States." If Jenner had any evidence of his, or the Fund's, violation of laws, Williams demanded that he undertake the appropriate criminal procedures. They would then be able to confront their accusers on the basis of evidence rather than rumor. Williams concluded with a challenge to Jenner to "step from behind the shield of your Senatorial immunity and make your charges directly rather than by inference and innuendo.[7]

Despite his confidence in the ability of the Fund to demonstrate the hollowness of Jenner's charges, Williams believed them to be a serious blow. He immediately contacted his acquaintances in Congress to enlist their aid. "It is a simon-pure frame-up between Jenner and Southern Tories like Talmadge and Jimmy Byrnes (concerning whom I warned our great friend FDR time and again)," he wrote Representatives John McCormack, Clarence

Cannon, and Franklin D. Roosevelt, Jr. Williams urged them to do what they could to "bring out the undercover character of the real forces involved." While personally confident, Williams was apprehensive of the effect that Jenner's charges might have on the board of the Fund.[8] He emphasized the organization's work against segregation as the underlying reason for the Jenner attack, and, stressing the partisan issues involved, thought "it should be grist to the mills of Northern Democrats if they are alert to what is really being done."[9]

Highlander Folk School director Myles Horton, a Fund board member and fellow witness, sought Tennessee Senator Estes Kefauver's help in getting the investigation dropped or at least conducted in an ethical manner.[10] Montana's Democratic Senator James E. Murray, noting the Republican concern for their narrow margin of power in the House of Representatives and the proximity of elections, counseled that some pressure on Northern Republicans by Fund supporters might have a softening effect. He was optimistic that such pressure on urban Republicans would bring prompt results, perhaps "in the form of some sort of White House or top Republican statement praising the Southern Conference Educational Fund, Inc."[11]

Radio-TV broadcaster Martin Agronsky, sympathizing with the plight of Williams and the Fund saw the affair as "typical of Mr. Jenner and his operations and of the loyalty investigations." He urged Williams as his best recourse, to fight back hard instead of relying upon Congress. After a long talk with Senator McClellan, Agronsky, much to his disappointment, was convinced that "the Senate really was not interested in curbing any of its wayward members." McClellan put the responsibility on the Republicans and ultimately with the voters, "and that means tolerating a bad situation for a long time," he advised Williams.[12]

Sensing the need for wider support, Williams appealed to black leaders and in so doing emphasized the Fund's interracial character. He asked NAACP legislative director Clarence Mitchell to "do some heavy visiting for me." Williams attempted to gain Mitchell's confidence by informing him that, upon accepting the presidency of the Fund, he had made it understood that he "would not tolerate any communists or any of their activities." Jonathan Daniels, who did not often agree with Williams on "the social issue," thought this approach "wise."[13] Williams hoped that his old friend, Mrs. Mary McLeod Bethune, would use her column in the Chicago *Defender* to alert Northern blacks to Jenner's attack on white opponents of segregation.

When little public support was forthcoming, Williams privately expressed his resentment that many black leaders had not spoken up in the Fund's behalf. "John Wesley Dobbs, a Republican at that, is the only one outside of the Baltimore *Afro-American* which has done anything," he informed Mrs. Bethune. And he added that "I don't mind saying I am pretty burnt up about it." After writing to a black member of the Democratic National Committee and receiving no reply, Williams decried the failure of black leaders, including a number he regarded as good friends, to reciprocate for Fund support over the years.[14]

Toward the end of February, 1954, it was clear that the officers of the Fund would soon be called before the Senate committee. Accordingly, the Board met to decide on what approach to take in that eventuality. Williams had made up his mind to give an emphatic "no" to queries about his membership, past or present, in the Communist party. Simultaneously, he would refuse to inform "either by opinion or otherwise," on others, even if he had to "take refuge behind all of the amendments there are."[15] James Dombrowski, however, while affirming his non-Communist affiliations and agreeing to answer fully all questions about himself and the work of the Fund, thought it a violation of the First Amendment to answer even those questions under duress. A long debate ensued, and Morehouse College president Benjamin Mays objected to a Board proposal to support its officers whatever their answers. He wanted them fully to cooperate with the committee and answer its questions. Rebuffed in these demands, Mays resigned as vice-president of the Fund, stating that he no longer had "great enthusiasm" for it.[16]

Williams expressed sadness that Mays' action seemed to indicate a willingness to go along with present trends, taking lightly "those basic freedoms written into our Bill of Rights which have given meaning to our democratic birthright in this country." He believed that the reasons for upholding the First and Fifth Amendments were as good today as when they first were inserted into the Constitution. It was the "temper of the times" that permitted the ascription of guilt to persons who claimed immunity under them. The resulting fear of public obloquy by invoking constitutional privileges, Williams wrote Mays, would result in the surrender to a "would-he totalitarian dictator because our actions are determined more by fears of public opinion than by a love for basic freedoms." Noting that the Fund had maintained unaltered its leadership, program and ideals, and that Mays had stood by it despite segregationist pressure, Williams was a bit disheartened.

He was beginning to agree with Robert Hutchins that "the sum total of civil rights traditionally enjoyed by Americans is dwindling with such rapidity that when the Negro has acquired all the rights of the white man, he may not have acquired much after all."[17] Mays' resignation was the first break in the Fund's ranks, and one of the first casualties of the Senate committee's attack.[18]

The decision by the Fund's officers to answer questions about their political and social views was a departure, under pressure, from a consistent civil libertarian stand of total refusal to comply with the committee's requests. Claiming the Fifth Amendment, in public eyes, was tantamount to admission of "subversive" views and activities. To safe-guard whatever effectiveness the Fund retained, they accordingly declared their own non-Communist affiliation, while refusing to discuss other persons, either on the Fund board or one-time associates.[19]

Arriving in New Orleans, Williams expressed his pride in the Fund and his association with it over the years. He emphasized that it was solely for its work in behalf of racial justice and equality that it was now under attack. Because racial equality was, at least in theory, acceptable to most Americans, the Fund's opponents could discredit both the organization and its goals only by linking them to "Communism." The mere announcement of the investigation was sufficient for this connection to be made in newspaper headlines and, consequently, in the popular mind. "Objective" reporting thus accomplished the purpose of the investigators --to smear the Fund and other Southern liberals. Williams trusted that these techniques would soon be repudiated by Americans, much as some newspapers had recoiled from McCarthy.[20]

Congressional sniping and committee attacks were not new to Williams. As a New Deal official, he had come in for more than his share of detraction as one of the first targets of the Dies Committee in the thirties. Williams regarded Dies and his successors, including Eastland, as "implacable enemies of everything the New Deal stood for: that concept...which held that what happened to people was a primary concern of government" in its republican form.[21] The present hearing, he thought, was but a continuation of attacks begun twenty years before with the object of driving every reformer out of government. In the new witchhunt at New Orleans, "the liberals of the South were being 'fingered,'" Williams was convinced, and he had the queer feeling of what those at old Salem must have felt when they were 'fingered' as witches."[22]

Williams' fears were justified. The hearings opened in a small, stuffy room of the 1890-vintage Federal building in New Orleans. The room was jammed with newspapermen, photographers, TV apparatus, police and the "usual clusters of well-dressed men talking casually or earnestly in corners." At front center was the massive, high bench where the Senator and his counsel, Richard Arens, sat. Directly below them was a small table with a radio speaker. To the left of the table was a kitchen chair and a piped radio speaker for witnesses' counsel; with no table, the latter were to manage their briefs and papers as best they could. Williams saw this as an intentional arrangement to place the subpoenaed at a disadvantage in the eyes of the spectators and the press. Senator Eastland seemed unusually nervous as his broad face followed his hands sifting the papers in front of him. Moments before, fraternizing with friends, he seemed the picture of ease and amiability, but once he had taken his seat on the high bench and had grasped the gavel, he became the agitated presiding officer. Committee counsel Arens sat on Eastland's right, behind a stack of papers a foot high through which he and an aide continuously rummaged.[23]

The first witnesses were two officials of the New Orleans Young Men's Business Club, who greeted the Committee warmly. They commended the investigators, and promptly described their own anti-Communist activities as far back as the early forties. They noted that as early as 1946 their own organization had tagged the Southern Conference for Human Welfare with a "Communist-front" label. Moreover, they testified that the present Educational Fund was simply a continuation of the Southern Conference. It had the same officers and aims, and thus could also accurately be described as a "Communist front."[24]

These conclusions were based upon, if not entirely lifted from, a *Report on the Southern Conference for Human Welfare*, issued by the House Committee on Un-American Activities in 1947. Released just four days before a major address by Henry A. Wallace in Washington, D.C., sponsored by the Conference, this report had been an obvious attempt to discredit the Conference, and through it, Wallace. Columbia Law School Professor Walter Gellhorn had subjected the Report to a withering analysis in 1947 as a mixture of falsehoods, half-truths, and an occasional accuracy.[25] It was, as an historian of the House committee noted, "the weakest of the [committee's] reports...gotten together in great haste" to be released on the eve of Wallace's speech.[26]

After this prologue, Arens called James Dombrowski to the table, and Eastland promptly asked Dombrowski to deliver to the Committee the names of Fund members and financial contributors, as ordered in the subpoena. Dombrowski furnished him with the names of the officers of the Fund and its financial statement. The Fund was not a membership organization and had no other members aside from those on the Board of Directors, declared Dombrowski. Dissatisfied, Eastland pressed Dombrowski for the names of the financial contributors, some three thousand in all. After disputing the meaning of "all financial records," Dombrowski refused to hand over the names of contributors and, in addition, challenged the Committee's authority to inquire into his speech, ideas and associations. Citing the First Amendment and that part of the Fifth Amendment forbidding deprivation of property except by due process of law, Dombrowski made clear that he saw nothing wrong with taking the Fifth Amendment and that doing so did not, in his mind, imply guilt.[27] Aware that Dombrowski was relying primarily on the First Amendment, Eastland ordered him to answer the question relating to contributors, and specifically whether fellow witness Leo Sheiner was among them. By refusing to answer, Dombrowski had put himself in jeopardy of a contempt of Congress citation. After Dombrowski denied membership in the Communist party, Arens called two informers to the stand, professed ex-Communists John Butler and Paul Crouch.

A sixty year-old former miner from Bessemer, Alabama, Butler had at one time been expelled from his union on charges of embezzlement, and had also been run out of town for assaulting his foreman. With Eastland frequently interrupting to admonish Arens not to lead the witness on, Butler stated that he had once met Dombrowski "on a Sunday," in 1942. According to testimony the meeting had taken place at the Thomas Jefferson Hotel in Birmingham, in the room of Mine, Mill and Smelter Union official Alton Lawrence, who, Butler claimed, was a Communist. The purpose of the meeting was to "discuss the party line." Lawrence allegedly had stated in answer to Butler's request to identify Dombrowski that "he was upper ten. He was a big boy...we were the lower class."[28]

Paul Crouch then took the stand. He was a smoother performer, and in contrast to Butler, obviously had his heart in it. A former Communist party official in the South, Crouch had been engaged in Party activities since the early twenties and had been court-martialed in 1925 for Communist activities in the United States Army.[29] He confidently recounted his "association" with Dombrowski for more than a decade after 1937. They frequently met, he stated, at Highlander Folk School in Monteagle, Tennessee, which was operating "ostensibly as an independent labor school, but actually working in close cooperation with the Communist Party." Dombrowski was an instructor at the school. Though not "formally" a member of the Party, Dombrowski was "under Communist Party discipline," Crouch declared. Party official Charles N. Smolikoff, alias Charles Dorraine, *Daily Worker* correspondent in the South, knew him well and thought highly of his work. "Mr. Arens," Crouch interjected at this point, "I should add for the record that Mr. Dombrowski told me on several occasions that he preferred to be called left Socialist rather than a Communist and that he could serve the revolutionary movement better under the Socialist label than he could under the Communist label."[30]

Unable definitely to affirm or deny being in a Birmingham hotel some twelve years before, Dombrowski firmly rejected Butler's contentions. Moreover, Dombrowski declared, had anyone ever introduced him as a Communist, he would have set the person straight forthwith; but the incident was a fabrication pure and simple.[31] As a staff member at Highlander Folk School, Dombrowski had met hundreds of people over the years; though it was possible, he could not recall ever having met Crouch. As for Highlander's reputation, Dombrowski referred to the opinion of John Dewey. Dewey, he asserted, had the "highest praise" for Highlander Folk School as an educational and community center.[32]

Dombrowski, however, affirmed that he vaguely remembered meeting Crouch for the first and only time in 1946 at a public meeting held in Miami to protest a "white supremacy law" passed by the Florida legislature. Crouch had been in a group of people along with Charles Smolikoff, who had introduced himself as the CIO director for Miami. The meeting itself had been sponsored by several hundred prominent people, "headed by a minister that [sic] had no connection with the Communist movement." Pressed by Eastland as to how he could remember one meeting in Miami years ago, Dombrowski replied that he was doing so only with some difficulty. Crouch had been writing articles attacking Dombrowski and the Southern Conference for Human Welfare for eight years, describing places where the two had allegedly met. Though hesitatingly recalling such encounters, Dombrowski replied, "when I see him today I do vaguely remember him." At one point, when Crouch testified that he, Dombrowski, and Leo Sheiner had discussed the hideout of top Communist leaders who had evaded imprisonment after their Smith Act convictions, Dombrowski shot back, "That is a lie, sir."[33]

Taking another tack, Eastland began a series of questions relating to Dombrowski's signing a petition of amnesty for the eleven Communist party leaders currently imprisoned under the Smith Act. His judgment and motives called into question, Dombrowski stated he would sign any petition to keep civil liberties inviolate, and insisted that the Communists were convicted of teaching and advocating, not of attempting to overthrow the government. After thwarting Dombrowski's attempt to describe the activities of the Fund, Eastland pressed him again to deliver the names of the Fund's contributors. When Dombrowski refused to comply, Eastland ordered him removed by the marshal.

Arens then took the chair and proceeded to read into the record a lengthy statement, allegedly by top Comintern official Georgi Dimitrov, expounding on the uses of non- Communist "friends" and sympathizers who are "generally worth more than a dozen militant communists...who don't know any better than to get themselves beaten up by the police...." Since non-party members enjoyed greater freedom of action, their "dissimulated activity" awoke no resistance and was "much more effective than a frontal attack by the communists." Our friends, Arens quoted Dimitrov, "must confuse the adversary for us, carry out our main directives, mobilize in favor of our campaigns people who do not think as we do, and whom we could never reach...."[34] This confirmed the Committee's case against Dombrowski, at least to Arens' satisfaction.

Eastland and his counsel next turned to Mrs. Virginia Durr, one-time officer in the Southern Conference for Human Welfare. Mrs. Durr proved to be the most difficult of victims, preferring not to reply to the Committee's interrogation. When she had taken her seat, her lawyer attempted to read a statement of defiance, stating that Mrs. Durr refused to answer any questions on grounds that the Committee had no valid authority to probe her political beliefs and associations. Her statement concluded with a declaration of "total and utter contempt of this Committee." The only remarks she made were to deny charges of being a Communist or "under Communist discipline."[35]

Mrs. Durr's performance was meat for the press, and in part what Eastland had set out to achieve. The Washington *Daily News*, on March 19, front-paged in a double headline, JUSTICE BLACK'S KIN DENIES RED CHARGE. Datelined New Orleans, the story stated that Mrs. Durr, sister-in-law of Justice Black, "denied today that she was a Communist or was ever under Communist discipline, but two former Communists accused her of 'plotting with the Reds.'" That same afternoon, the Washington *Star* announced, EX-COMMUNIST NAMES SISTER-IN-LAW OF BLACK AS PARTY AIDE. The New York *Herald Tribune*, the Baltimore *Sun*, and the Philadelphia *Inquirer* followed suit, as did the New York *Times*, which carried a story headlined BLACK'S RELATIVE IS LINKED TO REDS, and subtitled, JUSTICE'S SISTER-IN-LAW AND HUSBAND DENY CHARGE AT HEARING.[36] All these stories relied upon the testimony of Crouch and Butler, both of whom admitted to doubts that Mrs. Durr was a member of the Communist Party, but insisted she was "under Communist discipline." Crouch defined the meaning of this phrase as

> various strata of important people at high levels who accept Party discipline, who work with the Communist Party, who cooperate consciously in its activities for a limited or wide range of purposes, who are so important to the Communist movement that in some cases ...and especially the people who are connected with the Soviet espionage apparatus...they don't even pay dues to anyone, but simply are recognized...[37]

This vague, catch-all "definition" was the basis of the testimony against all of the witnesses.[38]

The fireworks continued after Highlander director Myles Morton took the witness chair. When he attempted to elucidate his thoughts and activities, but refused to name others involved in Highlander affairs, he was summarily ejected from the hearing room. In an executive session prior to the public hearing that day, Horton had ruffled Arens and Eastland by refusing to cooperate, and his interrogators, in turn, vented their displeasure by thus evicting him from the hearing.[39]

The star witness, because of his prestige and association with the New Deal, was Aubrey Williams. Though Eastland allowed Williams the opportunity not given to previous witnesses of cross-examining Crouch and Butler, he too was the object of assaults on his character and past associations. The old rumors, hearsay, and outright fabrications concerning the New Deal relief program and the National Youth Administration, which had first been aired in the thirties before the Dies Committee were again put on display. Only intermittently was Williams able to describe the Fund's work against segregation and Jim Crow before being compelled to spend the rest of the time, to little avail, refuting allegations of Communist associations and sympathies. Both Crouch and Butler, the Committee "authorities" on Communism, interrupted his testimony, on Eastland's request, to place him at certain meetings, even as a New Deal official, with top leaders of the Communist party in the South. At one point, Williams challenged Butler to remove himself from Committee immunity and make the same charges before the press, whereupon Williams threatened to sue him. Eastland, however, refused to permit Butler to be cornered.[40]

Despite the weakness of its case, the subcommittee succeeded in linking the Southern Conference Educational Fund to "Communism." The hearings, nevertheless, were a distinct disappointment to its sponsors as far as press and public reaction was concerned. Even Eastland admitted to Montgomery *Advertiser* reporter Fred Anderson his own disbelief that "either of the Durrs or Aubrey Williams are Communists," though he regarded them as "dupes" of the Communist "conspiracy." Richard Arens asked newspapermen their opinion of the Committee's case. They informed him that it was overwhelmingly hearsay evidence inadmissable in a court of law; nor were they impressed by Butler and Crouch as witnesses. Reportedly, Arens replied that "it would be lovely if we could offer a witness against these people that would be the kind of witness we want--such as Sunday School teachers or clean-cut FBI boys. But we have to take what we can get to make people understand what these people are."[41] The Montgomery *Advertiser* told of a press poll taken of the nine reporters attending the hearings, each queried as to "who of the principals represents the greatest threat to American ideals." There were four votes for Senator Eastland, two for Paul Crouch, one for Richard Arens, and one each for James Dombrowski and another witness.[42]

Aubrey Williams later observed that the reporters' sympathies for the witnesses, and the rather favorable newspaper coverage of the hearings in the South resulted from his, Dombrowski's and Virginia Durr's choosing to answer the lead question concerning Communist party membership, and standing upon First Amendment grounds to refuse further inquiries. The Committee had apparently counted upon their taking the much maligned Fifth Amendment. The First Amendment had no self-incrimination safeguard for the respondents against Congressional contempt citations, and thus seemed the more courageous and principled position for those genuinely "innocent" of Communist connections. By answering forthrightly, they "killed the show, before it had started" for the Committee.[43]

Another factor that discouraged further hearings by Eastland in the South at that time was the competition of his colleague, Senator McCarthy. McCarthy had just aroused a flurry of criticism from Secretary of Defense Charles Wilson over the Senator's charges of Communism in the U.S. Army. He had even earned a veiled rebuke from President Eisenhower for his unscrupulous methods and groundless charges.[44] Eastland's tepid performance in Dixie was no match for this in national headlines.

A coda of pathetic humor followed the New Orleans affair. So odious had the role of government informer become that even the Republican Administration, which had much to gain politically from testimony against former Democratic officeholders, began to question the credibility of the professional tattlers. Paul Crouch, one of the more prominent in the Justice Department's troupe of paid informers, had broadened his field of operations and, reportedly, had loaned his services to Senator McCarthy. McCarthy had included Crouch's revelations among his reasons for investigating the U.S. Army's Fort Monmouth installation, a decision that led to Administration charges that McCarthy was undermining the authority of the Executive and dividing the Republican party. Accused of giving conflicting testimony against various individuals, Crouch himself became the subject of an investigation by Attorney General Herbert Brownell and his deputy, William P. Rogers, in June, 1954.[45]

A Justice Department brief against Crouch revealed discrepancies in his testimony at various hearings as well as outright fabrications concerning his activities in Florida, Texas and elsewhere. A Federal judge in Texas, to whom Crouch had supposedly recanted his Communist ties in 1946, swore that he had never known Crouch and that no recantation had ever been made in his presence. A search of Crouch's testimony revealed that he had once stated he had broken absolutely with the Communist party in 1942. Yet elsewhere he had discussed dropping in at Party headquarters and other Communist offices in New York in 1946 on social visits, and, in 1947, had received a membership book. He testified, and later denied, that he had received secret military information for the Soviet Union; and that he was state publicity director for the CIO in Florida in 1947, despite a sworn affidavit by the Florida CIO director that no such position existed since his coming to the state in 1946. Crouch had charged that the wife of Leon Keyserling, former economic adviser to President Truman, was a Communist, although an investigation ultimately exonerated her of the charge. He also testified that there were over a thousand Communists in the U.S. armed services, with the only "evidence" being hearsay that Crouch had picked up in Moscow in 1920.[46]

Following the release of this report, Crouch publicly accused Brownell and FBI director J. Edgar Hoover of being "subversives" implicated in the "worldwide Communist conspiracy," and he demanded a Congressional investigation of them. In the ensuing uproar, the Justice Department faced a challenge to its entire practice of using paid informers before Congressional committees. The Department soon removed Crouch from its payroll and spirited him away to the Hawaiian Islands to keep him out of reach of the courts and the persons he had pilloried.[47]

In an affidavit to Aubrey Williams, union official Alton Lawrence repudiated John Butler's testimony that Lawrence met Dombrowski in a Birmingham hotel, and also that he introduced Butler to Williams in the early forties. Lawrence charged that Butler's testimony incorrectly placed him in Bessemer, Alabama, in early 1941. He declared that he had not arrived there until after December 1, 1941; that another man reported to have been present at the meetings, Mike Ross, did not move to Bessemer until 1943; and that Lawrence had never met Aubrey Williams until sometime after 1946.[48]

The Eastland Committee's red-baiting, inept though it was, constituted a severe blow to white people who supported the black struggle for equality in the South. Since the end of Reconstruction, the conservative South had always set great store by the thesis that all Southern white people thought alike on "the Negro question." Williams had faced attacks for his maverick views for many years, most bitterly during the debate over his confirmation as REA Administrator in 1945. Mississippi Senator Theodore Bilbo, Eastland's colleague, had upbraided Williams for his views at the time, commenting that "you should know better. Henry Wallace is a Northerner, you were born and reared a Southerner."[49] When Williams confirmed his part in the drafting of President Roosevelt's Executive order creating the Fair Employment Practices Commission in 1942, Senator Bankhead of Alabama went over to the opposition and helped to kill Williams' nomination.[50] While most Southerners were accustomed to blacks publicly claiming their rights, they often viewed white men who agreed with blacks in a different light, commonly as traitors to their kind.[51] By any standards, the group of white Southerners gathered together in the Fund were an uncommon lot. Aubrey Williams, the president of the Fund, was of old Scotch-Irish stock whose family had come to Alabama before the American Revolution, having been planters in South Carolina before then. Born in 1890, Williams had gone to work in Birmingham at the age of nine, and through hard work and some luck had received a scholarship to attend church-supported Maryville College in Tennessee. When World War I broke out, he volunteered in the French Foreign Legion; and on his return to the United States after the war,

Williams tried his hand at the ministry, preaching in a small Presbyterian church in Cincinnati. He soon incurred the displeasure of his superiors with his unorthodox sermons and religious classes and had to leave the ministry. Williams then turned to social work, and in the decade 1922-32 he worked for the Wisconsin Association of Social Workers to reform conditions in penal institutions and reformatories. In association with John R. Commons, Williams worked to improve state institutions for children, and obtain more rigorous state regulatory laws for state institutions generally.[52]

When the depression struck, Williams entered the employ of a private agency in Chicago, the American Public Welfare Association, through which President Herbert Hoover had attempted to coordinate relief activities of private charities across the country. It was during his service with this agency that Williams came to the attention of Harry Hopkins who, in 1933, called him to Washington to aid in the Federal Emergency Relief Administration. As Hopkins' trouble-shooter, Williams gained an intimate knowledge of the effects of the depression, particularly in the South and West. He made bitter enemies, as well as fast friends, among politicians, local officials, social workers and ordinary working people with his blunt, even-handed approach to their problems.

Most significantly for his later career, Williams developed an awareness of the problems unique to black people. Though born in the South, he had not given special attention or thought to blacks, even in his social work years in Wisconsin. As an insider in the Federal government and with responsibility for administering aid to states and localities, he could not avoid developing a deep appreciation of the enormous obstacles facing blacks, in both North and South. It was in his work with FERA and WPA, from 1933 to 1935, that he became "fully conscious and committed to the cause of the Negro."[53] Two black WPA advisers, Arnold Hill and Forrest Washington, kept him closely informed about the special problems of blacks in employment, wages and hours, and housing. Field workers in the WPA and later the National Youth Administration, kept up a stream of information, requests, pleas and warnings about discrimination on government projects. Williams discovered this discrimination himself while on tour, finding that it was one thing to make policy in Washington and quite another to carry it out on the state and local level. Often he overrode local administrators who persisted in discriminating against blacks, only to find them prevailing as soon as he had returned to Washington. He also learned how to carry on political horse-trading, providing more jobs for some politicos in return for guarantees of equal treatment of blacks. Williams often lunched with Walter White of the NAACP, who helped to shape his approach to black problems, and he began receiving invitations to speak before interracial organizations, such as the 1934 national NAACP convention in Philadelphia. These associations continued and deepened during Williams' tenure as head of the NYA, where he came to know "the one and only Mary McLeod Bethune."[54]

His World War II experience furthered Williams' understanding of the entrenched practices of discrimination against blacks in training and employment. He fought long and hard to gain entrance for blacks into war industry, where he met bitter opposition primarily from white controlled labor unions. His difficulties led him to seek the President's intervention to open the gates of industry to black workers. He thought it "a standing mockery" that the national vocational board in the Department of Labor never made a serious effort to secure apprenticeships for blacks to attain skills. He knew of no Secretary of Labor who had ever called this state of affairs to the attention of the nation or exhorted himself to bear down upon labor unions to open apprenticeship opportunities for blacks. Years before black workers themselves made this a matter of national concern, Williams thought that "until someone makes it their business to specifically get into this very important aspect of the Negro youth's problems, the white Unions and their leaders will succeed in keeping things as they are."[55]

Williams persuaded Mrs. Roosevelt to call a White House conference of those responsible for the letting of war production contracts, including the Secretaries of the Army, Navy, War, and other Administration officials. The attitudes voiced at that gathering surprised Williams. Former Farm Security Administrator Will Alexander, who was then a coordinator of youth employment and who, Williams thought, "always had one eye on the power structure," opposed any compulsory hiring and insisted on a policy of persuasion alone to end inequities. Secretary of War Henry Stimson sharply rebutted Alexander, contending that, on a voluntary basis, compliance would only be spotty; only an executive order making mandatory the hiring of qualified blacks would work. Sidney Hillman, CIO vice-president, agreed with Alexander and opposed Stimson's suggestion. The group as a whole ultimately concluded that the President should follow Stimson's suggestion.[56]

Shortly after this conference, when A. Philip Randolph announced plans for a march on Washington as pressure upon Roosevelt for concrete action on employment of blacks in the war industry, the President sent Williams and Mrs. Roosevelt to convince Randolph to ease his demands. After conferring with Stimson's assistant, Mrs. Anna Rosenberg, Mayor Fiorello LaGuardia, Walter White and Randolph, Williams and Mrs. Roosevelt urged the President to meet with Randolph at the White House. That meeting proved to be crucial, for Randolph, in a statement "as moving as any spoken words I have ever heard," recalled Williams, delivered an irrefutable argument that finally resulted in the President's agreement to draw up an executive order establishing a Fair Employment Practices Commission.[57]

His outspoken support of blacks led to Williams' ultimate departure from Washington. In 1943 the Anti-New Deal Congressional coalition cut appropriations of the National Youth Administration and forced its termination. Fresh from this victory, the same coalition proceeded to harass Williams and finally ended his official career by defeating his nomination to the REA post in 1945.

For a brief time, Williams harbored political ambitions in the belief that great changes were imminent in the South.[58] He found work with the National Farmers Union in Alabama and toured small rural towns to increase its membership. It was a logical pursuit in view of Williams' fondness for the American small farmers. He had endorsed their efforts to organize farm cooperatives in the twenties and thirties. He had also developed an abiding contempt for American business values which, he believed, overshadowed those of community, cooperation, and Christian charity much to the detriment of the nation as a whole.[59]

Williams had strong, though ambivalent, feelings about the poor white Southerners. In his eyes, they were the same people who "crossed the mountains and built democratic societies in the midwest with nice white villages, comfort, civilization and schooling." Victims of misfortune, they had settled in the poorer lands of the continent and had to compete with a plantation system built upon slave labor which finally crushed their spirit and corrupted their values. The Civil War ruined them, and the late industrialization of the South with its company towns, mill villages, anti-unionism and Negro-hatred, made the poor white "a very confused and deluded man." As a result, he thought they were "the likeliest material in the country for the lumpen proletariat, the mass base for a racist fascist movement." Having spread throughout the country in the millions, the poor Southern white man had also taken "his virus with him and has infected millions more with it." Williams was convinced that "he is a very dangerous man, and he must be cured, and during the process of cure he must be guarded from destroying others...."[60]

Williams returned to Alabama in 1945, after persuading Chicago department store owner Marshall Field and banker James P. Warburg to furnish him the capital to buy a rural publication, the *Southern Farm and Home*. He soon made it one of the most successful farm journals in the country, running its circulation up to a million. It was also unique among farm publications in that it challenged the fertilizer and implement interests, provided news about the problems of black people, and championed the United Nations. For these convictions, the journal lost much-needed national advertising, but still managed to maintain its circulation.[61]

Williams also undertook to build homes for middle-class Birmingham blacks. Upon inquiry of the Federal Housing Administration in 1947, he discovered that under the Federal Housing Act 29,000 homes had been constructed for whites in Alabama, but only 61 had been built for blacks. Sensing the great need and also the potentially profitable market, he prevailed upon Northern friends to advance him the capital to buy lots and begin construction. In the process, he discovered that banks, construction companies, and the FHA itself discriminated against him as a "poor credit risk." His success was outstanding, however, and encouraged local real estate interests to follow suit.[62]

Though socially ostracized by whites in Alabama, he did earn a grudging admiration from some. A Montgomery editor described him as "one of the few authentic radicals we have known who is not a solemn, humorless ass." He is "genial, genteel, a thoroughly companionable man who laughs all the way down to his transverse colon," the editor admitted. In view of his distaste for business values, Williams' ventures, ironically, made him moderately well-to-do, and he once mused that "making money is the easiest thing I ever tried to do."[63] Tall, gaunt, slow and laconic in speech, and graced with a ready wit, he often struck people as resembling Abraham Lincoln.

On good terms with the black community in the South, Williams was often critical of black leaders who shied away from the desegregation movement, and he complained frequently about Negro college presidents who kept their campuses off-limits to speakers opposing Jim Crow. The hostility of Southern whites and his enforced isolation notwithstanding, he remained soberly optimistic about the eventual vindication of his beliefs. He was an inspiration to like-minded whites in the South.

Associated with Williams in the Fund was James Dombrowski. Born in Florida in 1897, Dombrowski was the son of a prosperous Tampa jeweler.

His rather placid youth sharply jolted by the World War One, Dombrowski served as a non-combatant in the ambulance service, as did many young Americans who later became active in reform movements. Though maintaining from his youth a taste for the good life, Dombrowski turned toward the ministry after the war in search of answers that his received attitudes and values could not provide. Following his graduation *cum laude* from Emory University in Atlanta in 1923, Dombrowski wandered through academia, spending a year in Berkeley where he was deeply impressed by Methodist social gospeler Harry Ward's lectures on radicalism. Attracted to philosopher Alfred North Whitehead's classes, he spent another year at Harvard, and then went to Union Theological Seminary to study with Ward and with Reinhold Niebuhr. He eventually received a joint doctorate from Union and Columbia University with a dissertation, published in 1936, *The Early Days of Christian Socialism in America.*

Dombrowski's academic career mirrored his evolution from Methodism to Christian Socialism, which he retained throughout his life. For Ward's course on social ethics, he visited Elizabethton, Tennessee, to get a first-hand look at the bitter 1929 textile strikes. In 1932 he participated in the formation of the Highlander Folk School, and he remained its staff director until 1942 when he became an officer of the Southern Conference for Human Welfare. For thirty years he devoted himself to the gradual, peaceful change of Southern society, and under his influence a number of white and black clergymen of repute joined the Southern Conference Educational Fund.[64]

Quiet and dignified, with large, kindly eyes and a thin line of a mustache curving over his lips, Dombrowski, because of his family name, was often mistaken for a Bolshevik although his family was in a long line of American merchants and traders.[65] Dombrowski's work was notable for an absence of sensationalism, and an emphasis on solid, factual presentations of Southern social conditions. Often lending his name to petitions in behalf of peace, civil liberties and civil rights, his independence and magnanimity were taken as evidence of Communist ties by critics such as Eastland. Careful and meticulous, Dombrowski rarely made a move without the full approval and understanding of the board of the Fund.[66] "His honesty and integrity," Williams once remarked, "is so simon pure that it gets to be a bore at times."

Both men can best be understood as representative American liberals who insisted on taking the ideals of free speech and association, equality of opportunity, and a foreign policy of peace and international cooperation literally and without qualification. They were among those who made common cause with radicals in the thirties and forties in numerous popular-front organizations, and they suffered for continuing to do so when other reformers and former associates had retreated into a self-defeating anti-Communism after World War II. While it was no longer fashionable after 1945 because of the Cold War and general anti-Communist attitude in America, the popular front approach continued to be viable for some southern liberals in the struggle against segregation and white supremacy in the South. Much to their dismay, Dombrowski, Williams and the Fund became whipping boys in the domestic cold war, symbols of a political culture lag in the eyes of critics and detractors.

The Eastland hearing drastically altered the political climate for the Fund. The immediate reaction to the hearing, however, was gratifying for Fund supporters. Over two hundred blacks in the South, and a number of prominent whites, protested to Senate Judiciary Committee chairman Senator William Langer. They charged that the hearing had more of the characteristics of an inquisition than a legitimate, fact-finding legislative function of Congress." They strongly urged him to permit no more such inquisitions, especially the one-man variety by "a man from Mississippi, known to have spoken disparagingly of the Negro who fought and died for their country and ours." Among the petitioners were Mrs. Eleanor Roosevelt, Mrs. Mary McLeod Bethune, Reinhold Niebuhr, Oklahoma publisher and NAACP leader Roscoe Dunjee, Ben Shahn, and Dr. Herman Long, a leading black clergyman and faculty member at Fisk University.[67] Fund supporters rallied to the organization, many taking a more active role in its affairs, and over one hundred others gathered together as an advisory committee to further its work in the South.[68] Financial contributions to the Fund picked up considerably, and actually showed an increase over the previous year.[69]

Disturbed at the treatment Williams had received at Eastland's hands, some of his friends on Capitol Hill encouraged him by their responses. They informed him that they were attempting to work out "fair and effective rules of procedure" for Congressional committees.[70] Senate Democratic leader Lyndon B. Johnson, who had been Texas director for the NYA under Williams, "took an hour and went into everything with thoroughness."[71] Little of substance materialized from these sentiments, however. It soon became clear that Congressional Democrats were as unwilling to take effective measures to discipline or restrain Eastland as Republicans had been to move against McCarthy.

The Eastland committee did not immediately make public a report on the New Orleans hearings but leaked its "findings" to the American Legion, which in May, 1955, published smear articles in its journal, *Firing Line*. Williams was infuriated, and wanted to sue the Legion or, at least, force it to retract the articles.[72] Because of the rigidity of libel laws and the fact that the Legion was using material in the public domain, misleading though it was, Williams took neither course. As soon as the articles appeared, he wrote Eastland demanding that the committee publish its report on the Fund so as to scotch rumors that the organization was pressuring the Committee to keep it under wraps. Having already leaked its contents, Eastland complied. As expected, the report accepted the testimony of Crouch and Butler which had linked the Fund to the Southern Conference for Human Welfare as "operating with substantially the same leadership and purpose as its predecessor," and thereby also shared its "Communist" affiliations. It recommended that the Attorney General present the matter before the Subversive Activities Control Board "in order that a determination can be made as to the status of the SCEF." The U.S. Attorney General, however, never listed the Fund or the Southern Conference for Human Welfare as a subversive organization. Nor did the Subversive Activities Control Board order the Fund to register with it.[73]

Attacks on the Southern Conference for Human Welfare for being Communist-directed or a Communist front plagued it from its inception in 1938. Such charges came from a variety of sources ranging from right to left on the American political spectrum. The journal *Alabama*, organ of the "Big Mules," the leading corporation business interests of Birmingham, first publicized the charges after the founding convention of the Conference. Other groups hostile to the labor movement and the CIO in particular took up the theme, understandably since the Southern Conference for Human Welfare worked closely with labor unions and sought to win Southern workers and the general Southern public over to an acceptance of unionization in the region's industries. The Conference also had its left-wing critics, including a number of Socialists who participated in its affairs, serving on its executive board in the early forties. Among them Frank McCallister of the Southern Workers Defense League, Howard Kester and H. L. Mitchell of the Southern Tenant Farmers Union, and Kenneth Douty, constantly criticized the Conference for allowing what they considered excessive Communist influence to color the organization's affairs. There were three SCHW officers against whom suspicions were strongest: Joseph Gelders, executive secretary of its Civil Rights Committee, Howard Lee, executive secretary of the Conference from October, 1939, to mid-1941, and John B. Thompson, chairman of the Conference from 1940-1942. Communist publications at times referred to Gelders as "comrade Gelders" and he worked with them in a number of ways including efforts to end the poll-tax, the campaign of which he was an initiator in 1938. Opinions about Lee and Thompson derived from their participation in the American Peace Mobilization, an organization which opposed American entry into World War II on the side of Britain and France in 1939-1941 and which included a heavy Communist representation both in its membership and leadership. No concrete evidence of actual Communist Party membership on the part of these men during their years with the Conference ever materialized. None of them were ever active in the Southern Conference Educational Fund.

Aside from identifiable Communists in the activities of the SCHW, the relationship of the organization to the Communist Party must rest upon the programs of the two organizations. In the period 1935-1945, the American Communist Party adopted the popular-front line elaborated by Georgi Dimitrov, a Comintern leader, in 1935. Henceforth, fascism replaced capitalism as the most immediate and principal enemy of the proletarian revolution and Communists were to work with all who opposed fascism including non-Communists in the labor movement, liberal and reform organizations, religious and civic associations. Rather than forming separate Communist organizations or factions within such groups, Communists worked as bona-fide members carrying out the policies of such groups as long as they shared the Communist view toward fascism. In the United States, Earl Browder, the party chairman, went so far as to renounce the Communist belief in the necessity of a revolutionary overthrow of capitalism in favor of a belief in the improvement of capitalism by reforms which would provide "a more peaceful, less difficult and less painful transition to socialism when the time comes."[74] Following this line, Communists became hard-working members of reform organizations like the Southern Conference for Human Welfare working to make their programs effective and, in effect, dropping revolutionary militancy and the anti-capitalist program that had marked the Communist Party up to 1935. Many non-Communists accepted the Communists as valuable allies in a common struggle against fascism abroad and what they considered its home-grown variety in the form of anti-Negro, anti-labor and anti-New Deal organizations, spokesmen and policies. In view of the drastic revision in Communist strategy and tactics in the popular-front period, it would be as accurate to interpret the Communists as a "liberal" or "reform-front" within the radical left as to regard reform organizations, such as the Southern Conference for Human Welfare as "Communist-fronts." The SCHW, and the Southern Conference Educational Fund after it, were reform organizations working within the American political and economic system for peaceful social change. Neither were Marxist or revolutionary in aim or methods. To the extent that Communists participated in their activities they did so as conscientious reformers and there is no convincing evidence that they dominated the policies or activities of either organization.[75]

While their treatment at the hands of the Legion and Eastland was understandable, Williams and the Fund were not prepared for the reception they received from their own allies. Even before Eastland's investigation, Southern moderate Ralph McGill, editor of the Atlanta *Constitution*, had disavowed Williams and Dombrowski as "fellow travelers."[76] As early as 1950, the Fund had been critical of both McGill and the *Constitution* for their gradualist approach to desegregation, as well as their pro-Talmadge stands.[77] The *Constitution* printed articles, particularly on occasions of Fund gatherings in Atlanta, purporting to reveal the organization's ties with Communists. All attempts by Dombrowski and Williams to persuade the paper and McGill to desist from their sniping failed.[78] Both the *Constitution* and its friendly rival, the Atlanta *Journal*, had a rather cozy relationship with Governor Herman Talmadge, supporting his attacks on the U.S. Supreme Court as well as his moves to close the Georgia public school system as a strategy for avoiding desegregation. They had also played important roles in causing the defeat of Governor Melvin Thompson in 1948, which turned Georgia over to the Talmadge-Roy Harris segregationist faction for the next two decades. Despite this, both newspapers, and Ralph McGill particularly, enjoyed a wide reputation in the South, and more importantly, in the North. Their views on Southern politics and personalities carried weight with liberals nationally, and McGill's red-baiting of the Fund was most damaging.[79]

By mid-1956, the Board of Directors seriously questioned the Fund's ability to continue because of the estrangement between it and other Southern white reformers and even black organizations. There was general agreement on the board that the Fund's program in the South was unique and ought to continue. But the board doubted that it could gain the cooperation of other civil rights organizations. Nevertheless, the Fund resolved to continue to make available to others the organization's "technical and spiritual resources," and it set up a committee to explore the possibility of finding common ground with other groups associated in the Leadership Conference on Civil Rights, a clearing house of integrationist organizations.[80] Attempts by Aubrey Williams to interest A. Philip Randolph, prominent in the latter group, in the Fund's situation proved fruitless. Williams soon confided to Dombrowski that Northern integrationists were "simply not interested in the little handful of us that are down here." It was "just as well that we [should] make up our minds to that for once and all," he advised.[81] In August, the Fund established a Committee on Relationships with other Agencies under the chairmanship of Emory University Dean Albert D. Barnett to carry out its resolution. Dombrowski urged Barnett to give precedence to establishing contact with the Leadership Conference, headed by Roy Wilkins of the NAACP. By clarifying the Fund's ties with the Conference, he informed Barnett, "we will also serve the purpose of clarifying our relationships with the NAACP."[82]

Accordingly, Barnett wrote Wilkins to accept a prior invitation from Alan Knight Chalmers, chairman of the NAACP's Committee of One Hundred, to join that group, despite the fact that doing so "might be personally costly in view of the campaign in Southern states to brand the NAACP as subversive, and on that basis to outlaw it." Barnett assured Chalmers that the NAACP "can count on me." He then proceeded to his main concern on behalf of the Fund. Recounting its activities and the careers of Dombrowski and Williams and noting their performance before Eastland's committee, Barnett requested Wilkins to invite Dombrowski to the January, 1957, meeting of the Leadership Conference and to list the Fund as one of its constituent organizations. Declaring that the Fund had been the object of a campaign of slander similar to that waged against the NAACP, Barnett stressed that it "would go a long way to strengthen the hand of liberal white Southerners to have "the confidence of organizations outside the South such as the NAACP and the Leadership Conference on Civil Rights."[83] He added that the Fund "would be the one distinctly Southern member of the group, and our inter-racial character would add some strength to the Council."[84]

It was February 4, 1957, well after the January meeting of the Leadership Conference, before Wilkins briefly replied, stating that the group had decided against admitting the Fund for fear of making the Conference unwieldy.[85] Stung and amazed, Barnett could not understand how raising the number of participating organizations from forty-eight to forty-nine could make it unwieldy. He stressed again the contributions the Fund could make to the Conference. As an organization subjected to attack by Eastland, Talmadge and Byrnes, the Fund understood the political nature of such attacks and "how to take it," whereas identical assaults upon the Leadership Conference "are more apt to succeed" because it was composed of "outsiders." Inclusion of the Fund was thus an offer of assistance rather than a bid for recognition.[86]

Barnett soon dropped his defensive posture and strongly questioned the implications of the Conference's decision. He wondered whether that decision meant a vote of "no confidence" in people like Negro Baptist Bishop S. L. Greene and John Wesley Dobbs, a vice-president of the Republican National Committee and of the NAACP, as well as others on the Board of the Fund who were active in the NAACP in the South. Stressing the need for unity in behalf of civil rights to give maximum effectiveness to Supreme Court decisions, Barnett reiterated the contributions the Fund could make to that cause, and its disinterest in attempting to "ride anybody's coat-tails." It did not, however, wish to be excluded from the Conference or the civil rights cause generally, "on a basis of misinformation or misconception of our organization," particularly since "smears" of the Fund emanated from the identical sources from whom "comparable smears against the NAACP have stemmed." Barnett asked for a list of the member organizations of the Leadership Conference so that the Fund could inform them in detail of its work. He concluded with an appeal for "as much light as possible" in the matter.[87]

Not much more light was forthcoming, however. John Morsell, a Wilkins aide in the NAACP, took a different tack in asserting that the Conference was organized for the purpose of putting pressure on Congressmen to advance civil rights legislation. Under these conditions, the Fund's membership had been rejected because "it is assumed that little or nothing can be done to bring pressure upon Southern Congressmen for favorable action on civil rights bills."[88] Barnett countered by informing Morsell that, in the thirties when Barnett and a group of white Southerners had testified in support of the Costigan-Wagner Federal anti-lynching bill, non-Southern Congressmen considered their testimony most impressive and more influential than the views of their own constituents. As white Southerners in favor of civil rights legislation, they ought for that very reason to be included in the Leadership Conference.[89]

The real basis for the Fund's exclusion soon became apparent, i.e., the "Communist front" tag that Eastland had attached to it.[90] Williams regarded the entire dialogue with Wilkins as an "outrage" and "unbelievable." It was, he thought, "an example of high handedness of an absolutely unprecedented character--on the part of a group which had arbitrarily set itself up as the judge of who shall be allowed to participate and who shall not." The implications for the Fund were quite serious. Unless it could assert itself at meetings to formulate overall civil rights strategy, Williams feared it could not long survive. Under circumstances of increasing isolation from other integrationist organizations, the Fund would not be able to hold the interest or respect of people like John Wesley Dobbs, Bishop Edgar A. Love and other important black, as well as white, leaders in the South. Williams was in favor of having "a show down" and, failing that, either reorganizing under new leadership, relocating to better advantage in Washington, D C., or liquidating. Williams was painfully aware that he had taken up his tasks in the South only after consultation with Northern friends; their support had weighed heavily in influencing him to return to Alabama in 1945.[91] Had he remained in Washington, he doubtless would have found some place in official life or carved out a career in politics. Having taken on the burden of stimulating liberal efforts in the South and thus exposing himself to public scorn, Williams began to think that Northern reformers had deserted him. He no longer wished to be in what he described as "the equivocating position of undertaking to represent emancipated white folks of the South," and yet largely denied that opportunity "by those selected by the liberal forces of the nation to manage the fights or conduct the battles."[92]

Journalist Alfred Maund, a former Southern associate, confirmed Williams' worst fears about Northern organization. Maund informed Williams that when he joined the staff of the CIO Rubber Workers Union in Ohio its officers advised that he disassociate himself from the Southern Conference Educational Fund and disavow its leaders. Tracing down the source of the attack on the Fund, Maund had turned to a local labor leader whose Washington contacts had discovered the existence of an AFL-CIO "subversive list" of organizations, with the Fund conspicuously upon it. The compiler of the list, Maund stated, had worked closely with Senator Eastland; a name that kept cropping up in this connection was one Ben Segal, an officer of the American Federation of Teachers and also of the Fund for the Republic. A prominent supporter of reform projects, the Fund for the

Republic also considered the Southern Conference Educational Fund to be a "Communist Front," Maund reported.[93]

In an angry letter to Fund for the Republic president Robert M. Hutchins, Williams expressed his amazement at this information. He informed Hutchins that it made almost impossible the work of any white person on behalf of blacks in the South. Williams could understand why an Eastland or a Talmadge and "the propertied interests" for whom they spoke would brand him and the Fund. But when Hutchins, Roy Wilkins, and the leaders of fifty organizations giving direction to the civil rights movement "turn their backs upon us," in effect, accepting the label placed upon the Fund by Eastland, "then I begin to despair that any white person down here will be willing, or for that matter able, to carry on the fight in behalf of Negroes." Moreover, Williams chided Hutchins, "haven't you people who have put organizations and individuals on 'front' lists been engaging in a little J. Edgar Hooverism, or McCarthyism?"[94]

As the Fund came under increasing attack from Southern segregationists, it could no longer depend upon important civil rights organizations or their leading figures for appreciable support. With the important exception of Mrs. Eleanor Roosevelt, who until the early 1960's continued to give financial aid and public support through her syndicated newspaper column, most of the notables Williams had been associated with in the New Deal ceased to support the Fund. Not a few adopted a hostile attitude as they submitted to the domestic red scare. In the process, they also contributed to the impotence of liberal organizations as a force for effective social change in America.

SIX

The *Brown* Decision and Southern Compliance: Failure of an Effort

"We conclude that in the field of public education the doctrine of 'separate but equal' has no place. Separate educational facilities are inherently unequal." Ninety-one years after the emancipation Proclamation, Chief Justice Earl Warren thus delivered the unanimous judgment of the United States Supreme Court on May 17, 1954.[1] The Court further noted that "whatever may have been the extent of psychological knowledge at the time of *Plessy v. Ferguson*, this finding is amply supported by modern authority." Even if physical facilities were equal, because racial segregation produced feelings of inferiority in the segregated minority it was inherently unequal and, therefore, unconstitutional.[2] The variety of local school conditions affected by the decision, however, compelled Warren to order further arguments concerning proper methods of implementation, and he invited all affected states to submit briefs and participate in arguments. In addition to the four original defendants, South Carolina, Virginia, Delaware and Kansas, six states of the upper South joined the United States as *amici curiae* before the Court: Arkansas, Florida, Maryland, North Carolina, Oklahoma, and Texas. The NAACP continued to represent the litigants.

The Southern Conference Educational Fund was particularly gratified by the *Brown* decision. Six months earlier it had looked optimistically toward the Court's deliberations, hoping that "the harsh graven face the traditional South presents to the world will twitch with dismay."[3] By interring the "separate but equal" doctrine in education, the *Patriot* declared, the Court had, for the first time in half a century, reunited ethics and legality. "The spiritual schizophrenia that resulted from the credo: 'one nation indivisible, except into white and Colored in 17 states,' is now ended." Opponents of segregation were no longer virtual outlaws. Until 1954, the integrationist had

101

urged action contrary to law that had been upheld, at least tacitly, by the highest constitutional authority. Now the screw began to turn against the segregationist. "Having long ago rejected the institutions of the Twentieth Century," the *Patriot* asserted, "he is left without refuge at this breach of the Black Codes." Wryly, the journal hoped that the "law-abiding traditions of the South," manifested in the region's long and faithful adherence to segregation laws, though they flouted "all common sense, all common good, and ethical teachings," might now be reasserted in behalf of legal provisions "which promote prosperity and good conscience." Already the school boards of Washington, D.C., Greensboro, North Carolina, and Baltimore, Maryland, had chosen to comply purportedly as models for others.[4]

There were, nevertheless, formidable obstacles in the path of school integration. Perhaps the most subtle was the fact that school districts were based upon the neighborhood principle. Thus despite the ending of legal segregation, black ghettoes would produce ghetto schools, integrated in name only. Southern Senators were debating the merits of scuttling the Federal housing program, fearing as they did its use as an instrument for integration. For the first time in over a year, flames were burning on "Dynamite Hill" in Birmingham, Alabama, at the home of a black dentist who had moved "too close" to a white neighborhood. Despite the 1948 Supreme Court ruling that restrictive housing covenants were legally unenforceable, real estate interests maintained extra-legal barriers to interracial neighborhoods, thereby profiting from racial phobias. A blatant example of this was in Louisville, Kentucky, where a white couple had deeded a private home to a black electrician and his family in a white neighborhood. Subsequently, the white couple faced indictment for violation of the state sedition law after white law-breakers, purportedly including the real estate developer who had built and sold the house, shot out the windows and dynamited a part of the home to force the black family out. The city of Louisville used its resources against those who had attempted lawfully to breach the segregated customs of that Southern community, rather than against those who sought by violence to uphold segregation. Even the enlightened Louisville *Courier-Journal* commiserated with the segregationists, asserting that they were "entirely within their rights, we believe, in protesting the purchase of property in their subdivision by Negroes." Publisher Barry Bingham supported this position by accepting the claims of realtors that black purchasers in hitherto all white areas would decrease the value of the property. In rebuttal, the *Patriot* quoted a national survey report from a prominent business journal, the *U.S.*

News and World Report, indicating that "mixed neighborhoods usually provide a better long-term investment" because sales to minority groups broadened and strengthened the market.[5] The *Patriot* saw the Louisville case as a barometer of the course of school integration. If politicians eager to capitalize on white prejudices cooperated with short-sighted realtors to perpetuate black ghettos in the cities, the *Patriot* feared "any effective meaning will be gutted from the ending of segregation in schools and elsewhere...."[6]

With these problems in mind, the Fund's board of directors met in Atlanta on June 12 to discuss ways and means of implementing the *Brown* decision in the South. Bolstered by the Court's action, the black members of the board in particular expressed great interest in stimulating a Southwide movement in behalf of speedy enactment of the desegregation ruling. John Welsey Dobbs, Mrs. Bethune, Houston NAACP member Mrs. Lulu White, and educator Dr. Rudolph Moses moved that the Fund draw up a statement encouraging Southerners to work for its implementation. They also proposed that the Fund organize a regional conference to encourage compliance by the white South. Dobbs offered to cooperate with leading Southern black churchmen to raise funds for the conference.[7]

Adopting a firm policy statement heartily endorsing the *Brown* decision, the Fund saw the task of securing full integration henceforth to be largely the task of private citizens and local officials. School administrators had to be reminded that their oaths of office and professional training prescribed compliance with the new ruling, and also "reassured that they will he the better public servants for doing so." Emphasizing the positive, the Fund believed that most Southern communities had persons with the courage and moral vision to challenge and convince their fellows, and it pledged itself to seek out and support these persons. Expanding upon the intent of the Supreme Court, the Fund claimed that a major premise underlying *Brown* was that education as "democratic living" rather than an end in itself implied that the schools should not become "isolated showcases of functional democracy." Other goals were necessary if the schools were to integrate; the larger society itself must take steps in that direction, and the organization accordingly proposed such goals for the South. They included enactment of a Federal Fair Employment Practices Act; State fair educational practices legislation barring discrimination in all educational institutions, private as well as public; thorough establishment of a single standard of requirements for voting and jury service; integration of medical and hospital facilities, with access determined simply on the basis of need; availability of housing on the basis of individual choice and ability to pay, without legal or extra-legal restrictions aimed at minority groups; and integration of congregations and religious assemblies. As did the Southern Conference for Human Welfare before it, the Fund long had agitated for these goals, though it did not claim its program to be unique. The Fund believed its distinction lay in a "determination to achieve its goals expeditiously, and thus forestall further human suffering and waste."[8]

The *Brown* decision also aroused opponents of desegregation. Unlike the Fund, however, they were in a position to put their views immediately into effect. Barely had the Court's decisions gone to press, when the states of the deep South took steps to foil its intent. On executive recommendation, the Georgia and South Carolina legislatures adopted measures to prevent the use of public money on any school undertaking to integrate its student body; and they prepared the way for abolition of the public school system itself if necessary. In Mississippi, Governor Hugh White called a conference of white and black leaders to announce support for continued school segregation. Expecting their "rubber stamp" approval, Governor White was astonished when the predominantly accommodationist spokesmen of the black community insisted upon compliance with the Supreme Court ruling. The Fund was delighted at this development, though disappointed that Percy Greene, a black newspaper editor who had once been associated with the Fund, wavered.

The Fund suspected that representative of the Governor had approached Greene prior to the meeting to gain his support. Aubrey Williams reported to Dombrowski that he had been perplexed by Greene's statements in his newspaper to the effect that there was "no such word as Integration in the Constitution," and that "there were many ways short of violence to get fair play for the Negro." Dombrowski soon confirmed Williams" suspicions. He noted that he had received reports from Mississippi to the effect that Greene "had sold out politically to the white politicians." Dombrowski found it "hard to believe that a man who has been such a consistent fighter could go sour," but he did not know how else to interpret Greene's actions. While the performance of the larger group of blacks meeting with Governor White "was tremendous and stirring as they vigorously stood their ground," Dombrowski regretted that he could not say the same for "our friend, Percy." Though "he did not go so far as one Negro in the group to defend

Segregation," Dombrowski remarked, "he did come up with a proposal for a compromise....["9]

Recovering his poise, Governor White recalled the committee. Under his watchful eye, it drafted a "last resort" constitutional amendment to abolish the public schools or permit local school authorities to abolish parts of it; provide tuition grants to school children; and authorize the leasing, renting or selling of school property. The committee submitted the amendment to a special session of the Mississippi legislature in September, 1954, which approved and sent it to the voters for their sanction in December. Prior to this, Mississippi had taken the high road of resistance to the Supreme Court ruling by becoming the first state to initiate a grass-roots rebellion against desegregation. Spurred on by Senator James Eastland who, on May 27, had condemned the Court for being "indoctrinated and brainwashed by left-wing pressure groups," a number of businessmen in Eastland's home county in July, 1954, formed the first White Citizens Council in the town of Indianola. The Citizens Councils were the "militant reflex" of the blackbelt county seat elite. They rapidly became an influence in the state legislature, where the powerful Dixiecrat-Old Guard headed by Speaker of the House Walter Sillers of Bolivar County took up their cause.[10] During the legislative session to approve the public school amendment, several legislators took the opportunity to announce the formation of these Councils. They made note of their disassociation from the Ku Klux Klan, but also emphasized that should the councils fail "public sentiment might force the formation of something like the Klan." Beyond using economic pressure to keep black people in line by denying them credit, refusing to gin their cotton, and ousting them from their rented houses, some Council spokesmen in the legislature reportedly asserted that "a few killings" might also be called for "in order to prevent more bloodshed later."[11]

The Fund attempted to offset these ominous developments by encouraging white Mississippians to make a public show of support for desegregation. The organization had the cooperation of a number of white clergymen, including an official of the Episcopal church in McComb, Mississippi. The clergymen placed advertisements in state newspapers reprinting an outspoken editorial by Jeanette C. Carmichael, editor publisher of the Bay St. Louis *Light*. While announcing her support of Senator Eastland for re-election, Mrs. Carmichael chided him for his views. Declaring her opposition to public school segregation she argued that full and equal opportunities are the right of every American regardless of race or creed. Social relationships are for individual choice.... Under segregation there is no chance of equal opportunities, the segregated person is handicapped primarily by the creation of an inferiority complex.... Senator Eastland talks of "the People of Mississippi." Always remember one-third of these people are Negroes. Senator Eastland represents them also.

Mrs. Carmichael hoped that Eastland "and other misguided Mississippians" would "do a little soul searching and come up with a deeper love of their fellowmen of all colors, creeds, race and class."[12]

Recalling favorable past experiences, Dombrowski proposed taking a confidential poll of Mississippi school teachers to ascertain their views on the proposed school amendment. He was encouraged by a meeting of the teachers with Governor White. In a show of hands, over one-third of the teachers courageously voted against the proposal to abolish the public schools. Dombrowski wrote to a Fund supporter to finance a poll of teacher attitudes about compliance with the Supreme Court ruling; the specific state constitutional amendment abolishing the public schools; and their personal views about teaching in an integrated system. He proposed sending the questionnaire to about 20,000 white Mississippi public school teachers.[13]

While the voters of Mississippi overwhelmingly approved the amendment in December, two out of every three white teachers who responded to the poll opposed it, understandably so since the amendment endangered their pay, pensions and retirement benefits. More discouraging, the teachers, by a 3-1 vote, objected to an integrated system. Seeking light in the surrounding gloom, the *Patriot* noted that since the question was still hypothetical in Mississippi, "the answers do not indicate how hard the teachers would object if practical considerations on the side of integration were placed before them." The poll further indicated that the core of the opposition to integration, as with support for the Citizens Councils, centered in the Delta and the fertile eastern counties. Opposition to public school abolition focused in the major cities and the counties of eastern Mississippi from the Tennessee line to the Gulf of Mexico, an area with a long tradition of antipathy to the Delta planters.[14]

The teacher poll helped to crystallize the Fund's thinking about the organization of a Southern compliance conference. Bishop Sherman L. Greene, head of the African Methodist Episcopal Council of Bishops, and John Wesley Dobbs had agreed to raise $5000. Bishop Greene also invited Dombrowski to attend his Council meeting in Jackson, Mississippi, on the occasion of the national convention of the A.M.E. church "to sell his Bishops on the Conference and the fund." [15] With Greene as chairman, a group of 200 sponsors met in Atlanta in November 1954 to hasten plans for the Southwide conference. The participants agreed that many parents who might otherwise agree to integrated schools were moving toward segregation because of widespread reports and publicity given to those districts where difficulties had been encountered. The conferees sought to develop a plan of action to shape public opinion for integration.

Explicitly disavowing any intention to compete with the NAACP, the Atlanta conferees directed their efforts primarily at religious, educational, professional, parent, and youth groups. They had three purposes in mind. First, they wanted to prepare a statement which would receive the endorsement of "a considerable body of representative Southerners." Second, they hoped that the proposed Southwide conference would attract leaders in communities where integration was being attempted, or where planning committees and local citizen groups were engaged in efforts to prepare for it. A meeting ground for the exchange of ideas and experiences would, it was hoped, promote favorable action in other communities. Finally, such a conference would have wider significance in manifesting to the Supreme Court, as well as local school administrators, the degree of public support for integration, especially in the deep South. This would be critical in helping the Court establish a timetable of compliance in its next session.[16]

Preceded by meetings in New Orleans and Richmond, the main conference gathered in Houston, Texas, on May 17, 1955, the anniversary of the *Brown* decision. The Houston conference was notable for its good interracial attendance, which indicated that, given some effort, lines of communication could open in the South. The conference firmly opposed "gradualism," and voiced the belief that despite great hostility "integration, once put into effect, will win over its foes by its obvious blessings." The participants did not subscribe to the view that time alone would prove a remedy.

> Only through constructive action can equity prevail. Segregation has proved itself socially, an evil; politically, undemocratic; economically, a waste; religiously, a sin. It must be met immediately on all these levels.[17]

Noting advances in areas other than education, the conference recommended further legal action. While favoring FEPC laws, however, it recognized that they were not as yet feasible in most parts of the South. In order to create a more favorable climate, the conference urged the formation of state and local human relations councils representing both races as a means of coordinating their efforts. The conferees agreed that cooperative endeavors would accomplish "much more, more effectively and more rapidly, than can be accomplished unilaterally by a minority group," and emphasized the need for white people to take responsibility for dismantling segregation. The Houston conference was critical of Southern churches. It explicitly declared that "the matter of integration has became a problem only because the church, the body of Christ, has failed. The true church will have no problem over race...." Urging the cessation by the church of derisive terminology such as "Negro work," the conference called for the "race church" to give way to the "neighborhood church," particularly in communities that were changing in racial makeup. It saw a great need in every large city for a pioneering congregation whose existence, however, "should not afford an avenue of escape for those who would see integration working in the church." Rather, those who believed in "a raceless, classless church" might do their best service by remaining with their own congregations.

As for school integration specifically, the conference stressed the need for cooperation by white and black parents and firm, clear school policies. It advised administrators that they would not have "an easy time" and warned them to expect attacks from segregationist groups. A clear, unequivocal statement of school policy by administrators would make for success. School authorities must refuse "to evade the principles and the fact of desegregation, and make "an appeal to the public in terms of our traditions of democracy, fair play, and equal justice."[18] With these guidelines, the Houston conferees announced plans for a broader Southwide conference to be held in Atlanta in November, 1955. Houston was the last of the compliance meetings the Fund convened, however, for the segregationist counteroffensive prevented it from gaining enough white support to hold the Atlanta conference.

On the heels of the Houston gathering, the Supreme Court, on May 31, 1955, concluded its deliberations with regard to *Brown*. It remanded to local authorities the primary responsibility for "elucidating, assessing, and solving" those problems arising from its 1954 decision, and turned over to lower district courts the authority to conduct hearings on proper enforcement. The Court ordered the district courts to assure full compliance with its ruling "with all deliberate speed."[19] Acting contrary to the desires of the NAACP which had argued for a specific decree with a definite time limit to assure rapid compliance with the original decision, the Court, in substance, accepted the Southern position by adopting the most indirect method of implementation. Black spokesmen were angry at the Court's apparent retreat from the full implications of its original ruling. The Chicago *Defender* declared that, regardless of the good intentions of the judges, "they are now in the position of the cow that gave a full bucket of milk and then promptly kicked it over. What is worse," the *Defender* concluded, "the milk was supposed to be for us, the undernourished, underprivileged and underestimated...." The Oklahoma City *Black Dispatch* went further; it termed the edict "a complete surrender to states rights and local self-government."[20]

The *Patriot*, however, found some justification in the Court's procedure. Since the Court had no militia to back it up, issuing unenforceable edicts would have "risked ridicule...rather than have achieved integration in the states ruled by the more reckless Dixiecrats." The *Patriot* nevertheless questioned the wisdom of holding endless compliance hearings lest fruitless deliberations embolden "repressive groups" such as the Citizens Councils who already were claiming that their threats of violence had forced the Court to back down. In a deeper sense, the *Patriot* believed the Court's decision marked the end of the route for legal procedures alone. Future litigation would attempt simply to consolidate the gains already won. The next advances had to come "through persuasion and inspiration" of the people of the South to "exercise the freedom the court has decreed." The patient had to summon the will that no doctor could prescribe.[21]

The climate of many parts of the South in 1955, however, was not auspicious for the recovery of reason. Instead, the region entered upon a bitter period of white resistance to the *Brown* decision. By the end of 1955, the White Citizens Councils were the most vocal of the more than fifty segregationist pressure groups that had mushroomed in the region immediately after the 1954 ruling. Through 1956, the peak year of their influence, an estimated 300,000 white Southerners joined the Councils and Council influence pervaded the political and economic infrastructure in much of the region. A grass-roots movement, the Councils provided the cadres of "massive resistance."[22]

The largest and best organized Councils appeared in Mississippi where they dominated the political life of the state to such a degree that Southern Regional Council director Leslie Dunbar observed: "Mississippi is experimenting with a Soviet style of government, with the Citizens Council paralleling the state machine in emulation of a successful Communist Party."[23] Alabama's Councils organized first in Selma, the heart of the black-belt, in October, 1954. They soon spread to Montgomery after the black populace of the city initiated a boycott of the city's buses in December, 1955, to protest brutal treatment and segregated seating arrangements. The Councils were also powerful in Birmingham where they attracted support from the "Big Mules," the corporation elite of that industrial center, as well as from leaders of the Farm Bureau Federation, spokesmen of the wealthiest agricultural business interests of the state. In addition, elements of the Ku Klux Klan entered Council ranks providing important urban white working class support prone to open violence and voicing blatant anti-Semitic, anti-Catholic sentiments reminiscent of the Ku Klux Klan of the twenties.[24]

Unlike White Citizens Councils in Mississippi and Alabama, in Louisiana the control and organization was from the top down. State Senator William G. Rainach, chairman of the Joint Legislative Committee to Maintain Segregation, was president of the Association of Citizens Councils of Louisiana. Later, Representative John Sidney Garrett, Joint Committee spokesman in the lower chamber, took up the mantle of leadership, while William M. Shaw, the committee's general counsel, served as executive secretary. Rainach, Garrett and Shaw were all from the black-belt parish of Claiborne in northern Louisiana, where the first Citizens Council organized in Homer, in April, 1955. They established close ties with a prominent urban segregationist group, the American Association for the Preservation of State Government and Racial Integrity. Leading figures in the latter group included a member of the Louisiana State University Board of Supervisors, an ex-president of the Louisiana Medical Association, and the president of the Louisiana Farm Bureau Federation. The two groups eventually united to form the Association of Citizens Councils with Rainach and colleagues using their positions effectively to intimidate other legislators into support of Council policies and activities. So effective was their control that the Louisiana Citizens Councils continued to expand after the movement declined in other Southern states. Citizens Councils were also effective and influential in South Carolina and Virginia. They were less raucous and emotional in style, however, befitting the more aristocratic tradition of the Old South.[25]

Impressive as the grass-roots character of the Councils was, leading neo-Bourbon politicians[26] influenced their direction through their public support. Herman Talmadge, Harry F. Byrd, Strom Thurmond, and other old Dixiecrats of 1948, led the new crusade. Most strident of all was Senator James O. Eastland, dubbed "the Voice of the South" in Citizens Council literature.[27] Eastland was the most influential individual shaping the direction of the white supremacy movement, a relentless crusader "who was never far from where decisions were being made."[28] Epitomizing the contradictions and belligerence of Southern white resistance, Eastland ardently propounded an "Americanism" which was a blend of biology, regionalism, and nationalism. In his eyes, real southerners were white, for "the Negroes were only living in their midst." Eastland's South had a vital service to perform. "The future greatness of America, he asserted, "depends upon racial purity and maintenance of Anglo-Saxon institutions, which still flourish in full flower in the South." State rights was the most important bulwark against Communist subversion, he insisted; it rested so firmly upon a Southern foundation that, "when state sovereignty falls in the South, it automatically falls elsewhere."[29]

In a Memphis speech in June, 1954, shortly after the desegregation ruling, Eastland had sketched out a campaign to mobilize public opinion for a reversal of the decision. He called for the founding of

a people's organization, an organization not controlled by fawning politicians who cater to organized racial pressure groups. A people's organization to fight the Court, to fight the CIO, to fight the NAACP and to fight all the conscienceless pressure groups which are attempting our destruction.

Reaching out for support beyond the South, he pledged that

our organization will carry on its banner the slogan of free enterprise and we will fight those organizations who attempt with much success to socialize industry, and the great medical profession of this country.... Generations of Southerners yet unborn will cherish our memory because they will realize that the fight we now wage will have preserved for them their untainted racial heritage, their culture and the institutions of the Anglo-Saxon race.[30]

Sparked by Eastland, the Federation for Constitutional Government formed in December, 1955, designed to serve as a central agency for the state rights movement. It was to plan strategy for "massive resistance" in the South and for carrying the fight to the North. Its stated aims included coordination of the efforts of "literally hundreds of patriotic organizations" across the nation, maintaining a lobby in Washington, publishing a Federation magazine, undertaking large-scale public relations programs, and conducting field organizational work. In the minds of a number of its supporters, it had an unstated objective: the initiation of a third political party. The Federation failed to achieve many of its goals. It was never able to incorporate the

111

Citizens Councils into its structure, in part because of suspicion of professional politicians. Yet the Federation was a landmark in the rise of "massive resistance." Four months after the Federation's appearance, the Citizens Councils of America took the field to coordinate the various state associations, their activities duplicating much of the Federation's own program. Compared to the latter, however, the Citizens Councils were quite provincial in outlook. Eschewing many of the other aims of the Federation, the Citizens Councils preferred to concentrate on maintaining racial segregation and, in time, became "the largest effective coalition of white supremacy groups...the closest thing that existed to an institutionalized cockpit of massive resistance strategy." Eastland and other leaders of the Federation soon accepted this new situation and maintained an alliance with the Councils.[31]

In parts of the deep South the frenzy stirred up by the Citizens Councils, aided and abetted by leading Southern politicians, created a climate of hate reminiscent of the anti-black savagery of the early years of the century. After several years without reported lynchings in the South, Mississippi witnessed four killings in 1955. In one incident, a group of whites including a deputy sheriff forcibly abducted a fourteen-year old Chicago black boy from the home of relatives he had been visiting in Tallahatchie County, allegedly because the boy had whistled at a white woman. Emmett Till's bullet-filled body later appeared in a nearby river. Although two white men admitted in open court to having participated in his kidnapping, an all-white jury absolved them. Two other blacks shot to death were Lamar Smith of Brookhaven, and a minister, the Reverend George Lee of Belzoni, Lee in broad daylight on the Lincoln County courthouse lawn. Both Lee and Smith had refused to remove their names from the voter registration list after the local White Citizens Council had so insisted. One of Lee's co-workers, Gus Courts, fled the state after recovering from serious wounds in a similar incident.[32] Though the FBI knew the men who killed Reverend Lee were employees of a white service station in Belzoni, the Department of Justice refused to issue a warrant for their arrest; the Attorney General claimed that the incident was "purely a local matter."[33]

In addition to extra-legal intimidation, most Southern legislatures pushed through statutes outlawing the NAACP. They penalized with dismissal all state employees who were members of the organization, most notably public school teachers, and they forbade the future employment of NAACP members by the state. Mississippi also attempted to forestall Federal legal activity within its borders by assessing penalties against all persons, including agents of the FBI, whom it held to be " interfering with state law under the color of federal authority."[34]

Lacking strong popular support in Mississippi, the Southern Conference Educational Fund helped to organize a delegation to Congress. Made up of black and white Southerners and headed by Methodist Bishop Edgar A. Love of Baltimore and Dean James L. Hupp of Virginia Wesleyan College, both members of the Fund, the delegation called for an investigation of the infringement of Federal rights of Mississippi citizens. Presenting a petition signed by nearly 3000 persons from all 48 states, they urged Senator William Langer, chairman of the Senate Subcommittee on Human Rights, to conduct hearings in Mississippi to determine whether new Federal laws were needed. By throwing light on events in that state, the petitioners hoped to marshal public opinion which would "encourage the fair-minded white people of Mississippi to exercise their own constitutional liberties and help to establish the orderly supremacy of law.[35] In the absence of a Federal presence, they argued, there was little either black or sympathetic white Mississippians could effectively do to protect themselves, since both had been "condemned to silence by the same lawless forces that have turned the whole apparatus of state government" against the black people.[36] But these pleas failed.

The Fund had somewhat greater success influencing events in Louisiana. For many years, James Dombrowski had operated out of New Orleans, and the Southern Conference for Human Welfare had been very active there. Soon after the *Brown* decision, Fund members began to encourage sympathetic persons in New Orleans to put desegregation into effect in the public schools. After many months of delay by school authorities, Fund members, led by Rabbi Julian B. Feibelman, presented a petition challenging the policy of the Orleans Parish School Board. The petition garnered the signatures of 180 leading citizens, including 30 clergymen of all faiths and 20 university professors from Tulane and Louisiana State University, as well as lawyers, union officials, parent-teacher officers, and newspapermen. Dombrowski was elated at the response, a result of more than three months' effort. He saw the petition as a model for other Southern cities and wished the Fund had resources to put a full-time person to work on similar efforts in Atlanta, Birmingham, and Columbia, South Carolina.[37] He thought it "no coincidence" that the very day the desegregation petition appeared, the Eastland committee publicly released its report on the Fund,[38] and that the following day, a White Citizens Council formed in New Orleans and circulated its own petition to preserve school segregation.[39]

Seizing the initiative for an appropriate observance of Human Rights Day, the Fund and its supporters sought permission from the Orleans School Board to hold in the Rabouin School auditorium a public forum on desegregation featuring speakers from cities where school desegregation had already taken place. At first, acting Mayor Victor Schiro agreed to proclaim December 10-15, 1955, as Human Rights Week, but then he reneged, stating he had no authority to issue such a proclamation. Mayor DeLesseps Morrison, engaged in a difficult campaign for the governorship, sought to keep his flanks free from assault. The proposed meeting also came under attack from the Young Men's Business Club. It called upon the citizenry to boycott it, and it sent all forum sponsors copies of the Eastland report, smear articles on the Fund from the American Legion's *Firing Line*, and editorials from the ardently pro-segregationist New Orleans *States-Item*. Caving in to the pressure, the school board rescinded its prior agreement to use of the auditorium, although it had agreed to allow use of another school facility to the White Citizens Council. Reaffirming its support of the Fund, the integration group decided to reapply on an individual basis for use of the auditorium. After continued public pressure and the arguments of an American Civil Liberties Union attorney, the school board relented. On December 15, the Fund's "Citizens Forum on Integration" marked the first time that a public school facility in New Orleans had been available for public discussions sympathetic to school integration.[40]

Taking advantage of its limited success, the Fund kept up its criticism of the Orleans School Board. It assailed its obstructive tactics and its arguments against desegregation. A South Carolina editor, Thomas R. Waring, presented the school board's case to a national audience in an article in *Harpers*, in January, 1956. Waring cited the board's affidavits alleging that black pupils scored lower on progress tests than white pupils and that state public health statistics evidenced higher rates of venereal disease and illegitimacy among black students. He included as evidence physicians' statements claiming that integration would harm the health of white pupils and spread venereal disease among the white population. He also cited psychiatrists' assertions that integration would be "psychiatrically traumatizing to the children of both races." Waring added social class differences and comparative crime rates to the list of negative effects of integration.[41] Anticipating the use by other school boards of similar arguments appealing to medical and social "facts," the Fund asked its Medical Advisory Committee to undertake a full inquiry into the subject.

The Advisory Committee discounted the school board's statistics with regard to venereal disease. It claimed that with school children venereal disease was predominantly congenital, not contagious. It was spread only from intimate sexual contact, and most authorities considered it to be a socio-economic rather than racial problem. Moreover, in recent reports, public health officials had not mentioned venereal disease as a problem in the Orleans Parish schools; while in four years of parochial school examinations of white and black children, there had been no evidence of venereal disease as a health problem. In addition, the Committee questioned statistics purporting to show higher rates of venereal disease, crime, and other negative features among the black population than among the white. Blacks relied more heavily upon public institutions where statistics were gathered, and that alone could distort the figures. From their own experiences in other cities such as Denver and Philadelphia, members of the committee reported no health problem as a result of school integration, either among students or the general population.[42]

The medical committee's report and the Fund's lively presence in New Orleans helped to create a climate in favor of the *Brown* decision which enabled Federal district courts to press for its implementation. In March, 1956, Federal District Judge J. Skelly Wright voided the Louisiana statute placing the public schools under the police power of the state, a device segregationists had used to nullify *Brown*. A native of New Orleans, Judge Wright also negated the provision remanding to administrative hearings each complaint of law violations against segregationist school authorities as a "travesty in which this court will not participate." Though he set no timetable for integration and also did not comment upon the "public health" arguments of the school board, Judge Wight rejected a plan permitting school superintendents the right to assign pupils to schools.

The case had broad regional import for it was the first time a Federal court had scrutinized one of the state segregation laws devised to circumvent the *Brown* ruling.[43] In retaliation, Louisiana attorney general Fred S. LeBlanc, in an effort to suppress the NAACP, the Southern Conference Educational Fund, and other integration organizations, invoked a 1924 statute aimed originally at the Ku Klux Klan and requiring virtually every type of organization to file membership lists with the state.[44] The Louisiana events, however, were only the calm before the storm of the segregationist counter-offensive against the Supreme Court's desegregation decision.

The paucity of results from its efforts to gain voluntary compliance to desegregation compelled the Fund to look in other directions. The hardening of white attitudes, both a consequence of, and an encouragement to organized segregationist activity, doomed attempts to convene a regional compliance conference. The hoped-for Southern white support for integration failed to materialize. Toward the end of 1956, therefore, the Fund turned to the black community and the Federal government to effect the changes that white integrationists had been unable to accomplish.

SEVEN

The Second Reconstruction: Beginnings

In the spring of 1956, the segregationists achieved their most signal victory in the effort to win the South over to a program of "massive resistance" to desegregation. After weeks of backstage maneuvering and after five redrafts to accommodate moderates, Senators Strom Thurmond of South Carolina and Harry F. Byrd of Virginia, led an overwhelming proportion of the Southern delegation to Congress, 101 of the 128 national legislators from the region, in proclaiming a "Southern Manifesto." The "Declaration of Constitutional Principles" was an outright challenge to *Brown v. Board of Education*. Condemning "the unwarranted decision of the Supreme Court" as the substitution of "naked power for established law," the Declaration commended "the motives of these states which have declared the intention to resist forced integration by any lawful means." It appealed to "the states and people who are not directly affected by these decisions to consider the constitutional principles involved against the time when they too, on issues vital to them, may be the victims of judicial encroachments."[1] In the Senate, Democratic leader Lyndon Johnson, who was not asked, and Albert Gore and Estes Kefauver of Tennessee alone refused.[2] Though less dramatic than its originators intended, the Manifesto achieved for the white supremacy crusaders the blessings of some of the South's most respected leaders.

The *Southern Patriot* termed the Declaration "a document of pure political expediency," calling on the signers to consider changing realities lest the South face further tragedies.[3] Fund president Aubrey Williams sent a strong letter to his friend and former political ally, Senator Lister Hill, the day after the Manifesto appeared. "You must have had a hard time uttering phrases like, "No man or group of men can be safely entrusted with unlimited power" Williams declared, knowing as you do how in Alabama the whites have held the Negroes in utter subjection for all the years you and I have lived here, which is all of our lives. What group of men have exercised more unlimited power over other men than the white farm owners over the Negro farm laborer or sharecropper, or the white building contractors, or the white gas station operators or the white employer of what-so-ever business, trade or profession.... It is and has been the accepted right of the white man, for a hundred and fifty years, to exercise undisputed power over the Negro. In common honesty let's not bring up the question of unlimited power.

You speak of 'abuse of' this power, that is 'judicial power.' Where has there been more flagrant abuse of judicial power than right here in Montgomery, your home. I have not heard you speak out against that....[4]

With the Montgomery bus boycott in mind, Williams noted that a grand jury had indicted ninety blacks, twenty-four of them ministers, for conducting the boycott. Meanwhile the White Citizens Councils had not so much as been threatened with an indictment, even though they had widely publicized through the newspapers an economic boycott of blacks signing petitions in favor of school integration. Williams also cited case after case of blacks driven from their homes, forced out of established businesses, and finally out of their communities by the white boycott. "You know I state the facts," he wrote Hill, who did not respond, "when I say there is one use of judicial power when Negroes are involved and another use or more often non-use of it when whites are involved."[5]

The Southern Democratic-Republican coalition had an effective grip on Congress, however, and President Eisenhower's reluctance to enforce the *Brown* decision bolstered their control. By choice of the President, implementation of civil rights legislation devolved upon Federal courts whose judges were either pro-segregationist or were under social pressure and increasingly isolated in the South, much as the British royal governors were before the American Revolution. Thus, the task of making desegregation a reality fell upon integrationists, including members of the Southern Conference Educational Fund. The attacks of the White Citizens Councils and their political allies, on the one hand, and the tepid support and disavowal of the Fund by liberals on the other proved to be immense obstacles for integration.

Fund members and other integrationists were under heavy pressure to cease their activity. In New Orleans, the Chamber of Commerce fired Robert Barnes, a young editor of its *News Bulletin* after he had rebuffed demands to quit the Fund and desist from further integration activity. Unable to find other employment in New Orleans or the South, he moved to Philadelphia.[6] Another journalist, Ewing Poteet, drama and music critic of the New Orleans *Item*, lost his position for having signed a Fund-sponsored petition urging desegregation of the city's buses and trolleys.[7] A tragic victim of segregationist harassment was Juliette Hampton Morgan, a white librarian in Montgomery. Not an activist but an avid letter-writer, she had aroused the fury of segregationists by a number of her letters-to-the-editors of the Montgomery *Advertiser*, the Tuscaloosa *News*, and other Alabama newspapers. Over the years, she criticized Southern racial mores and dealt scathingly with the alleged psycho-sexual deviations of white Southern men, which she attributed to their double standard for white and black women. Miss Morgan had, on the other hand, earned the praise of the black community for publicly admiring the Montgomery bus boycott. In a letter to the *Advertiser* on December 12, 1955, she compared the boycott to Gandhi's famous "salt march" for India's freedom. Purportedly the first public reference to Gandhi in that context, her analogy stimulated Martin Luther King to endorse Gandhian methods for the struggle of black people in America.[8] As an alumnus of the University of Alabama, she had supported Autherine Lucy, the first black student at the University, when Miss Lucy was the object of white violence on that campus in 1956. A member of an old, respected Southern family with roots in Alabama reaching back to its frontier days, Miss Morgan was ostracized by the white people of Montgomery ostracized Miss Morgan and Mayor Gayle, once a close family friend, threatened her with loss of her job. After persistent badgering by the White Citizens Councils caused her health to decline, she died from an apparent overdose of sleeping pills in July, 1957.[9]

The Fund also felt the blows of the Citizens Councils. Having managed to operate a successful printing business along with his journal, *Southern Farm and Home*, Aubrey Williams lost some of his largest accounts, which forced him to sell the journal, and ultimately the printing end of his enterprise as well.[10] New Orleans banks handling the Fund's accounts became hostile, and some bank officers participated in efforts to "run them out" of New Orleans.[11] James Dombrowski discovered that the FBI, claiming suspicion of "potential subversion," was investigating white Fund supporters who entertained black people in their homes.[12]

Agreeing with the NAACP's Roy Wilkins, the *Patriot* noted that the main victims of the segregationist purge were young white Southerners. Of the

119

twenty-nine persons reported shot or wounded in racial incidents in the years 1955-1960, eleven were white.[13] A Mississippi State College professor reported that 81,000 persons, predominantly of working age, were leaving Mississippi annually and, despite the high birth rate, the population of the state in 1960 was likely to drop below that of 1950. The *Patriot* found further evidence for its belief in the fact that 40 per cent of the emigrants were white, and it placed the onus for the state's declining economy upon "the wild men" of the White Citizens Councils who were "'preserving' a 'way of life' that is intolerable to almost as many whites as Negroes."[14]

In the face of continuing persecution, the Fund continued to give moral support to critics of segregation, such as the black president of Millsaps College in Jackson, Mississippi, who publicly resisted Citizens Council intimidation.[15] In some cases it provided financial aid, as in its subsidy to P. D. East, a white Mississippi editor of a satirical anti-segregationist journal, the *Petal Paper*, in Petal, Mississippi.[16] It also commended politicians such as Winthrop Rockefeller, who called for an end to hate as an answer to social problems, and Governor Leroy Collins of Florida, who favored regional action against terrorist bombings.[17] By 1956, the Fund began to turn toward a more effective answer to the totalitarian politics of white segregationists: the development of black political power in the South.

Early in the year, James Dombrowski and Aubrey Williams had discussed the possibility of opening an office in Washington, D.C., supervised by Williams in order to make the best use of his numerous contacts in the capital. They agreed on the need for building national support for civil rights legislation and changing the Senate cloture rule, the real bottleneck in the way of effective legislation.[18] Baring resort to an outright police state which it found unlikely anywhere save Mississippi, the *Patriot* thought that the ballot would eventually silence "the racist demagogues" in the South. Once the Southern black community achieved its proportionate voting strength, the outmoded and unrepresentative political structures used as a sanctuary and source of power by segregationists would "change faster than litmus paper." It was no mere chance that the White Citizens Councils in Mississippi had acted to rig voting requirements even before "hedging the schools with legalistic bunkers."[19]

Others in the South also recognized and opposed the voting frauds that kept white supremacists in control. In Louisiana, for example, the White Citizens Councils had particular success purging voter registration rolls in twelve parishes and causing a drop of 10-11,000 black voters in 1956-57.

All twelve parishes were in the northern half of the state. Four of them had black populations of over 50 per cent; three had 16-33 per cent black populations; and the others from 33-50 per cent.[20] A former governor and Huey Long supporter, James A. Noe, discovered a Citizens Council maneuver in Monroe that resulted in the challenge and removal of 4,000 black voters from the election rolls. He financed a re-registration drive that restored the voting rights of 1000 blacks in that city. In the same parish, a white woman registrar who took seriously the educational requirements for voting enforced them equally against whites and blacks with the result that more whites than blacks failed the test. When outgoing Governor Kennon removed her from office, she appealed and gained sufficient time to permit the new governor, Earl Long, to reappoint her. Long also introduced a bill in the legislature eliminating the literacy requirements for voting. The *Patriot* commended Governor Long, commenting that for all the Longs' other shortcomings, they were not race-baiters a la Bilbo. Earl's brother Huey had, through quiet pressure, begun the removal of obstacles to black political participation in that state. As governor, Earl Long continued to oppose the White Citizens Councils and other staunch segregationists in Louisiana, though he never allied himself with outright integrationists such as those in the Southern Conference Educational Fund.[21]

The White Citizens Councils and kindred groups carried on a concerted effort in the South to prevent blacks from registering and voting, with growing effect from 1954, but particularly from 1956 to 1958. In Mississippi, Louisiana and Alabama, registrars dodged black applicants, often by declaring the registration offices vacant. In North Carolina, registrars used the literacy requirement to the same end by requiring blacks to "interpret" the Federal and state constitutions. The *Patriot* quoted a report from an assistant United States attorney general to the effect that in several Louisiana parishes registrars challenged blacks and ordered them to appear within ten days to prove their qualifications. They compelled black applicants to bring three witnesses who were voters in the same ward, but challenging all black voters in a ward meant that no one could serve as a witness.[22]

So effective were these tactics that in the four years following the *Brown* decision the Southern Regional Council concluded from its own intensive surveys that the number of black registrants fell between 1956 and 1958. In the eight states considered to have fairly reliable figures, the Council noted that in 1958, black registration was 1,028,827, compared to a 1956 total of 1,074,672.[23] In some sections of the South, according to the Council, "an attempt to exercise their right of franchise as Americans seemed a greater risk...than at any time since the outlawry of the white primary in 1944...."[24]

White supremacist strategy manifested itself in 1956 in several violent incidents which tested the will of Southern moderates and the Federal government to uphold the law and the courts. In February, Autherine Lucy entered the University of Alabama after winning a three-year battle to gain admission. Soon after she appeared on campus, segregationists whipped up a violent campaign of verbal abuse and physical harassment. They pursued her through several University buildings and prevented her from attending classes. The University administration did little to protect her, while Tuscaloosa city police and the Alabama state highway patrol were under orders to arrest no students despite the violence. Under pressure from white mobs and the segregationist-minded board of trustees, the University soon capitulated and suspended her in order to preserve "law and order."[25]

In September, when the Clinton, Tennessee, high school opened its classrooms to twelve black students, John Frederick Kasper, head of the white-supremacist Seaboard Citizens Council, appeared in the town to stir segregationists to action. Other outsiders did likewise. Governor Marvin Griffin of Georgia sent money; "Ace" Carter of the North Alabama White Citizens Council, and Senator Eastland, in an Alabama speech, bolstered their cause. Several days of rioting resulted in Kaspers' indictment in Federal court for incitement. The jury acquitted him, however, and his release contributed to the boldness of Clinton followers. After National Guard troops appeared to restore order, moderates in the town bestirred themselves. The school principal took a firm stand for the black children; a white minister walked with them through the town to the school and, after an attack by a white crowd, the great majority of the white population, alarmed at the course of events, resoundingly defeated the White Citizens Council ticket by a vote of 4-1 in the election for mayor and aldermen. Calm returned to Clinton.[26]

In an effort to bring national pressure to bear against the intimidation of blacks and white sympathizers, Aubrey Williams and Martin Luther King, Jr., leader of the Montgomery Improvement Association directing the bus boycott in that city, appeared before the platform committees of both the Democratic and Republican parties. They hoped to convince them that "the federal government has a clear duty to guarantee to all Southerners the rights and privileges of full citizenship." Offering petitions signed by residents of all the Southern states, they were the only Southerners to press for strong civil rights planks at the major party conventions. They called for a five-point program to include enforcement of Federal court decrees guaranteeing protection to all American citizens; enactment of legislation to implement the *Brown* decision and the pledging of Federal financial, technical and moral aid to compliant local officials; guarantees of the right to vote without threat or hindrance; revision of court procedures for redress of abuses against individuals; and revision of the Senate cloture rule so as to permit passage of civil rights legislation.[27]

Neither party, however, was willing to adopt a strong civil rights program. The campaigns of both Adlai E. Stevenson and President Eisenhower, with their vacillation on civil rights, caused dismay among Fund members and like-minded Southerners. "However you vote November 6," the *Patriot* commented sardonically, "you can vote with a clear conscience: either party's presidential candidate is likely to do as much as the other in regard to gaining enforcement of the Supreme Court's desegregation decrees. Both have displayed an equal lack of zeal on the issue."[28] The Democrats' civil rights plank was weak, asserting that "force" should not be used to carry out school desegregation decrees. In the House of Representatives, Howard Smith of Virginia kept the Rules Committee locked up on the civil rights bill until it was forced out by a Northern Democratic-Republican coalition and passed on the floor of the House, only to die in the Senate. Senate Majority leader Lyndon B. Johnson used his authority to prevent civil rights legislation from reaching the floor by keeping the Senate in recess, a tactic that prevented the calling of new bills which could only be done on a new legislative day. While expressing indignation about violence in the South, President Eisenhower displayed ignorance as to how Southern authorities were defying court orders to desegregate, and he did nothing to exert Federal pressure to implement such orders. "By contrast," asserted the *Patriot*, "tons of rhetoric have been expended on the farm problem, on Alger Hiss, and on who did or did not appease Juan Peron."[29]

Some movement on the question of civil rights began after the 1956 elections. With a margin of victory greater than 1952, the Republican administration took a firmer stand in the face of rising white violence in the South. In Clinton, U.S. Attorney General Herbert Brownell decided to prosecute those blocking integration of the town high school. A Federal judge found chief inciter of the mob, John Frederick Kasper, guilty, sentenced him to one year in jail for contempt and the violence then subsided. Brownell's action outraged segregationists, but it heartened supporters of the *Brown* ruling and put new life into the effort to frame a

Federal civil rights law in the 1957 session of Congress. The effectiveness of the contempt procedure in dampening violence in Clinton, together with the fact that it could be applied by a Federal judge without recourse to a jury trial, gave civil rights forces the incentive to include the contempt provision as a major feature of new legislation. The failure of juries to convict whites accused of intimidating blacks to deprive them of the vote had frustrated all legal action to secure integration in the South.[30] The jury-trial provision, however, now became the critical issue in the Senate debate over the 1957 civil rights bill.

In April, 1956, Brownell placed President Eisenhower's civil rights program before Congress. Largely a reiteration of former President Truman's civil rights proposals of 1948, it was limited to protection of the right to vote and did not strike against discrimination in general. The program called for establishment of a Federal Civil Rights Commission to study charges of voting violations and intimidation of blacks; the creation of a new Civil Rights Division in the Justice Department; and two new proposals permitting the Federal government to assume a more active role as guardian of civil rights. These included the strengthening of existing Federal statutes by eliminating the requirement that all state court remedies be exhausted before a Federal court could intervene in a civil rights case, and authorization of the Federal government to initiate court action protecting civil rights without the necessity of waiting for a court suit by an injured party. Blocked in the 1956 Congressional session because of Southern objections and the reluctance of both major parties to make a campaign issue of civil rights, the program reappeared in the 1957 session. Civil rights supporters added a new provision allowing Federal prosecutors to obtain Federal court injunctions without the necessity of a trial against real or threatened violation of court orders on pain of fine or imprisonment for contempt. Title III of the bill, in addition, gave the Justice Department and the new Civil Rights Commission authority to investigate and prosecute for violations, not only of the right to vote, but also of a wide range of civil rights infringements in employment, housing, public accommodations, and school desegregation.[31]

No sooner did the legislation reach the floor of the Senate than Southerners attacked the measure. They claimed that deletion of a jury trial in contempt proceedings was an assault upon fundamental constitutional protection of due process. Unable to filibuster the entire measure because of growing national pressure for some civil rights legislation, the Southerners prevented passage of the bill in its original form and whittled away at its provisions all through the spring and summer. During the height of the Senate debate, the Southern Conference Educational Fund gathered the signatures of eighty-five Southerners of both races to an advertisement in the Washington *Post and Times-Herald* in support of the bill *without* the jury trial provision.[32] The Fund clearly spelled out its views in an exchange of letters between Aubrey Williams and Senate Democratic leader Lyndon B. Johnson.

As a spokesman for the residents of border states who wanted tranquility and were ready to accept token desegregation, Johnson played a key role in guiding the bill through the Senate. He added a jury-trial amendment to placate the deep South, and he also permitted the elimination of Title III. He thus gained Southern acquiescence to a vote on the bill without a filibuster.[33] In a reply to Williams, Johnson argued that a number of Senators, such as Clark of Pennsylvania and Kefauver of Tennessee, "whose devotion to the 'civil rights cause' cannot be questioned," had grave doubts about the elimination of jury trials "through the use of a legal subterfuge." He could not, in all conscience, "juggle with the concept of equity in order to by-pass one of the fundamental concepts of our liberties." He did not think that an effective voting rights guarantee rested upon the denial of a jury trial in injunctive proceedings.[34]

Taking note of Johnson's argument that at least something would be gained through passage of the measure as it stood, Williams nevertheless thought that his Texan friend was not "thinking the thing through to the actual local situations where any civil rights law would have to prove itself." With Montgomery as an example, Williams wondered what would happen if, after a court ordered a registrar to register blacks with as much dispatch as he registered whites, the registrar continued to obstruct speedy registration. If a court found the registrar to be in contempt, Williams inquired if under Johnson's amendment, he could then demand and be entitled to a jury trial. If so, "then you can pass civil rights bills until you are blue in the face and you will not help Negroes in Montgomery, Alabama, get the right to vote," Williams declared. The jury trial provision was "sprung as a defeating move...now as our good friends from these deep south states see this thing coming down on them," he informed Johnson. "It was a clever stratagem but it should be seen for what it is and disowned and fought for that reason."[35]

The bill passed in its weakened form and, despite this, some considered it to be the "most significant piece of legislation in the field of civil rights since

125

the original Civil Rights Act of 1875." It was a herald of changing national attitudes to the role of the Federal government in protecting the voting privilege for black people. Yet it had little effect upon race relations in the South.[36]

Sensing the changing attitude toward southern events, both in Washington and the North, the Fund endeavored to expose to a national audience the segregationist denials of voting rights. Initially, it planned to launch a campaign for a change in the Senate rules so as to eliminate filibusters.[37] Stepping up its own activities, the Fund also added to its staff Carl and Anne Braden, a white couple long active in interracial activities in Louisville. The Bradens were the principals in the 1954 house-bombing incident that resulted in Carl's conviction and imprisonment for sedition in 1956. Newspaper reporters of many years' experience, they were also active in a number of church groups and labor unions in the Louisville area. The Fund requested them, as field directors, to give special attention to the voting problem and to organize Southern support for civil rights legislation at national and state levels.[38]

The Fund's program gained in relevance when a new crisis developed over the implementation of a school desegregation plan in the public schools of Little Rock, Arkansas, in September, 1957. As in Clinton, Tennessee, the year, before, white supremacists organized to foil the school board's plans. By forming jeering mobs outside the school selected for token desegregation, they persuaded Governor Orville Faubus to declare his opposition to both the school board and the courts. When Faubus sent Arkansas National Guardsmen to Little Rock to prevent the entrance of a handful of black children into the school, he forced President Eisenhower's hand. Having failed to plan or prepare for such an eventuality and having manifested a lack of zeal in enforcing desegregation, Eisenhower suddenly ordered U.S. Army troops into the city, bayonets drawn, to open the school to the city's black children. The incident aroused the nation, for the moment, to the clash of forces involved in the whole desegregation conflict, but it did not put an end to the crusade to keep the South in line with segregationist ideas. Rather, throughout the South it emboldened White Citizens Councils to continue their defiance of the Courts and the Federal government.[39]

The little Rock events, in the Fund's view, were a vindication of its work in the South. Aubrey Williams wired his congratulations to the President for his "firm stand" in the matter. He was pleased to see that Eisenhower had discovered what many in the South had known for a long time: "that the only time states rights are used is to obstruct the rights of minorities which are powerless and have practically no rights or protection under so-called states rights."[40] On the other hand, the Fund was convinced that mere capitulation to desegregation was inadequate and self defeating. Without acceptance of the moral validity of desegregation, and without confidence in the intellectual and emotional worth of integration for white as well as black children, the purely legalistic approach would fail to enlist majority white support. The Little Rock school superintendent, Virgil T. Blossom had for years discouraged all attempts by sympathetic whites in the city to help him develop plans for desegregation. His resistance to anything more than meeting the letter of the law was a prelude to the calamity that overtook the schools in 1957.[41] Recognizing that many white people in the South were ready to accept token desegregation simply on the basis of respect for law and order, the Fund viewed such acceptance as inadequate to the challenge integration involved for the white South. It held that there must be "a new crusade" to convince more white people that desegregation was "the right way." Failing this, there would be more Little Rocks or, equally unfortunate, a situation already existing in Northern cities and a danger in some border cities where token desegregation was in progress: "desegregation by law, but segregation still in fact."[42]

Stiffened in their determination to secure the entry of blacks into Southern politics, the Fund was convinced that had blacks been more active politically Faubus would never have dared to flout court orders and the Federal government in the interests of a small minority of vocal white supremacists. It therefore continued its financial support to several voter registration projects in the deep South in 1957 and 1958. While such projects were modest affairs, the Fund believed them to be the most important remedy in the long run.[43]

To involve more Southerners in its day-to-day activities, the Fund announced formation of a 102-member Advisory Committee with representatives from 18 Southern and border states and the District of Columbia. In support of its overall program, Northern friends of the Fund organized formal "Friends of SCEF" committees to increase financial, moral, and organizational support for the Southern program. The first group to organize was in Chicago where a noted neurologist, Dr. Roland P. Mackay, arranged meetings and house parties for Fund board member E. D. Nixon. Other committees formed soon after in New York, Detroit and Los Angeles. The organization also announced a sizeable increase in its budget for 1958,

127

planning a total expenditure of $41,185 as compared with $25,500 the previous year. The increase was primarily for new staff, additional publications and educational material, and more travel for staff members. The new plans called for the organization of a hearing in Washington, D.C., in the spring of 1958.[44]

The Washington hearing, set for April 27, had among its aims the encouragement of public pressure on Congress for the quick and early acceptance of nominees to the newly created U.S. Civil Rights Commission, and the airing of evidence of voting right violations in the South.[45] Coordinated by the Bradens and a number of black community leaders in the capital, the organizers hoped to have Attorney General William P. Rogers and an official of the Justice Department's Civil Rights Division as main speakers and well-known Southerners as reporters.[46] At one point James Dombrowski thought to invite the President himself to address the conference. Aubrey Williams readily agreed to write Eisenhower adviser Sherman Adams for his assistance, and Dombrowski proposed forming a delegation to visit Adams requesting an interview with the President.[47] More realistic considerations soon dispelled these musings. On reflection, Williams thought that it would be a mistake to invite government officials just for prestige purposes for fear that they "would use this for political purposes and give insincere tone to the meeting." He thought it better to have someone "direct from the struggle," and he singled out Dean Charles Gomillion of Tuskegee, attorneys Arthur Shores and Austin T. Walden, of Birmingham and Macon respectively, and Martin Luther King, Jr. One of the Washington black sponsors suggested as headliner Williams himself.[48] Though sentiment for a "name speaker" persisted, the sponsors preferred instead to rely upon the reports themselves to attract the public.[49]

More pressing than the celebrities problem was that of guaranteeing the interracial character of the meeting. Anne Braden spent much of her time attempting to drum up white attendance for the gathering. Since it was to be held in a black church, there was reason to expect a sizeable black turnout.[50] Dombrowski, however, cautioned her not to take black attendance for granted since it had been his experience that black people "do not attend functions sponsored by whites or even a mixed group." He advised her that should they fill the house "it will be feathering your cap and that of the Committee"; he suggested contacting student Americans for Democratic Action groups who had expressed a desire to cooperate.[51]

In the early planning stages, the Fund received assurances of support from many church groups whose good offices were crucial for success. The Jewish community of the capital also looked favorably at first upon the meeting. Noted Washington Rabbi A. Balfour Brickner, Isaac Frank of the Jewish Community Services, and representatives of the American Jewish Congress and B'nai B'rith all promised support.[52] The assistance of Jewish leaders was particularly desired in order to counter criticism that "Jews in the South were not doing their part in the integration movement." This criticism had been reported to exist among Southern blacks, Carl Braden asserted, and it had been "played upon by the white supremacists to encourage anti-Semitism among Negroes and thus further divide the minorities in the South."[53]

Important assistance came from Mrs. Eleanor Roosevelt's highly successful fund-raising affair held in honor of Williams at the Hotel Delmonico in New York City on February 26. Mrs. Roosevelt urged her listeners to "support these organizations and these people who are doing the work that we in the North are not able to do." The well-attended luncheon garnered $13,000 for the Fund, and it also provided valuable publicity for the Washington hearing.[54] Williams informed the gathering that the South was going through "one of the worst periods I can recall. It has brought into being forces that we thought were on the decline," with many moving from the White Citizens Councils into the Ku Klux Klan because they regarded the Councils as too mild. In a hopeful note, he saw among southerners a "mass decency" which had to be encouraged "to keep the white South in the struggle." Williams was seconded by E. D. Nixon and Dean Gomillion. A warm telegram from Martin Luther King, Jr., praised both Williams and the Fund as "very helpful and very much needed in this period of transition."[55]

The publicity and efforts of its supporters notwithstanding, the Fund had difficulty with several of the larger, well-known organizations such as the NAACP and the Americans for Democratic Action, whose national offices, wary of the "Communist" tag on the Fund had decided against cooperating with it. While local officers of both groups were cooperative, Anne Braden reported a coolness in the national office of ADA. Efforts to reason with one of its officers floundered because it was "awfully hard to talk to somebody who's still living in the 1930's when it's almost 1960."[56] A black NAACP official told the chairman of the local arrangements committee that he could not afford to operate with the Fund because it had been labelled "pink" and he had to protect his organization.[57] The NAACP attitude particularly hindered efforts to gain support from white liberals in the city since they tended to take the word of the NAACP "as final on what efforts of this kind they should support." Local people thought that NAACP coolness would have little effect on black attendance, however, because that organization was peculiarly ineffective among blacks in the District.[58] The Bradens and their associates were anxious to prevent open or even disguised attacks upon the Fund by those liberal groups critical of it. Such attacks might dampen the effect and perhaps even disrupt the hearing.

Some supporters dropped out. Most painfully, Rabbi Brickner demurred just prior to the opening of the meeting and thus prevented other Jewish notables from replacing him; but the Fund was pleased with the support it retained. Several hundred local and national church, civic, and civil rights organizations received announcements of the hearing. Aubrey Williams sent letters to Lyndon Johnson, Sam Rayburn, Lister Hill, John Sparkman and Allan Ellender on April 15, noting that while they "probably wouldn't want to be caught dead with me at the meeting," he wished it were possible for them "to avail yourself of some of the information" to be presented.[59] James Dombrowski suggested to Anne Braden that the conference organizers consider sending an invitation to all Southern governors to come personally or send an observer.[60]

The conference assembled at the Asbury Methodist Church in Washington, D.C., before an interracial audience of almost 1000 people. After an invocation by a white Unitarian minister and a brief statement of the aims and nature of the Southern Conference Educational Fund and its hopes for the hearing by bishop Edgar A. Love of Baltimore, Aubrey Williams warned Americans of dangers to their own freedom in selective enforcement of the Constitution. However poor relations between black and white had become since the May, 1954, Supreme Court ruling, he saw little reason for complete despair because of a new spirit among black people of the South. A new generation, brought up with the admonition to "keep peace with the white man at any price," had now decided to possess their freedom; the Montgomery bus boycott and the Tuskegee Civic Association's struggle for the right to vote were highlights of this new mood. Williams considered it a "great sadness" that black people carried on their struggle in "naked aloneness." They engaged the white supremacists of the South and the political, educational, and law enforcement institutions and a considerable number of the churches of the region. Also they often found the Federal government helping to keep them from "the enjoyment of the rights vouchsafed under this self-same federal government." Disparaging the

130

Administration's retreat from enforcement of Supreme Court decisions after Little Rock, Williams remarked that there was more concern in the Federal government and on Capitol Hill "that there be no more Little Rocks than that justice be done."[61]

Placing the attainment of voting rights in a larger framework, Williams thought it quite probable that black political emancipation had begun a major political realignment. This emancipation he said "could be the activating agent that threatens to explode the present ill-mated political setup." Depending upon the determination of Southern blacks and the political weight of their Northern and Western brothers, the combined pressure of black people would finally force the "Southern Oligarchy" into the Republican party to join its conservative counterparts in efforts to preserve the "present power structure in control in our country." Liberals in both the major parties would eventually be forced to recognize their own self interest in uniting behind "their respective professions and promises." The common interest of progressive Americans of both races was to bring about the opportunity for a fundamental realignment in American politics. "We must recognize the Negro's struggle for what it is," Williams concluded, "the spearhead which...if it succeeds, can clear the ground of the creeping fascism and totalitarianism which is inherent in the thinking of the power elite and their supporters, the conservatives and reactionaries of both parties."[62]

Moving on to the reports from the South, the audience at times gasped at accounts of the often maddening obstacles put up by local authorities and state governments to black registration. Again, the deep South states of Mississippi, Alabama, Georgia, Louisiana, and parts of Florida were the bedrock of white supremacy. A white minister from St. Petersburg, Florida, described how the power structure of that state, faced with the first victory of a black man in a North Florida county primary election for justice of the peace, simply had the legislature declare the election illegal, rewrite the laws increasing the number of positions, and force a new runoff in which the black candidate lost by a fair margin. In North Carolina, though blacks in the larger cities had a somewhat easier time, the black-belt eastern counties faced the insurmountable hurdle of tortuous literacy tests and a complicated chain of appeals which discouraged most from even attempting to vote. Other reporters from Virginia and Louisiana narrated at some length cases of intimidation and loss of economic livelihood for those blacks who registered or attempted to get others to do so. Dean Gomillion detailed how Alabama registrars delayed registrants, avoided them or closed their offices and posted no notices for further registration, and in other ways violated the law. There were some bright spots. After leaders of both parties in Maryland publicly declared that the black vote was of no significance and refused to pass civil rights legislation in the state legislature, supporters of such measures organized a highly successful voter registration drive that netted 15,000 new voters in Baltimore alone. White supremacists in South Carolina, where the NAACP had been active for years, feared further legal actions by blacks and avoided more obvious tricks to deprive them of the vote. In all states, in addition to political manipulation and outright fraud, other factors such as poor education and low income, largely consequences of black powerlessness, furthered general political apathy among black people.[63]

James M. Nabrit, Jr., of Howard University, summed up the report and urged three types of action: political pressure for a strong, decisive report by the new Civil Rights Commission; a southwide state-by-state registration campaign to increase the number of blacks on voter rolls; and an educational campaign to raise the level of political understanding among blacks. He emphasized that though this might boomerang if alarmed whites should register and vote in greater numbers, he thought it more likely they would remain indifferent. In either case, increased black registration alone would be a strong inducement to white politicians to seek the black vote and make it politically hazardous to ignore it. [64]

After the hearing, Aubrey Williams, Bishop Love, and Francis A. Gregory, assistant superintendent of Washington schools and chairman of the local arrangements committee, led a delegation to present the reports to George Tiffany, staff director of the Civil Rights Commission. Tiffany was responsive. He invited the reporters to continue supplying the Commission with information, and he also agreed to work with them in unearthing additional facts. The delegation received a similar response when calling upon members of the Civil Rights Division of the Justice Department. They then lobbied among members of Congress to urge confirmation of the Commission and more teeth in the civil rights law.[65] After calling upon the Commission to send members of its staff South to hear for themselves the stories of intimidation and vote deprivation, the members of the delegation entreated Congress and the President to provide a remedy "while there is still time."[66]

The Fund's new emphasis upon gaining Federal support for black voting rights in the South met with greater success than its appeals to white Southerners. Its new approach coincided with growing support among non-Southerners for civil rights action, as expressed in the revival of Congressional activity for new legislation. With the establishment of the U.S. Civil Rights Commission, the Fund found valuable assistance and a new voice within the Federal government for civil rights. Encouraged by this new turn in national opinion, the Fund was hopeful about the success of desegregation, though it was prepared for a difficult time in view of continuing segregationist opposition.

EIGHT

Subversion and SCEF: Carl Braden and Others

Fresh from its successful Washington vote hearing the Fund again came under fire. Field director Carl Braden now became the personification of subversion to Fund opponents. The house Un-American Activities Committee announced its own hearings for Atlanta on July 29-30 purportedly to uncover the operations of the Communist Party in the South. The score of witnesses subpoenaed included Carl Braden and other white integrationists; only one witness was black.[1] Aubrey Williams wrote to Representative Emmanuel Celler of the House Judiciary Committee claiming the hearings were a design by Richard Arens, Committee counsel, and its chairman, Francis Walters, "to publicly pillory any white person, Jew or Gentile, who openly favors and works" for desegregation. Charging that their purpose was to intimidate whites working for integration, Williams urged Celler to bring the matter before the full house "and force a showdown," since Celler had only just concluded testifying before the Judiciary Committee deploring mounting violence against "certain races in the South," and in favor of increased governmental protection for them.[2]

The Fund president telegraphed Lyndon Johnson and Sam Rayburn to call Walters and Arens off, "or you are going to find yourselves minus the Negro vote in those Northern states you have got to have if you want to win in 1960." He informed them that black newspapers were replete with stories of the Committee's hobnobbing with Georgia's Governor Griffin and Attorney General Cook, leading segregationists favoring a "states rights" party in the South.

Griffin and Cook were among Southern politicians who were hauling the NAACP into court, attempting to jail its leaders for membership in it, and now branding white friends of the black man in the South as "communists" and "traitors" "disloyal" to their country. Williams dismissed the charge of "communism" as "of absolutely no moment" in the South. The targets he saw were Southern liberals and others, like Rayburn, who had power and

135

were above dictation by die-hard white supremacists who wished things in the South could be "left as they were in McKinley's time."[3]

While the Fund circulated an open letter to Southern black leaders emphasizing the Un-American Activities Committee's assault upon integrationists, Carl Braden sought to arouse community concern at the Committee's appearance in Atlanta.[4] Williams continued his efforts to get Congressional floor action against the Committee. He volunteered his services to Representative James Roosevelt of California, who was sympathetic, offering to testify in Washington, if necessary. Williams wanted an investigation into the Committee's activities in Atlanta, its relations with other government agencies, and "most important of all who are they working with down here." Noting the wave of bombings, maimings, and other terror incidents in the South against Jews and blacks, which the Committee apparently did not consider "un-American activities," he questioned its sincerity of purpose. What they were doing in reality, he advised Roosevelt, was taking up the white supremacists' equation of "communism" with integration and defense of the rights of minorities. "It is a common knowledge," he asserted, "that down here advocacy of equality for Negroes makes one a Communist, in fact that is a Ku Kluxer's and white citizen council member's definition of a Communist."[5]

The Fund's efforts were effective with Southern black spokesmen and the black press. For the first time, prominent blacks publicly stood with Southern white integrationists and called upon Congress to keep the Un-American Activities Committee out of the South. Two hundred black notables, including clergymen, college presidents and educators, editors and publishers, and other professionals and civil leaders, took a full page ad in the Washington *Post and Times Herald* expressing their concern at the Committee's failure to investigate the recent wave of police terror in Dawson, Georgia, the bombings of Jewish synagogues and black churches in several Southern states, and the repeated intimidation and violation of the right of blacks to register and vote. The signers strongly condemned the Committee's harassing and "subversive" labeling of "any citizen who is inclined to be liberal or an independent thinker," and of "any liberal white Southerner who dares to raise his voice in support of our democratic ideals." In reference to President Eisenhower's appeal for greater communication between white and black Southerners, they declared that attacks by Eastland and the Committee "spread [terror] among our white citizens," making it

136

increasingly difficult to find white people who are willing to support our efforts for full citizenship. Southerners, white and Negro, who strive today for full democracy must work at best against tremendous odds. They need the support of every agency of our Federal Government. It is unthinkable that they should instead be harassed by committees of the United States Congress.

Congress, they demanded, should use its influence to keep the Committee out of the South "unless it can be persuaded to come to our region to help defend us against those subversives who oppose our Supreme Court, our Federal policy of civil rights for all, and our American ideals of equality and brotherhood."[6]

Attempts to have the statement placed as an advertisement in the Atlanta *Constitution* failed because the journal feared repercussions from politicians and white supremacists in Georgia.[7] Nationally, the black press gave much attention to the projected hearings, some commenting that the primary target "appears to be the Southern Conference Educational Fund, a group of predominantly white liberals who try to discharge their moral responsibility on the question of integration." The question was not Communism, wrote well known Los Angeles black journalist Jack Tenner, but whether the laws of the land were to be upheld. He urged the abolition of the Committee as well as a strong protest against its use of the power and prestige of Congress "to aid segregation."[8] The Baltimore *Afro-American* and spokesmen for the Negro Newspaper Publishers Association expressed similar sentiments.

More specific reasons for the Committee's subpoenaing of Braden was his activity in organizing opposition to a bill in Congress to revive state sedition laws declared void by the Supreme Court in the 1956 *Nelson* decision. That decision had reversed Carl Braden's conviction under the Kentucky law arising from his purchase, and the subsequent bombing of a house for a black friend in a Louisville white neighborhood. Braden had spent eight months in prison until the Supreme Court's decision freed him. The *Nelson* ruling aroused criticism in Congress, and Un-American Activities Committee members led efforts to curb the Court.[10] The Bradens believed that the Committee had been piqued at the "somewhat less than honorable role" in which Anne Braden had cast it in *The Wall Between*, a book about the Louisville case, published eight days prior to the Atlanta hearing.[11]

At the inquiry, Braden refused to answer questions about the policy-making process in the Fund, persons active in it, or the activities of other Southern integrationists and Northern civil libertarians. Six of the seven questions put to him, covering the seven counts of his indictment, specifically

137

concerned civil rights activities. The other inquired if Braden was a Communist Party member at the time of the previous board meeting of the Southern Conference Educational Fund. To all of them, Braden declined an answer and concluded his appearance declaring that "my beliefs and associations are none of the business of this committee."[12] Another witness, Frank Wilkinson, who had advocated the Committee's abolition and had been asked by the Bradens to come to the hearing as an observer, was subpoenaed moments after arriving in Atlanta. He took the First Amendment with Braden. Congress cited both for contempt on August 13, 1958.[13] Only newly-elected black Representative Robert C. Nix of Philadelphia voted against the citations, on the strength of the statement of black leaders in the *Washington Post*.[14]

Furious at this second Congressional attack on the Fund, Aubrey Williams asserted that Chairman Walter had consorted with Governor Griffin and others who had "by word and deed, day in and day out, defied the Government of the United States" for the purpose of destroying or driving from the South any organization upholding the Constitution's equal rights provisions. He also linked Richard Arens, of Walter's staff, to Roy Harris, Griffin and Cook, all ardent white supremacists. Williams charged that Arens had been in constant contact with them before and during the hearings and that Arens had used pictures of Fund members attending a Board meeting the previous December in Atlanta. Presented as exhibits during the hearings, they had been surreptitiously taken by the Georgia Education Commission, which Cook headed. When Walter replied that Williams' complaint convinced him that the hearings "must have been very good and effective," Williams challenged him openly to debate their value and significance. Walter did not seize the bait.[15]

The hearing and resulting contempt citation, along with the threatened imprisonment of Carl Braden, affected the Fund in ways the Eastland hearing of 1954 did not. In the course of many discussions evaluating the significance of this latent attack and the need for a response by the Fund, the relationship of civil liberties to the organization's civil rights program absorbed the attention of its officers. At first, the Bradens proposed that the case be handled by the Emergency Civil Liberties Committee (ECLC), a civil liberties defense organization to the left of the ACLU,whose director was Clark Foreman. The ECLC had offered to take up the defense of Braden and of Wilkinson, who until recently had been an ECLC board member. A strong incentive in favor of such a decision was the high cost of legal briefs, educational material, and the services of leading constitutional lawyers Leonard Boudin and Victor Rabinowitz. The Bradens feared that the costs of legal defense and the diversion of energies into a civil liberties issue would impair the work of the Fund. They therefore suggested that either they be temporarily relieved of connection with the Fund, or that it give only moral support to Braden while leaving the defense burden in the hands of the ECLC. Besides, they were uncertain as to the attitude of Fund supporters toward his case.[16]

Braden's co-defendant, Frank Wilkinson, vigorously refuted this reasoning. He thought that Braden's defense should be handled by the Fund as "an anticipated defensive battle in an over-all offensive campaign," the first of many skirmishes the fund must expect in the near future. Wilkinson viewed the Southern connections of the Fund as an asset. He also regarded Fund attorney John N. Coe as an effective civil liberties lawyer, especially in view of Coe's National Lawyers Guild ties. Basically he wanted to steer Braden clear of reliance upon the ECLC. Formerly a member, Wilkinson had broken with it and switched to a Los Angeles organization, the Citizens Committee to Preserve American Freedoms, which included several current and ex-members of ECLC. The Los Angeles group disliked the essentially legalistic, defensive posture of the ECLC and favored a more vigorous, offensive strategy to combat the House Un-American Activities Committee and other crusaders against "subversion" who, they believed, were rapidly destroying the Bill of Rights. Wilkinson informed Braden that the ECLC, though it had offered to undertake the expense of defending him, would rely upon Braden's good name and that of the Fund to raise considerable sums in the New York area. Judging from past experience with others in similar situations, Wilkinson believed the money would then be diverted to general expenses of the ECLC. He argued that because of Braden's integration activity and subpoena, the Fund could raise at least as much in its own behalf. He urged Braden to stress his Southern identity as a staff member of a Southern organization, and a person defended by Southerners. Wilkinson made light of Braden's belief that some Fund contributors might not approve of their money going into anything but the "direct fight for integration." "What happened to you in Atlanta," he asserted, "*is* the direct fight for integration "[17]

Wilkinson's argument impressed James Dombrowski. Though he preferred the Fund to be on the offensive, Dombrowski realized that it would have to fight important defensive actions in the coming years. In fact, merely to stay alive would take some doing, for he was convinced that "the principal attack" would continue to be harassment by the junior versions of the House Committee in the Southern states. He expected, specifically, assaults from the Johns Committee in Florida and the Rainach Committee in Louisiana, among others.[18]

As a result, the Bradens accepted the offer of Leonard Boudin to head Carl's defense and tactfully informed Clark Foreman that the Fund had decided to undertake the Braden case for its own educational purposes in the South. Braden persuaded John Coe to enter the case as an associate with Boudin and received Boudin's consent to add a black Louisville attorney and Fund member, A.M.E. Zion Bishop C. Ewbank Tucker, to the defense battery.[19] Another black attorney, Conrad Lynn, offered his services and they were accepted. Lynn had worked on the Wade-Braden case in Louisville, and he had connections with the NAACP and the Southern Christian Leadership Conference, an important organization of Southern black ministers.[20]

The decision to make Braden's defense an integral part of the Fund's program did not sit easily with all of the organization's supporters. A long-time Fund supporter and staunch liberal, Albert Barnett, emeritus dean at Emory University's School of Theology, pledged his cooperation; yet he thought that Braden should have answered the questions of the House Un-American Activities Committee. He argued that rather than attacking the Committee's legitimacy, Braden would have done better to criticize its misuse of authority so as "to go on with the business in hand which is integration." He recalled this as the course Dombrowski and Williams had taken at the Eastland hearing which stand he believed, "met favorable reaction."[21] Others less confident than Barnett wanted assurances that the Fund was not a "Communist front" or even in sympathy with the Communist Party.[22]

Anne Braden sought to reassure her husband's critics. Barnett's position had the virtue of reasonableness and common sense in distinguishing between civil liberties and civil rights. She, however, defended Carl's refusal to answer questions on First Amendment grounds arguing that it was the indispensable protection for those who would attempt to improve "our very imperfect society." Congress did not have to pass a law negating free speech or association for it effectively to silence dissenters. The mere inquiry into beliefs, she argued, created a climate of fear which would have the identical result without incurring the onus of scrapping the Constitution itself. By granting to Congress or governmental agencies the right to question private citizens about their beliefs, Barnett would soon concede the right of the state to regulate private lives. The investigation itself shaped public attitudes, and soon people would begin to accept the proposition that certain ideas and associations were henceforth proscribed; before long it would become common knowledge that to step over the line would cost one his livelihood, his friends, his very right to pursue his chosen field of work. In such an atmosphere, the first victims would inevitably be those working for social change, since their efforts required as a precondition the very freedoms the First Amendment guaranteed and which the Un-American Activities Committee so blithely ignored. In the face of governmental violations of free speech and association, the individual under attack had several courses of action: attempt to oppose the government by talking against it; organize to change its officials and enact different laws and procedures; or refuse to cooperate with it when it struck at one directly. Braden had adopted the latter course, in effect one of passive resistance.[23]

Though not directly criticizing the stand Williams and Dombrowski had taken in 1954, because under the circumstances of that time they might very well have acted similarly, the Bradens did question the effectiveness of their position. They had met numerous persons who refused to cooperate with the Fund claiming that its officials had been accused of being "communists down in New Orleans." Of all who had raised this objection, "not one...had ever heard that Aubrey and Jim both testified they were not communists. The answer just never catches up with the question," Anne Braden asserted.[24]

The dialogue with Barnett convinced the Bradens of the need for the Fund to undertake greater efforts "to get the First Amendment back into people's consciousness."[25] As a perceptive and courageous Southern liberal, Barnett was typical of those who condemned the Un-American Activities Committee's failure to investigate atrocities against blacks while accepting as legitimate the Committee's investigations of opinions and beliefs. The Fund would have to enlighten Southerners on the connection between civil liberties and desegregation.

A manifestation of deeper conflicts in American politics, the Atlanta events drew attention to the central issue of American society as it entered the sixties. The increasing pressure for full equality for black people was developing explosive potential. The 1957 Civil Rights Act intensified black demands for broader, more effective measures now that an end to their long exclusion from the benefits of American life seemed to be in sight. These pressures extended constitutional rights and by lifting the oppressive restrictions of segregation strengthened the libertarian features of American society. At the same time, efforts to restrict the liberties of all Americans in the interest of "national security" were approaching a climax.

The Supreme Court under Chief Justice Earl Warren was the focus of this contradiction. Beginning with the *Nelson* decision in 1956, the Court began to clip the wings of investigating committees of Congress and their counterparts in the states which sought to make national security and "loyalty" the test of political legitimacy. Individual rights of free expression and association were under severe attack throughout the fifties. Congressional committees badgered, censured, and imprisoned witnesses for refusal to surrender their right under the First Amendment to remain silent about their beliefs. State officials and lawmakers similarly abused many persons in and out of government employment for refusal to submit to political inquisitions directed at Communists and their sympathizers. The Cold War had effectively muted social criticism by radicals. To national security alarmists and others opposed to the orientation of the Warren Court, Congressional legislation appeared to be the most effective recourse.

The *Nelson* decision, by claiming that Federal laws had preempted the field, precluded the states from prosecuting state citizens for sedition. It thus had invalidated laws in over 40 states, Alaska and Hawaii, and jolted those in Congress deeply concerned with the problems of subversion. Joining with segregationists in a strong coalition, they sponsored a score of bills to upset the decision. This coalition settled upon a House measure, H. R. 3, which, besides excepting state sedition laws from Federal preemption, attempted to undo the preemption doctrine entirely by excluding all state laws from Federal interference unless expressly overruled by Congress. The proposal had wide ramifications and imperiled the interests of many groups, particularly labor unions and interstate businesses, whose opposition was of indirect aid to civil libertarians.[26]

National security and segregationist advocates returned to the fray in 1957. In June, the Supreme Court, by a 6-1 margin in the *Watkins* decision, attempted to limit the powers of Congressional investigating committees. Subjecting committee questioning of witnesses to the test of pertinency to legitimate legislative purposes, the Court declared that First Amendment rights had priority on such occasions. In the *Sweezy* decision, handed down the same day, the Court upheld the same limitations for state legislative investigations, particularly restricting intrusions into academic freedom. Both rulings provoked the Court's critics to respond by introducing the

Jenner-Butler bill in the Senate. The bill drastically curbed the appellate jurisdiction of the Supreme Court by extending to Congressional committees the authority to decide for themselves the question of pertinency and, thereby, punishment for contempt of Congress. The bill also allowed Congressional committees the authority to control their own investigations subject to the will of the House or Senate; restored enforceability to some forty-three state anti-subversion statutes voided by *Nelson*; and amended the Smith Act to make it applicable to current activities of the Communist Party.[27]

Like the anti-*Nelson* H.R. 3, the Jenner-Butler bill was part of a wide-ranging attack upon the powers of the Supreme Court. This thrust of "massive retaliation" against the Court was almost assured of success because of the coalescence of anti-Communists and segregationist opponents of the *Brown* ruling.[28]

Both measures were a direct threat to the Southern Conference Educational Fund. In 1954, Braden, prosecuted and convicted under the Kentucky state sedition law, had received a 15-year sentence. He had served eight months when the *Nelson* decision voided the statute and effected his release. The House bill now threatened to put white integrationists into their earlier position, for in the eyes of its opponents integration was tantamount to subversion and sedition. In 1958, the bill seemed assured of passage after easy sailing through the House and an apparently solid coalition of Republicans and Southern Democrats in favor of it in the Senate. Even liberals such as New York Republican Senator Jacob Javits favored the measure. When a Fund supporter had written Javits about segregationist intentions, Javits, a former state attorney general, replied that "a state has the same right to protect its sovereignty against subversive influences as the Federal Government has to protect the sovereignty of the United States."[29]

In a near panic at the possibility of passage of H.R.3 and similar bills, Aubrey Williams wired Senate majority leader Lyndon Johnson that "if you pass the *Nelson* decision bill they will put people like me in jail for advocating the right of Negroes to vote."[30] Johnson urged Williams to take his advice and "keep your shirt on. The Senate in my judgement is not going to do anything that will wind up by throwing innocent people into jail."[31] In a close vote on August 21, the Senate voted 41-40 to send the anti-*Nelson* bill back to the Judiciary Committee, thereby killing the bill for the 1958 session.

Pressure for adoption of both measures built up again in the 1959 Congressional session. Supporters of the bill permitting states to prosecute for sedition now adopted a new tactic. They separated the first and second sections of the bill. The first one embodied the broader provision giving states concurrent jurisdiction with the Federal government over all legislation unless expressly denied by Congress. This section had stirred the greatest misgivings among business and labor groups, and thus served as a lightning rod for opposition. The second section specifically exempted state sedition laws from Federal preemption and threatened to slip by unnoticed. The strategy confused opponents who were not alert to the new development. James Dombrowski wrote Mrs. Roosevelt informing her of the progress of the sedition bills in Congress and urged her to use her influence with the NAACP to oppose their adoption.[32] Fund lobbyists in Washington discovered that NAACP officers Roy Wilkins and Henry Moon, who had opposed the adoption of the anti-*Nelson* bill, were unaware of the new tactic separating it into two measures. AFL-CIO lobbyists were also unaware of the tactic and Fund representatives quickly furnished copies of the new measures to both groups.[33]

Aubrey Williams button-holed his Capitol Hill acquaintances. In an hour-long talk, Lyndon Johnson confided to Williams that "the situation is worse than it was last year." The lineup on the Senate Judiciary Committee was about even, with Senators O'Mahoney of Wyoming and Alexander Wiley of Wisconsin doubtful.[34] At a loss as to how to approach Wiley, Williams contacted "some old stalwart friends" in Wisconsin for their advice.[35] He then attempted to meet O'Mahoney and wrote him a long letter expressing his fears about the impact of the proposed legislation upon integrationists in the South. Stressing the need for greater communication between the races in the South, Williams informed O'Mahoney that "the inevitable result" of giving the states concurrent jurisdiction in the sensitive and vague field of sedition would be a rash of legislation that would wipe out the small amount of interracial communication still existing. Any inquiry into sedition would lead to inquiry into speech, thought and writings and, in the present climate of political opinion in the South, such inquiries were "as likely to be into stories about black and white rabbits or the 'Three Little Pigs' as into the writings of Lenin and Stalin." By the time the Supreme Court could re-assert the fundamental principles, integrationists and others willing to abide by the desegregation decisions would have been "silenced and herded into conformity with the racial fanatics and the damage will have been done."

Aware of O'Mahoney's state rights beliefs and no "champion of an all-encompassing Federal power" himself, Williams maintained that without the rights thrown around the individual by the Constitution, "our form of government cannot long continue."[36] Besides informal pressure, the Fund helped to organize a public mass meeting in Louisville on May 22, 1959, at which Southern black leaders called upon Kentucky Senators Morton and Cooper and the Kentucky Congressional delegation to oppose the anti-subversion bills. Martin Luther King and ministers from all black church denominations issued a similar appeal to Congress.[37]

Debate on H.R. 3 in the House of Representatives revealed the intense Southern interest in the bill. House Judiciary Committee Chairman Emanuel Celler strongly opposed the measure, claiming that it was "an attempt to tell the Supreme Court of the United States how to conduct its business;" while Representative Byron Rogers of Colorado saw in it an "expression of discontent with the liberal decisions of the Supreme Court...." Barratt O'Hara of Illinois declared that "everyone knows that the real issue here is civil rights. H.R. 3 is the rock. The Supreme Court of the United States is the target." O'Hara declared that his Southern colleagues, fully aware that they were fighting "on the last foothold of what they know is a lost battlefield," had wrapped themselves in the "brilliant robes of the dear old doctrines of Federal preemption" to preserve their social order. The Southerners were fully aware, if others were not, that "this is the civil rights battle in the 85th Congress when trial by jury was the battle cry."[38] Despite strong opposition, the bill passed the House on June 24th, 1959, by a vote of 225-192, with 114 Republicans and 111 Democrats in support. Again, however, it failed to pass the Senate. In fact, most of the other Court-curbing and anti-civil liberties legislation also failed of passage in 1959.

The principal reason for the turn of events against these measures in Congress was a reversal in the attitude of the Supreme Court. By two 5-4 decisions on June 8, 1959, *Barenblatt v. United States* and *Uphaus v. Wyman* the Court undid the restrictions it placed upon Congressional investigating committees and their state counterparts in *Watkins* and *Sweezy*. The change of attitude in the high court sharply reduced Congressional enthusiasm for Court-curbing legislation.[39]

In *Barenblatt*, Justice Harlan speaking for the majority made a far-reaching declaration about Congressional power to legislate in the field of Communist activity. He declared that such activity was, by its very nature, an illegitimate conspiracy outside the bounds of accepted political discourse in this society. As such, it was a threat to American institutions and constitutionally a legitimate subject of Congressional inquiry, exposure, and legislation. In balancing the competing private and public interests at stake, Harlan declared, Congressional power in the last analysis "rests upon the right of self-preservation, 'the ultimate value of any society.'" Hence, the witness's First Amendment right not to answer gave way to the government's right of self-preservation and its right to have information about subversion. Abuses by legislative committees were not to be remedied by what Harlan regarded as parallel abuses by the judicial authority. The remedy lay "in the people, upon whom, after all, under our institutions, reliance must be placed for the correction of abuses committed in the exercise of a lawful power."[40]

In the *Uphaus* decision, the Court reversed the *Sweezy* ruling by upholding the conviction of clergyman Willard Uphaus for refusing to divulge guest lists at his summer World Fellowship Camp in New Hampshire. The Court accepted the state's argument that "subversives" were known to have attended the camp and the state had a need to know this and proceed against them. The Court, implicitly rebutting *Nelson*, held that the state could prosecute on the theory it might find evidence of sedition against the state alone. These decisions constituted notice to Congress and to the states that they need have little concern about judicial limitations on their investigatory powers; they also opened the door to Southern segregationists to use the full power of the state against their opponents.[41]

In November, the Florida state legislature cited three black ministers who were leaders of the NAACP for refusing to turn over names of NAACP members to the Florida Legislative Investigating Committee. Thus Florida put the *Uphaus* decision to use in the desegregation controversy.[42] The *Barenblatt* decision placed Carl Braden's case in jeopardy since he had taken essentially the same approach as Barenblatt, claiming First Amendment protection when refusing to answer the questions of a Congressional committee. Although Barenblatt had refused to reply concerning his membership in the Communist Party, and thus came within the purview of the Court's decision, Braden was in peril because he had refused to answer questions relating to his integration activities. The government argued that the *Barenblatt* ruling applied to Braden because Committee counsel had information "that defendant was a Communist or cooperating with Communists." Under this interpretation, all that was needed to evade First Amendment restraints was for the Committee to claim that it was investigating Communist activity. Anything could be labelled "Communist activity" since part of the anti-Communist mystique was that the Communists were ubiquitous, if not omnipotent. There was no way to check what "information" the Committee had to back up its claim.[43] Months of sparring between Braden and his attorneys, Leonard Boudin and John Coe, over appeal strategy came to an end as they found themselves forced to make a frontal assault upon *Barenblatt* in hopes of reversing its sweeping endorsement of unlimited Congressional inquiries into speech and association.[44] While his attorneys prepared to do battle before the U.S. Supreme Court, Braden worked to strengthen the Fund.

Embroilment with the House Un-American Activities Committee and the Justice Department ironically created new opportunities for the Southern Conference Education Fund. The Atlanta hearing elicited an outcry of protest from Southern black spokesmen against the Committee. It was "a big step," the Bradens believed, "toward building the kind of joint Negro-white movement we want to build in the South." Dependent as such cooperation was upon the willingness of blacks to work with whites, as well as the reverse, this new expression of support was welcome. Now that important segments of the Southern black community had reacted forthrightly in behalf of White integrationists the prospects for positive movement toward integration seemed brighter than at any time since 1954. Many in the Southern Conference Educational Fund looked to Anne and Carl Braden to provide the movement with creative ideas at this juncture.[45]

Both were native Southerners. Anne Braden had grown up in Mississippi and Alabama, while Carl Braden was a life long resident of Louisville. Their family backgrounds, however, were quite dissimilar. Anne came from a respectable, upper middle-class family of Anniston, Alabama, and, as many well-bred Southern women before her, she attended private schools, including Randolph-Macon College in Virginia. Carl Braden was born into a working-class family in Louisville. His father was a railroad worker, and the family knew grinding poverty in Braden's youth when his father joined thousands of other workers in the bitter railroad shopmen's strike of 1922. From his father, who was a devoted supporter of Eugene V. Debs, Braden developed a life-long attachment to socialism, to which his mother's Catholic faith added an ethical-religious dimension. The strong family ties of the Bradens created in Braden the inner strength to overcome poverty and other social obstacles facing a working class youth in the South of the twenties and thirties. At one point in his youth, Braden attended a Catholic seminary in Cincinnati with the intention of entering the priesthood, but his restiveness

147

led him away from the Church and he became a newspaper reporter instead. Active in the labor union struggles of the thirties, Carl Braden was a copywriter on the Louisville *Courier-Journal* at the time he met Anne in the mid-forties. After graduating from college, she also entered newspaper work, first in Birmingham and then in Louisville.

Carl's labor union activities involved him in interracial friendships, and he drew Anne into his orbit of relationships when the two met while working on the same newspaper in Louisville. For Anne, Carl's world was a shattering, albeit liberating experience. The emotional and intellectual walls that segregation and years of indoctrination in white superiority had built around her crumbled under the impact of sharing social, political, and simple human experiences on an equal basis with black people. These interracial encounters rekindled the religious ethos of her Episcopalian upbringing with its emphasis upon human brotherhood and helped to make Anne a fervent advocate of a truly interracial society. Partly motivating her zeal, admittedly, was a deep sense of guilt over the privileges that white people, such as her own family, enjoyed at the expense of blacks. Almost inevitably, these activities of the Bradens culminated in the house-purchasing incident of 1954 that transformed their lives.[46]

In the Spring of 1954, Carl Braden responded to a request from a black friend, Andrew Wade, to locate more adequate housing for his young, growing family outside the poor black ghetto of Louisville, Kentucky, where they both lived. Not fully aware of the risks, the Bradens purchased a home in an all-white Louisville suburb, as Wade had desired, and then resold the house to Wade. The Wades immediately became the object of racial attacks which escalated into gun-fire and, ultimately, the dynamiting of the house. In the subsequent uproar, a politically ambitious district attorney, with the overwhelming approval of "respectable" white Louisville and the fearful silence of much of the black community, indicted Carl Braden under the provisions of a nearly-forgotten state sedition statute. A search of the Bradens' home had uncovered "subversive," i.e., radical, literature which convinced the skeptical that "communism" was, as feared, at work insidiously undermining the otherwise excellent race relations of the city. In the prevailing climate of racial and anti-Communist hysteria, Carl Braden was convicted and sent to prison, serving eight months of a fifteen-year sentence. He was released from this ordeal only when the U.S. Supreme Court ruled such state sedition statutes unconstitutional in the 1956 *Nelson* decision.

By 1957 the Bradens were about to leave the South for Chicago to work with civil liberties groups in opposition to the House Committee on Un-American Activities. But Anne had misgivings, and a letter from Aubrey Williams persuaded her and Carl to forego the move and remain in Louisville and the South. Williams had urged them not to leave the city "where you have sown your very blood in the streets and in the courts and in the prisons...under any circumstances, except on a stretcher." He gave identical advice to other liberal Southerners who wanted to leave the South for "the cleaner land of forgetfulness in the north." Williams' plea, and an offer to join the staff of the Southern Conference Educational Fund as field secretaries, ultimately induced the Bradens to remain.[47]

Though optimistic about the potential for constructive action in the South, the Bradens were aware of the general frustration and isolation of white liberals. They were convinced that the main drawback to the developing integration movement was the near absence of communication between Southern white people, as well as between them and the black community.[48] After surveying integration activity in most Southern states in May and June of 1958, they concluded that there was little movement toward integration. Rather there were many individuals of diverse outlooks and similar goals going their separate ways, often without knowledge of others of like mind in the same community. Still there was activity in most sections in behalf of desegregation, among both races, enough to encourage them to propose that the Fund become a nerve center of inter and intra-racial communication in the South.[49] They suggested that the Fund hold at last one annual Southwide gathering around a timely theme dealing with integration. Such affairs would advertise the fact that there were whites in the South willing to stand up and be counted. They would also make the Federal government aware of Southerners who needed and desired its assistance. The 1958 Washington vote hearing had served this purpose well, and the Bradens favored holding a similar conference at Williamsburg, Virginia, in 1959, to celebrate the tenth anniversary of the Fund's Declaration of Civil Rights adopted at Jefferson's home. The Fund's semi-annual board meetings, they believed, should be held as workshops for members and others in the community invited to participate. The previous fall one such workshop had been held at Fisk University in Nashville where Aubrey Williams delivered an analysis of the program of the Fund. The organization's state committees could hold similar meetings more frequently to involve their own supporters and to create a tighter-knit group of activists.

149

Their proposals included expanding the *Patriot* in size and frequency of publication. They hoped to make it an effective Southwide newspaper, more thorough and accurate than the existing commercial press which was largely hostile or indifferent to integration in the South. The Bradens hoped to build a network of correspondents to keep themselves informed on regional developments, as well as to encourage activity by correspondents in the course of reporting upon events. Local people had a great need for the Fund to contact potential sympathizers and devise leaflets, pamphlets, radio and TV programs, and news releases. The Fund, largely because of the Bradens' knowledge of the newspaper world, was developing an effective information system for black, labor, religious and national newspapers.

In the matter of voter registration, the single most important concern of the organization, the Bradens suggested that the wisest course was to provide funds for better situated local people. Important as was the stimulation of white activity for integration, the Fund's best hope would continue to be black political participation. Recognizing that the Fund itself was too weak to make a real difference in the South, they nevertheless believed the commitment of its members made a profound difference by helping to develop the people "who will change history in the South." Like Lucy Randolph Mason more than a decade before, the Bradens viewed the Fund's educational function to be neither that of converting others, nor "trying to organize people according to a blueprint we devise." Instead it was "a catalytic agent" stimulating people "to find within themselves the strength of their convictions, and to determine through communication among themselves the best organizational forms for working toward the social change they seek."[50] They sought means of interaction to help create a larger sense of community among Southern integrationists, noting that the Ku Klux Klan and the White Citizens Councils "provide their followers with this feeling of belonging to something bigger than themselves, albeit something negative." Surely integrationists should inspire people "by providing them with a positive program based on their own deep feelings and traditions." The task had to be done by dedicated persons thinking about "integrating our society rather than their own personal glory."[51]

Traveling through Mississippi, Carl Braden discovered that despite an atmosphere heavy with violence and fear, black leaders were deeply involved in voter registration work. At first they gave their attention to the literate through voter clinics and then began thinking about an adult education program to reach the vast numbers of illiterate blacks in the Delta. Some black spokesmen informed Braden that the white landowners had mechanized their farms. Though this had created a surplus of black farm laborers, black leaders were encouraging their people to remain in Mississippi. Asked for his assistance, Braden requested the Fund to help finance a black service station operator in Cleveland, Mississippi, Amzie Moore. A Marine veteran, Moore was active in the voter project along with a black Roman Catholic priest, Father John LaBauve of Mound Bayou. At great risk to himself, Moore had directed a project in the heart of the Delta despite white economic pressure and the fear tactics of White Citizens Councils. He had also helped his wife operate a beauty parlor and another man a cafe on the same property, but he was in need of funds to keep up his mortgage and insurance payments. Moore told Braden of his plans for encouraging similar enterprises in Mississippi as part of the social, economic and political liberation of his people.[52]

That Moore and Father LaBauve had extensive contacts east of the Mississippi River augured well for the voter project, and Braden thought that keeping them and other black activists in Mississippi was also vital to the aims of the Fund. He attempted to persuade Fund leaders to support Moore. Braden had a difficult time, however, convincing Aubrey Williams. Visiting him at his home in Montgomery, Braden found him pessimistic about the possibility of locating significant black or white support. Furthermore, Williams was fearful that a grant to Moore would drain the Fund's small treasury. Assisted in his arguments by Montgomery bus boycott organizer E. D. Nixon, Braden informed Williams that many people in the North and West were wondering what the Fund was actually doing besides publishing quantities of literature. Because the Fund was already supporting a voter project in Alabama under Nixon's direction and there was no difference of principle involved, Williams finally assented.[53]

Years of social isolation and incessant attacks from fellow Southerners had taken their toll on Williams. Bitterness and disappointment, mingled with the realization that cancer was sapping his vitality, began to undermine his optimism and increase his irritation at imagined slights and disagreements with associates. Not long after the Fund took on the Bradens, Williams and Carl Braden, both of them blunt and outspoken, began to rub against each other's exposed nerves. Personality conflicts were only a part of the relationship; more significant were developing political or strategic differences. Though critical of the practices of the American business system and political structure, Aubrey Williams remained a firm liberal throughout his life. Racial equality, he believed, could occur within a capitalist system reformed in the direction of a welfare state. Braden, on the other hand, was a convinced socialist who viewed racial conflicts as inherent in the capitalist structure of American society. Relating race and class conflict, he believed unity of black and white workers to be the most effective instrument for resolving the ills of American capitalism. Where Williams took pleasure in the company of prominent politicians and upper-middle-class persons of both races, Braden felt at home with working people. An effective speaker and organizer, he would much rather socialize at simple church suppers, union meetings, and interracial gatherings than at the more formal fund-raising affairs Williams arranged in New York City. These differences manifested themselves sharply as fund-raising problems developed. The spring 1958 Hotel Delmonico affair in New York, chaired by Mrs. Roosevelt for Williams and the Fund, opened the way for more intense efforts to raise money for the Fund's activity in the South. In her talk Mrs. Roosevelt suggested that the Fund create a permanent fund-raising committee in New York.[54]

The Bradens and James Dombrowski immediately set about organizing a committee of New York supporters. Aubrey Williams, however, registered a strong dissent. He did not think that people of the stature of Mrs. Roosevelt, Justine and Shad Polier of the American Jewish Congress, and publisher Freda Kirchwey of the *Nation* magazine, all of whom had lent their support to the Fund's annual affairs, could be expected to meet regularly. He advised Anne and Carl Braden "to take what they are willing to give you and not push them" to any greater effort, lest they "soon wash their hands of you."[55] Braden was upset when he discovered that Williams had been telling people in New York that the Fund had no intention of establishing a permanent committee. The Bradens had been cultivating the field in the city at the time and were irritated at Williams' apparent ignorance of their efforts.[56] Braden wrote to Williams clarifying his plans and pointed out that there was no intention of having celebrities staff the New York committee. Rather, there were a number of lesser-known, though influential, people who had already formed a committee similar to those in San Francisco, Los Angeles, Chicago, Boston and Philadelphia. All they expected of Mrs. Roosevelt and the others was willingness to lend their names to the Fund's effort and to attend the annual benefits as they had in the past. Without a permanent committee, the Bradens would be forced to spend most of their time in Northern fund-raising to the neglect of their duties in the South.[57]

The Williams-Braden dispute was symptomatic of the different approaches, as well as the marked difference in the range of contacts of the two men. Williams was adept at getting contributions from wealthy sympathizers without having to undertake a systematic program of year-round appeals. One such contributor was an heir to the Woolworth fortune, George Pratt, who gave $10,000 to the Fund in 1958 and similar sums in later years.[58] The weakness in Williams' method was that it made the Fund, in effect, entirely dependent upon the reputation of one man; without Williams, the contributions from such sources would soon cease. For its future stability, the Fund required a more permanent, on-going operation. By the end of 1958, the chief problem was securing a person with experience, contacts, and dedication to the Fund's program who would serve as a full-time fund-raiser in the East.

Eventually, the New York committee and Braden settled upon the Reverend William Howard Melish for the position.[59] An Episcopal clergyman with long experience in interracial work, Melish had as a youngster caught the eye of millionaire philanthropist George Foster Peabody. Peabody brought Melish's father from Cincinnati in 1904 to be minister at Holy Trinity Church in Brooklyn, a post which the younger Melish later held. As a youth, Melish had mingled with many black intellectuals at Peabody's Saratoga home, and as a student at Harvard he had roomed with the son of the president of Hampton Institute. Active for many years in Cincinnati parishes, Melish involved himself in interracial youth work. He had toured the deep South visiting Tuskegee, Howard and other black colleges. After taking up his post at Holy Trinity in 1939, first assisting his father and then succeeding him, he had involved that church actively in the affairs of a community that had a growing black population.

Holy Trinity's vestry included black people, who also comprised 40% of the congregation. Melish encouraged the development of a regular Negro History Week program that brought noted speakers to the community; he developed an inter-faith exchange with other Protestant and Jewish clergy; and he took the lead in welcoming W. E. B. Dubois as a resident to the Brooklyn Heights area. He helped to spark a campaign to open up the swimming pool and other facilities to blacks at the Hotel St. George located in the Heights; and Melish's wife assisted the parish in maintaining a teenage program for some 400 black and Puerto Rican youth, in the downtown Brooklyn area. In addition to interracial activity, Melish was well known among left-wing circles as the national chairman, since its founding in 1942,

153

of the Council on American-Soviet Friendship. He was also active in the American Labor Party which had supported Henry Wallace for President in 1948. His activities drew criticism from the Protestant Episcopal Diocese leadership in Brooklyn. In 1949, the Diocese sponsored an effort to deprive both Melishes of their control of Holy Trinity, involving them and the largely pro-Melish congregation in a long controversy which was still simmering at the time of Melish's consideration for the Fund post.[60]

Melish's controversial reputation immediately increased the tension between those who feared connecting the Fund to a person of Melish's background and others, like Braden, who would brook no submission to red-baiting. Braden insisted upon judging Melish on his personal merit, experience, and dedication to the work of the Fund. Because a number of Fund supporters were close to Mrs. Roosevelt, James Dombrowski apprised Williams of the Melish application, and urged him to seek her impression of Melish. Dombrowski emphasized that he was the most qualified applicant who would consider working for the Fund at the relatively meager annual salary of $6,500.[61] In his correspondence with the former first lady, Dombrowski reiterated the Fund's need for a person of Melish's experience and willingness to work despite low pay. He also noted that Judge Hubert T. Delany, a Fund supporter and NAACP board member, had convinced him that Melish would be an effective fund-raiser.[62] Obviously piqued, Mrs. Roosevelt expressed her disagreement with Delany. Emphasizing that the Southern Conference Educational Fund "has a hard enough time now without employing such a controversial figure," she declined to speak or preside at the Fund's forthcoming benefit if Melish were present. Though agreeing to attend, she preferred "not to act in a capacity which makes me responsible for Mr. Melish."[63] Anxious to allay her distrust, Dombrowski sent her a copy of Melish's autobiography and urged her to give Melish a chance to prove himself in the position before passing judgment upon him. Noting the similarity in educational and ecclesiastical background between Melish and himself, Dombrowski regarded him as "a person who has been persecuted and deeply hurt because, and only because, he has been true to his deepest religious convictions as they applied to the struggle for peace, justice and freedom." Though he had never met him personally, Dombrowski sympathized with Melish because of their common social gospel background so out of step with what Dombrowski regarded as the straining for personal success and institutional advancement among contemporary churchmen. He thought Melish had "much to contribute to an area where there is so little leadership." When a similar controversy had developed over the retention of the Bradens because of their past, the Fund's decision to disregard all considerations except their personal merit "had been amply vindicated."[64]

Stressing that the Fund's best hope was for Melish to do a successful job, Aubrey Williams urged Dombrowski to go easy with Mrs. Roosevelt since he was not going to change her mind.[65] None too sympathetic himself with the Melish appointment, Williams thought that the best way to deal with the dispute was to place the best interests of the Fund before the feelings of either Mrs. Roosevelt or Melish. He did not, however, accept Judge Delany's argument that the Fund had to develop a grass-roots approach in its fundraising instead of the informal one hitherto practiced. Williams doubted that such an approach was realistic, since "after twelve years in the West, there are no grass roots [and] even in the South, the grass roots are relatively shallow." He argued that there "just isn't enough time and money to get that kind of widespread support. We must get as much money as cheaply as we can and send it down South. I can't see any city-wide grass roots movement."[66] After tightening its own structure, the New York committee agreed to retain Melish on a 6-month trial basis. Dombrowski was to handle the problem of smoothing over relations with Mrs. Roosevelt.[67]

Working enthusiastically in association with the New York committee, Melish arranged numerous parties in the city and also made the rounds in Connecticut, Massachusetts and New Jersey. In addition to raising money for the work of the Fund, the parties were educational affairs bringing together persons sympathetic to integration but otherwise inactive. Melish helped bring black activists to New York to speak about Southern developments. These meetings served to widen the horizons of Southern blacks and Northern supporters. They helped to develop a sense of common interest in desegregation, encouraging thought about the problems of an integrated society and the immense obstacles to be overcome. They also alerted Northerners to the deep crisis in the South: blacks were on the move there and needed support from outside the region. Melish's efforts were highly successful. By June 1, 1959, he had raised a total of $20,000 for the Fund, more than such parties had produced in all of 1958. As a result, he continued on a permanent basis.[68] The fund-raising efforts in New York were an important link in communications between Southern activists and Northern supporters of integration. With a solid basis of financial and political support outside the South, Braden now felt more secure returning to the South and pursuing his ideas with renewed vigor.

NINE

New Ferment in the South: 1958-1960

Attacks upon the Fund from the House Un-American Activities Committee and defection of powerful supporters did not deter it from seeking new opportunities to advance integration in the South. In two states, North Carolina and Florida, the Fund lent a hand to local people who had bestirred themselves and sought its aid. Widely held to be "moderate" in its racial attitudes, North Carolina was, unhappily for its reputation, under severe challenge from its black population. In 1956, Mrs. Louise Lassiter, a black teacher from Northampton County in the northeastern black-belt had attempted to register to vote along with twenty-five other blacks. She failed, however, to impress the white registrar, who rejected her on grounds of having "mispronounced several words" while being examined on the literacy test. Mrs. Lassiter filed suit in Federal Eastern District Court seeking a permanent injunction to restrain election officials from using the literacy test to determine voting qualifications. In April, 1957, seven days before the Federal court hearing, the North Carolina General Assembly amended the state statute in order to provide for appeals from the registrar's decision to the county board of elections and up the chain to the State Superior Court. On June 10, the three-judge Federal court declared the disputed article of the state constitution in violation of the 14th and 15th Amendments to the U.S. Constitution. But it did not declare itself on the new amendments and, retaining jurisdiction in the case, recommended that Mrs. Lassiter exhaust all administrative remedies and seek constitutional interpretation in the state courts. Following this procedure and again turned down by the registrar, the county board, and the state courts, Mrs. Lassiter took her case on appeal to the U.S. Supreme Court on July 1, 1958. She retained a black lawyer from the state, James R. Walker, Jr., who had the aid of local citizens in publicizing the case. Hostile whites, including law officers, harassed Walker and jailed and fined him on trumped-up charges. At this juncture the Bradens, on the request of the Walker-Lassiter Defense Fund, entered the case, preparing news releases and raising money for the group. The Bradens also sought and obtained the services of Leonard Boudin, Braden's counsel, to enter an *amicus* brief before the Supreme Court in the Lassiter case.[1] The Fund's publicity and legal efforts pressured the NAACP national office, which had previously declined assistance, to enter the case.[2] Though it received national attention as a serious constitutional challenge, the Lassiter appeal eventually lost in the U.S. Supreme Court, which refused to upset the literacy requirement in its 1959 session.

Concurrent with the Lassiter-Walker case was an incredible sequence of events in the town of Monroe, in Union County. In November, 1958, two black youngsters, aged 8 and 10, playing with several white friends in a ditch kissed a 7-year old white girl. The girl's parents panicked at this breach of Southern racial etiquette. Six carloads of police subsequently whisked the boys away to the county jail and held them without charges for several days. After a hearing before juvenile authorities, and after the briefest notice to the boys' parents, who had no benefit of counsel, the court sentenced them to indeterminate sentences at the state reformatory, the Morrison Training School at Hoffman. This occurred in a community alive with tension for over a year because of the militant desegregation activities of Union County NAACP president Robert F. Williams and Dr. A. E. Perry, a black physician and Williams' second-in-command. A Marine veteran, Williams had returned to Monroe determined to break down its color bars. He met with solid white hostility; the Ku Klux Klan organized demonstrations, parades and shooting incidents against him and Perry. Undeterred, they organized their own protective guard, and the town of Monroe teetered on the brink of open warfare.

Hearing of the boys' railroading, Williams contacted NAACP authorities. When the national NAACP and its North Carolina state officers kept hands off the affair, attorney Conrad Lynn entered the case. Lynn helped to form an interracial Committee to Combat Racial Injustice. Carl Braden served on the Committee, and within a month the Monroe "kissing case" became an international *cause celebre*, eliciting outrage from the European press and intellectuals who vigorously denounced the U.S. State Department's "white-wash" of the case as a "non-racial incident." Governor Luther C. Hodges reluctantly reversed the juvenile court's decision and the state authorities released the boys in the custody of their parents, welfare clients "rehabilitated" in new lodgings with the aid of the NAACP.[3]

The Braden's activities earned the Southern Conference Educational Fund a wealth of goodwill from North Carolina blacks. In May, 1959, they and sympathetic whites met at Shaw University in Raleigh to form the first "Friends of SCEF" organization in the South.[4] In response to an inquiry from Dr. Alexander Moseley, chairman of the "Friends of SCEF" and active in the Walker-Lassiter Defense Committee, Braden suggested that the group spearhead a campaign to establish a Federal voter registration commission. This had been proposed in H.R. 7957, a bill introduced in the House of Representatives. It would create and empower a commission to register voters under Federal law wherever state law discriminated on literacy or other grounds. Its importance for North Carolina blacks was obvious. An effective campaign in behalf of the bill, Braden asserted, "might do more than all the lawsuits you could file from now until 2000 A.D." They would also be a welcome addition to a campaign undertaken by the Fund and the Tuskegee Civic Association, as well as other groups in the South and nationally.[5]

The North Carolina events underscored the Fund's relationship with the NAACP. Because the Southern blacks were in the forefront of the desegregation struggle and they regarded the NAACP as their own, the Bradens considered the NAACP to be the most important organization in the integration movement. The NAACP had the Fund's support and in many areas Fund supporters were also members of the NAACP, although in the South relatively few whites were active in it affairs.[6] Despite disagreements with national NAACP leaders, Braden and other Fund members took pains to avoid competing with, or publicly criticizing, the organization. The events in Monroe sorely tested this policy. The "kissing case" had become a center of controversy within the NAACP because the North Carolina state chairman and the state field representative kept hands off until forced into activity by the vigorous stand of Union County leaders Williams and Perry. When the Committee to Combat Racial Injustice entered the case, North Carolina attorney general Malcolm Seawell began red-baiting to discredit the entire case against the state. A prominent consideration in his suspicion of the Committee was the presence of Carl Braden on its board. Reputed to be a racial "moderate," Seawell publicized Braden's Congressional contempt citation and his Louisville conviction.[7] In addition, the counsel for the Committee, Conrad Lynn, had a reputation for accepting unpopular cases. He had defended a number of Puerto Rican nationalists who had attempted to assassinate former President Truman, as well as several civil liberties cases involving Trotskyists and other leftists. The red-baiting gave the state NAACP officials further reason to undercut Williams and Perry, and rumors soon spread about their "intemperance" and "unreasonableness"; an NAACP national officer, Gloster Currant, reportedly referred to Williams as a "wild man" for his vigorous testimony in court when the case reopened.[8]

The attitude of the state and national NAACP and their half-hearted support of the Monroe blacks caused Robert Williams to contemplate leaving the organization. He made a number of public statements casting the Association in an unfavorable light. Braden advised Williams and George Weissman, chairman of the Committee to Combat Racial Injustice, not to create a dual organization, but to ignore the whispering campaign against them. He counselled them to keep to the matter at hand, the exoneration and release of the black youngsters unjustly incarcerated and taken from their parents. His main interest, Braden informed Weissman, was to avoid setting up an organization in competition with the NAACP. The "idea of being a gadfly is fine," he declared, "so long as it cannot be twisted into the appearance of being a horsefly."[9] Braden urged Williams to remain within the NAACP and fight for his ideas and policies there, because the association in Union County was in a strategic area of the South. Outside the NAACP Williams would lose his effectiveness. Having earned a national reputation for his militancy, Williams would not have to fear reprisals by national NAACP leaders; rather, in tandem with others in the organization, Williams could play an important part in moving the NAACP itself into a position of greater militancy.[10]

Braden had further opportunity for reflection after Williams publicly called upon blacks to meet "violence with violence," and to stop "lynching with lynching." The NAACP reprimanded Williams and suspended him for six months from his position as branch president in Union County.[11] Though cognizant of the reasoning behind Williams' position, Braden expressed his own preference for the nonviolent philosophy of Martin Luther King. He thought that "people have a distorted view of King's philosophy and I believe history is going to show this very soon." Contrary to prevalent conceptions of King's views as involving "cowardice or Uncle Tomism," Braden thought that it

> takes more real courage to participate in non-violent direct action than it does to take up a gun and fire back at an attacker. The latter is easy; anybody who can pull a trigger can do it. Only a person who has developed strength

through love of his fellow man can take the abuse, and perhaps even physical assault, that often goes with non-violent action....[12]

The Williams controversy was a portent of changing moods among blacks; Braden and the Fund were soon to face critical choices vis-a-vis the black movement and its relationship with white sympathizers.

Integration activity in Florida was in sharp contrast to North Carolina, where energetic local movements needed only the professional advice and assistance of Braden and the Fund. Integrationists in Florida were in disarray and often demoralized. Two Miami women active in community affairs wrote to express their dismay at the limited activity to desegregate public schools. While various social agencies engaged in "manipulatory, behind-the-scenes" moves, the absence of open public agitation encouraged segregationists and deepened the apathy and sense of impotence of integrationists. The Dade County Council for Community Relations, much like its parent Florida Council, contented itself with sponsoring neighborhood discussion groups and distributing literature on desegregation problems. The professionals in the organization placed the emphasis on a compliance with the *Brown* decision. They did not wish to antagonize powerful segregationists in northern Florida who sought to protect their pupil assignment laws and were, under threat of abolishing the public schools altogether, pressuring moderates to accept a parent-option bill. There was a woeful lack of leadership among blacks in the NAACP, while the Congress of Racial Equality (CORE), tend to be "timid and unsophisticated" in its approach.[13] In Miami, the American Jewish Congress took a more forthright position in behalf of desegregation, but its participation with other groups in a "unified agency" effort hampered its ability to take meaningful action.[14] Surmising that the mood of integrationists in other parts of the state must be similar, the women suggested that the Fund help organize "some kind of state-wide medium for communication and action." A meeting of people from as many counties as possible would determine the resources for action available in the state and begin the process of exchanging state-wide information. Possibly a steering committee would take shape as an instrument for further action and communication.[15]

James Dombrowski took up their suggestions and proposed a statewide meeting in June with carefully selected people as the nucleus of a planning committee. Informing the Miami pair of the Bradens' current visit to central and northern Florida, Dombrowski noted that the Fund staff had for some time looked upon Florida as "one of the most fruitful fields for action."[16] By the end of September a committee of persons from Miami, Jacksonville, and the University of Florida at Gainesville, met to plan a larger gathering for the Fall. Among its difficulties was locating a place suitable for an interracial meeting, particularly if it involved sharing meals.

These difficulties compounded a more serious problem of leadership. The Miami people wrote despairingly of the actions of CORE which had attempted a demonstration in Miami without proper planning and training. As a result of CORE's poor tactics, local sympathizers became embroiled in costly court action. The fiasco had convinced the Miami people that leadership and control henceforth must be in the hands of blacks themselves with whites in a supporting role "and in no way manipulatory." Blacks, however, were also divided among themselves, and existing organizations tended to have too narrow a base of support in the black community. Thus, white persons either left the existing groups or took a totally passive role in them.[18] This absence of initiative among Floridians was a serious impediment, and Carl Braden insisted that the local people organize themselves rather than wait for outsiders to do the job. The CORE experience was something the Fund did not wish to repeat.[19] As a start, the Bradens suggested that the proposed meeting arrange a realistic agenda for action so as not to discourage people by failing to attain goals that were as yet much too ambitious. They suggested some lobbying in the state legislature as a specific objective and as a program to present to others for concrete action.[20] Braden was to attend the proposed meeting, and Dombrowski asked William Melish to accompany him.[21]

On a journey in November, 1959, ranging over the width and breadth of the state, Melish and Braden began to comprehend the scale of the problems facing integrationists in Florida. John M. Coe, the Fund attorney who resided in Gulf Breeze across the bay from Pensacola, related the case of a condemned black man, John Edward Paul. Convicted of rape on the flimsiest evidence, Paul's conviction had drawn a strong dissent, unusual for a Southern jurist in a case involving a black man, from State Supreme Court Judge Drew. The white woman involved had identified Paul from a police lineup by "smell and the sound of his voice" alone. She testified that her child had been asleep in bed with her, her husband had been in the next room, and neighbors within fifty feet, and that she had called out and screamed numerous times; all to no avail. Governor Collins, a racial "moderate," had been impervious to appeals on Paul's behalf. In another part of the state, another black man, Willie City, also had been convicted on a

162

rape charge. Both he and Paul, were to die in the electric chair despite the fact that several white men recently convicted of raping a black co-ed at Florida A & M University in Tallahassee, had been sentenced to life imprisonment. Coe defended Paul, while the American Civil Liberties Union took up City's cause. Yet neither knew of the existence of the other case.[22] A Fund supporter, Reverend Ben Wyland, attempted to arouse the public conscience of St. Petersburg to a third rape case involving a black man. But Wyland, too, was unaware of the City case. Practically without public protest, the executions of both Paul and City took place on November 14, 1959.

Braden and Melish visited the courageous woman editor of the Mt. Dora *Topic*, Mrs. Mabel Reese, who had won a number of awards for her crusading efforts. They found Mrs. Reese locked in controversy with Lake County Sheriff Willis McCall, who rivalled Police Commissioner Eugene "Bull" Connor of Birmingham in his reputation for brutality toward black people. McCall had aroused public resentment for railroading a mentally-retarded teenage white boy, Jess Daniels, into a mental institution for life. After a white woman, fearing public notoriety, had withdrawn charges against a black man for allegedly raping her, McCall arrested Daniels when the woman charged her assailant was white. McCall kept Daniels incommunicado for four days, fired shots into his cell to intimidate him, and permitted the woman's husband to enter the cell with a rubber truncheon. By beating the wall the man forced a "confession" from Daniels, who had the mentality of an eight year old. A long-time foe of McCall, Mrs. Reese thought she now had an opportunity to terminate his career. She faced severe economic pressure, however, and had to seek other employment four days a week merely to keep her paper alive. Her plight was also unknown to integrationists elsewhere in Florida.[23]

Braden interpreted the plague of rape cases as a design to intimidate blacks. They were part of a pattern that included efforts by the Florida Legislative Investigating Committee to destroy the state NAACP, public threats by the Klan, and economic pressure by the White Citizens Councils. The rape cases were, he thought, an attempt to keep the races separate psychologically "by implying something animal and inhuman to the Negro."[24] Both Melish and Braden agreed that Florida integrationists were too individualistic and had little sense of the importance of communication with others of like mind. Moreover, the example of John Coe was symptomatic of a larger obstacle to an effective statewide movement. Deserving his reputation as one of the best lawyers in the South, sensitive and willing to defend blacks in difficulty, Coe had little contact with the NAACP in his own home city. He lived in a community which permitted no black person to enter except on a specific domestic or other employment assignment. This territorial and economic gulf between the races was a barrier that good will alone could never bridge. Far deeper than school integration or common transportation facilities, it was grounded in accumulated privilege, real estate, and inheritance. Real integration had "this basic Sahara desert of tangible property ownership" to reach over and cross. The very humanity of people like the Coes made Melish and Braden sense the difficulty of the total problem.[25]

In spite of many difficulties, the potential for leadership was encouraging. Among white people, in addition to Reverend Wyland in St. Petersburg, who was the moving spirit in his own Florida Council for Racial Cooperation, there was a professor of education, Hal Lewis, at the University of Florida at Gainesville. Lewis headed a Committee on Human Rights that brought together people of both races, including the first black student and his wife to be admitted to the University's professional school. There we a number of white students from Florida State University in Tallahassee who had joined black students from Florida A & M in the local CORE group and the NAACP youth organization. Most impressive were the black leaders Braden and Melish encountered. Tallahassee had the Reverend C. K. Steele, "a dapper, little man" who had led the bus boycott several years before as head of the city's Inter-Civic Council. One of the founders of the Southern Christian Leadership Conference, Reverend Steele was also on the board of the Southern Conference Educational Fund. In Miami and Coral Gables there were the three leaders of the Florida NAACP, all of them clergymen: Episcopalians Theodore Gibson and A. Leon Lowry and Baptist Edward T. Graham. Lowry was president of the state organization. All three impressed Braden and Melish with their intelligence and courage in the face of the attacks of the state legislature. Attesting to the reach of Fund supporters were a number of blacks in Jacksonville, including prosperous realtors and an elderly railroad clerk. The latter's fondest memories were of his days at Tuskegee; he had been part of the honor guard when Booker T. Washington returned from his historic dinner at the White House with President Theodore Roosevelt. This group of middle-class blacks contributed generously and regularly to the Fund; they made, for example, an important and sizeable loan to Amzie Moore's project in Mississippi.[26]

Difficulties persisted in bringing these different groups and personalities together, since none appeared willing to assume direction for all. Consequently, Dombrowski asked Braden to prepare a memorandum setting forth his ideas for a full board discussion and review of overall organizational policy in regard to affiliates.[27] A state-wide exploratory meeting was to be held in March, 1960, at Orlando, but the Fund, on Braden's advice, refused to locate and recruit people in Florida. The organization did not look with favor upon the creation of a committee that would wither on the vine, for it was much harder to organize on the basis of a previous failure. The Fund encouraged the Miami people, however, to attend another hearing on the voting problem to be held in Washington, D.C., later in January of 1960.[28] Guaranteeing the suffrage for Southern blacks did not become easier despite the passage of the Civil Rights Act that year. Once again the segregationist white South used its infinite capacity for delay, obstruction, and outright resistance to prevent enforcement of a Federal statute it abhorred. Consequently, the Southern Conference Educational Fund made preparations for yet another public hearing to expose the fraudulent nature of the electoral process in the South. By so doing, the Fund hoped that more vigorous Federal action would be forthcoming.

The Fund's emphasis upon opening the registration books and the polls to Southern blacks coincided with the efforts of the U.S. Civil Rights Commission to establish the facts about voting denials. In its attempts to gather information from Southern officials about registration procedures, the Commission faced a wall of resistance. In December, 1958, Alabama Attorney General John Patterson ordered county registrars and judicial officers not to comply with Commission subpoenas; Circuit Judge George C. Wallace officially impounded all registration records to keep them out of the Commission's purview. "They are not going to get the records," Wallace hotly declared. "And if any agent of the Civil Rights Commission comes down to get them, they will be locked up.... I repeat, I will jail any Civil Rights Commission agent who attempts to get the records."[29] When the Commission scheduled hearings on July 13, 1959, in Louisiana, after it received seventy-nine sworn complaints of registration denials from blacks, state officials proved equally uncooperative and tried to force the Commission to reveal the names of complainants. They also instituted a civil suit challenging the constitutionality of the Civil Rights Act itself, and finally appealed to a Federal district court for a temporary order enjoining the Commission from holding a hearing. Sixteen hours before the announced opening of hearings, Federal District Judge Benjamin Dawkins granted the order. Though it was of dubious constitutionality, the order forced the Commission to call off the hearings because of the cost involved in making an appeal to higher courts.[30]

Two members of the Fund's staff were in Shreveport to support sixty-seven blacks filing affidavits. When Judge Dawkins forced the cancellation of the hearings, the Fund blasted his action and helped to raise $16,000 to aid those subjected to economic pressures resulting from voter registration work.[31] The Fund also threw its support behind a campaign for Congressman Adam Clayton Powell's civil rights bill, which provided for Federal regulation of voter registration. The Tuskegee Civic Association had undertaken to arouse Southern blacks and asked for the Fund's cooperation.[32] The Bradens promised help in publicizing the bill expressing their belief that the campaign "is the key to opening many channels...." Even if the bill never becomes law, they saw it as a lever to force Southern states to liberalize their registration laws for, in line with recommendations of the Civil Rights Commission, it proposed to invalidate literacy requirements. They were certain that there had been leaks from the Commission "in order to get a campaign moving at the same time it made its report...."[33] As more black organizations enlisted in the drive for an effective Federal voter registration law, Carl Braden waxed enthusiastic. Writing to Dr. Charles Gomillion of the Tuskegee Civic Association, he insisted that lobbying in the halls of Congress would accomplish nothing. Grass roots pressure had to be built up in support of the measure; Braden saw a vital part for the various black voter leagues and interracial organizations in moving other groups such as labor unions and church organizations. "Together they can turn this into a new Populist movement, which is long overdue in this country," Braden declared.[34]

The campaign also succeeded in drawing attention to the strategic and tactical differences between the NAACP and other civil rights organizations. A conference in Atlanta in January, 1960, turned into a tug-of-war between the NAACP on the right and the Tuskegee Civic Association, the Southern Christian Leadership Conference, and the Southern Conference Educational Fund on the left. Through delaying tactics, the NAACP sought to steer all activity into the office of its Washington legislative director Clarence Mitchell and then adjourn the conference quickly. Led by Charles Hamilton, the Tuskegee group countered the Association's moves, while the smaller black voter leagues who looked to the NAACP for leadership were confused by its "do nothingness." As a result, the conference broke up without any new direction, the various groups more or less agreeing to go their own way. Braden thought the educational value of the conferences was "immense," for it "showed the Tuskegee people the real colors of NAACP, which will be a net gain in the long pull." He was confident that as "the folks from these small voter leagues learn more about the do-nothing policy of NAACP, as demonstrated in life, they will swing more toward TCA and SCEF and SCLC for help." Evidence of the touchiness of the civil rights establishment was the insistence of AFL-CIO representatives that there be no publicity of any kind about the meeting.[35] The conference afforded the Fund some satisfaction in view of the NAACP's latest refusal, in November, 1959, to admit the Fund to the Leadership Conference on Civil Rights. At that time, Bishop Edgar A. Love and Dr. Herman E. Long, leading black clergymen and officers of the Fund, had conferred with Roy Wilkins for two hours, only to find Wilkins adamant in his negative attitude toward the Fund.[36]

The conference helped to bring the Fund into a warm relationship with the SCLC and the Bradens into a similar relationship with Martin Luther King. The previous October, King had written to the Bradens expressing his gratification at Carl Braden's participation in an SCLC conference in Colby, South Carolina. He hoped the Bradens would "find it possible to become permanently associated with the Southern Christian Leadership Conference." Expressing his "firm belief that our movement must be interracial to be thoroughly effective," King declared that the Bradens' joining would help keep the struggle "over and above a mere racial struggle." It was King's conviction that "the tension in the South is between justice and injustice rather than white people or Negro people."[37]

Later that month King expressed his delight at Braden's interest in "becoming permanently associated with SCLC." While the Conference was not a membership organization, but an association of affiliated groups, all who attended its conference went on its mailing list. Thus, he stated, "in a real sense you are already a part of the Southern Christian Leadership Conference." King also hoped Braden could get some local group in Louisville to become an affiliate of SCLC.[38]

Along with joining other organizations pressuring for new Federal civil rights legislation the Fund sought to make use of the affidavits that were to have been presented before the Civil Rights Commission in Shreveport, Louisiana. Dombrowski suggested another hearing in Washington, D.C., in a form similar to the 1958 voting restriction affair. He suggested that it include testimony from counties such as Terrell County, Georgia, and Macon County, Alabama.[39] His idea received the enthusiastic support of Dr. Gomillion of Tuskegee and Reverend Martin Luther King. Fund supporters in Washington who had arranged the previous hearing once again enlisted in the effort.[40] No longer isolated as in 1958, the Fund received the support of the SCLC, the Tuskegee Civic Association and fourteen black voter leagues and civic organizations in the South.[41] The Fund worked closely with King in duplicating the procedures of the Civil Rights Commission, including a distinguished panel of six, a counsel, and witnesses.[42] Dombrowski attempted to include Mrs. Roosevelt as a panel member. She wrote declining the invitation, but Methodist Bishop G. Bromley Oxnam and former Maryland Governor Theodore McKeldin accepted similar invitations,[43] as did the President of the Council of Bishops of the African Methodist Episcopal Church, Bishop George W. Baber, and Reverend C. Ewbank Tucker, who held a similar post in the A.M.E. Zion Church.

Timing the hearing to coincide with the Congressional debate over the new civil rights bill, Fund leaders arranged for a number of liberal Congressmen to meet with a delegation of panel members and Southern black leaders attending the hearing.[44] United Electrical Workers Union lobbyist Russ Nixon, who arranged Congressional meetings for the participants, noted that such visits by black leaders closely involved in the Southern voting controversy would assist Congressional liberals who were being challenged by Southern Democrats to clean up their own house in the North. Representative Chester Bowles of Connecticut, for example, had written an article in a national magazine accepting the Southerners' challenge, which contributed to doubts that effective legislation could be passed in the current Congressional session.[45]

As the hearing preparations picked up in tempo, and as publicity in the Washington area spread, the inevitable red baiting also appeared. Fulton Lewis, Jr., devoted four consecutive radio broadcasts to attacks on the proposed hearing, specifically targeting Bishop Oxnam and Carl Braden for his choicest smears. These attacks persuaded Governor McKeldin to withdraw. A group of anti-Communist Methodists, called the "Circuit Riders," attempted to force Oxnam to sever his connection with the affair, but without success.[46] The pressure from anti-Communist groups did force the pastor of Vermont Avenue Baptist Church to renege on his commitment to host the hearing. The pastor of the Methodist Church, where the previous

1958 hearing had been held, spared the Fund further embarrassment at the last minute, however, when he offered his facilities.[47]

The hearings which took place on January 31, 1960, presented tales of intimidation, outright denials of the right to register and vote, and open violence against blacks determined to exercise their rights of citizenship. One witness from Louisiana reported that after attempting to discuss with a Louisiana state senator the problem of discrimination in registering, he faced indictment for "attempting to intimidate a member of the Legislature." A number of college faculty members from Tuskegee and Rust College, Mississippi, detailed their frustrating experience following the tortuous complications of filing and passing literacy tests, only to receive no notification of passing or failing. Tales of economic pressure, "whispering" campaigns, and violence involving the attempted murder of one man's mother, stunned the audience; one witness declared that, with the alternatives blacks faced in Mississippi, all but the absolutely fearless decided "that to live is more necessary than to vote."[48] The hearing drew an estimated crowd of 1,500 people who "gasped and laughed at times" as the witnesses related their stories about "the conspiracy to keep us from voting."[49] The black press gave the hearing excellent coverage and also delivered strong editorials "giving the FBI hell."[50]

Designed for maximum impact, the hearing coincided with a Congressional battle to discharge the civil rights bill from the Senate Rules Committee. While including the Civil Rights commission's recommendations for the appointment of Federal voting referees upon complaint of registration interference, the measure also provided for complicated legal machinery involving civil suits and court injunctions before referees could be called. In effect, as with the 1957 Act, the new legislation had few teeth in it. Contrary to the Commission's desire to preserve all registration records for five years, the 1960 bill provided for only a 22-month holding period.[51] Even this weakened measure failed to get the support of the Eisenhower Administration. Eisenhower stated that, while he had no objection to Congress studying the bill, he doubted its constitutionality.[52] The strategy, as Braden was able to discover, was for the House Rules Committee to report the "toothless" bill out no later than February 5 with a gag on it entailing limited debate and no amendments. After some maneuvering in the Senate, the bill would then be passed giving both parties the opportunity to say they had done something on civil rights and to tell proponents of civil rights "to go on home as Congress has done everything it is going to do."[53]

Despite passage of the bill, segregationists continued to put roadblocks in the path of black voters. The Fund discovered in June that Eastland, as chairman of the Senate Judiciary Committee, had forced Attorney General Rogers to shelve forty voting rights cases. In return Eastland allowed the nomination of the head of the Justice Department's Civil Rights Division to come up for a vote, as well as its entire appropriation and that of the Department itself.[54]

Casting about for means to put the hearings to good use, the Fund decided upon a stronger civil rights law to include Federal registrars for local and state, as well as Federal elections; urged its supporters to discover, assemble and report all violations of civil rights to the Civil Rights Commission; insisted upon appointment of black registrars to county boards; and called for public hearings by the Commission in the South.[55] The Fund sought to maintain and expand the personal relationship between liberal Congressmen and Senators and Southern blacks active in the voting struggle. It also promoted a tour by a delegation of "the voteless" to non-Southern states whose legislators had voted with the Southerners against civil rights measures.[56] Dombrowski discussed setting up an independent, tax-exempt foundation called "The Fund for the Voteless" to promote black political activity in the South. A wealthy New York supporter had shown an interest, and Dombrowski was confident that "some rather substantial funds" could be raised for the project. He proposed a board of directors for it including Williams, Martin Luther King, and Herman Long.[57] More concretely, the Fund took up the offer of a group of Detroit supporters who wanted to finance a pilot registration and voting project in the South.[58]

The Fund proposed to finance a registration project in South Carolina, mainly because, as a result of new laws, there had been a drop in black registration from 100,000 in 1956 to 58,000 in 1958. In the 1958 Washington hearing, Mrs. Modjeska Simkins, a black NAACP leader in the state and a long-time Fund officer, impressed Dombrowski with her comment that voter intimidation was not as overt or important a factor in South Carolina as it was elsewhere in the South.[59] After discussions with black leaders in South Carolina, the head of the Sumter County CORE, who was also on the local NAACP board and president of the county voters league, assumed direction of the project. Slated to run for a period of four months, the project included three black students from Claflin, South Carolina State, and Benedict Colleges as assistants. The sit-ins that had occurred in February had impressed the Fund, and Dombrowski believed that in "their deepest significance they are a spiritual manifesto from Southern

Negro youth that they will settle for nothing less than full citizenship and the total elimination of all forms of discrimination, whether bolstered by law or custom." And in that struggle, the Fund notified its supporters. "Southern youth has no instrument more powerful than the ballot."[60]

Soon after the Washington hearings, the Fund became involved in a bitter conflict in the West Tennessee counties of Fayette and Haywood. Blacks had allegedly not voted there since Reconstruction, and there were about 7,000 voting-age blacks in Fayette County alone. A young black grocer and filling-station owner, John McFerren, and twelve friends organized a Fayette County Civic and Welfare League in 1959 to begin registration. After winning a court suit for the right to register, the black tenant-farmers and share croppers faced economic pressure and intimidation by white landowners in the county. Major oil companies also boycotted McFerren and other blacks by digging up the metal oil containers in the county, thus denying black farmers the fuel to run their tractors. Many blacks lost their homes and farms, and McFerren, who testified at the Fund's Washington hearing, called upon it to publicize their cause and raise funds for their relief. Soon national press services and newspapers carried accounts of the plight of black farmers in West Tennessee. The Fund also contacted supporters with oil stock to pressure the companies involved. With a $1,000 donation from a New York sympathizer it bought a number of tents and helped to set up a "tent city" in Fayette County in September, 1960. The West Tennessee struggle went on for years eventually involving the Federal government on behalf of the black farmers.[61]

The Washington hearings stimulated the hoped-for activity in Florida, and the scheduled Orlando meeting took place in March with over sixty participants from many Protestant denominations, Jewish congregations, AME churches, the Florida Parent-Teachers Association, Councils on Human Relations, NAACP, and other groups. An information exchange followed to keep the various groups in separate parts of the state informed about civil rights and civil liberties developments.[62] In May, Carl Braden informed his Miami contacts that he would spend three weeks in the state to help expand the work of the Orlando group, and particularly to help in combatting segregationist measures of the new state administration. He also intended to combine this with work in behalf of the three NAACP leaders under indictment by the state legislature for their First Amendment stands.[63] By July, Braden's work began to show some results. After three hot, hectic weeks, the Florida Legislative Project appeared, acting as a watchdog on the

171

legislature and communicating news of new pro-segregationist legislation in the works in the state capital. Pledges of support for the new group had come from the state Parent-Teachers Association, the Unitarian Fellowship for Social Justice, and the NAACP. Writing to Dombrowski, Braden insisted upon complete secrecy for the list of Florida contacts, so as not to expose them to harassment.[64]

Repeating a pattern begun at the Eastland 1954 hearing, the Fund suffered a setback when Mrs. Eleanor Roosevelt tendered her resignation. In January she had inquired of Dombrowski as to "what is happening on the accusation that the Conference is communistic?"[65] And in April, 1960, she announced her separation from any further public sponsorship of Fund affairs. Stating her intention of "getting out of a number of activities," she offered, however, to "gladly help on individual things."[66] Williams and Dombrowski were deeply dismayed by Mrs. Roosevelt's sudden change in attitude, particularly since she had recently been the hostess, for the third consecutive year, at the Fund's annual New York reception. Williams wrote Dombrowski that the appearance at the reception of a man suspected of Communist ties during the thirties, had alienated her and caused her to question the political character of Fund supporters.[67] He also thought that Mrs. Roosevelt had been offended when the Fund retained William Howard Melish as its permanent fund raiser despite her advice that it was unwise and that contributors would refuse to see him.[68]

Williams did not urge her to reconsider, since he believed that while "slow to act," she was "firm" when she did. Writing for advice to a friend of Mrs. Roosevelt, Justine Wise Polier of the American Jewish Congress, Williams nevertheless reaffirmed his own position on Communists in the Fund. Always distrustful of the Communists, and insistent that any organization in which he participated be "free from Communist direction or divisive activities," he also refused to proscribe persons accused of Communist or left wing activities. Williams opposed a "loyalty" test for supporters or contributors to the Fund. He believed that others, such as the Americans for Democratic Action and the AFL-CIO, who indulged in this practice "have done the liberal element in this country irrevocable injury" by "splintering...the liberal front all down the line." Williams believed that Mrs. Roosevelt was doing the same to the civil rights forces of the South "by listening to some red-baiters who have filled her with a lot of talk about how many Communists are supporting the Fund." Declaring, without further elaboration, that the Fund's retention of Melish and Carl Braden had given hostile parties "some pretty obvious clubs to hit us with," he stood by them nevertheless, noting that "these people are really heroes, and are the kind of fighters...who had been tried, tested, and found not wanting in courage and commitment to the ideals we sought."[69]

The Bradens were even more strongly convinced that "the red-baiting has just finally gotten Mrs. Roosevelt." They were certain that the NAACP national office "has been working on her," just as it had several years before on other prominent people who had agreed to help raise money for the Fund.[70] In 1958 Carl Braden heard that Roy Wilkins had told Fund supporters in New York that the Bradens' "employment by SCEF" was part of a grand design by the Communist Party to revive SCEF as a vehicle in the South; and that the Party did this as part of its effort to stir up trouble in the South."[71] As a matter of principle, the Bradens opposed any thought of appeasing Mrs. Roosevelt by dropping Melish. They agreed with Melish and Williams in refusing to adopt a policy of "screening" potential supporters of the Fund.[72] On hearing of Mrs. Roosevelt's resignation, Melish thought it probable, and abhorred the fact, that "somebody is constantly watching and appraising our activities, meeting places, and the like." The "screening [of] people to whom one turns for interest and support is to me vicious," he declared, fearing that course as the logical end of Mrs. Roosevelt's reasoning. "I feel a little bit sick in the stomach at the thought."[73]

The Fund adopted no such policy, however, since none of its leaders were about to betray their principles in panic at the latest defection from its ranks. Mrs. Roosevelt's willingness to aid in a private capacity in the future, however, persuaded the organization's officers to see her move as possibly tactical, rather than a principled rejection of the Fund. Then active in the insurgent reform wing of the New York State Democratic Party, Mrs. Roosevelt most likely considered the severance of her Fund ties as advisable in order to free herself from "unnecessary organizational attack."[74] A more serious consequence of her resignation, however, was the fear that it would have an adverse effect upon blacks on the board of the Fund in the South.[75] The blow to the fund-raising efforts of Melish in New York was obvious, now that other groups, such as CORE and the SCLC, were increasing the competition for funds from Northern sympathizers.[76]

Although competition for funds increased, and was to make for a tighter situation in the future, the Bradens did not fear competition with other groups in the South. The NAACP and SCLC were primarily black organizations; CORE, interracial like the Fund, was essentially a Northern group and had a very limited program. Only the Southern Regional Council, and the Human Relations Councils affiliated with it, could in any way be considered competitive. The Bradens had often been asked to justify the Fund's existence in view of the fact that many whites interested in interracial activity more easily became involved in the Human Relations Councils. The Bradens, however, never regarded the Councils as rivals; in fact, they often encouraged whites to join them. They viewed the Councils as bodies that best met the needs of most Southern whites concerned to help their communities adapt to the changes which seemed inevitable in the period after 1954. The Fund, on the other hand, sought to pioneer in new directions, often aggressively so, and thus could not for the period immediately after the *Brown* decision attract the majority of Southern whites whose attitudes were in flux. Now that the situation in the South had drastically changed, with blacks in a dynamic push toward a desegregated society, the Fund answered the need for a new kind of activity among whites to parallel the new mood of Southern blacks. The Fund offered a program of action, instead of discussions alone.[77]

One manifestation of the new mood among blacks was the willingness of leaders in the Southern Christian Leadership Conference to cooperate more closely with the Fund. At the SCLC board meeting in Atlanta in June, 1960, the Bradens had discussed this and the problem of red-baiting with Martin Luther King and others. The basic problem was the antagonism that some members of King's board had for the older Southern Conference for Human Welfare and, as a carry-over, for the Fund. The Bradens regarded King's attitude, and even more that of Birmingham's black leader, Reverend Fred Shuttlesworth, as encouraging and suggested to Aubrey Williams that a conference be arranged between the SCLC and several Fund leaders. Discussion of the origins of charges against the Fund and its predecessor would be a prelude to discussion of practical ways to effect closer ties between the two groups. The Bradens disagreed with those who thought King to be weak; they believed "his heart is pure," and that he "has great strength."[78] Williams, however, did not at that time share their sentiments in regard to King. His attitude had been shaped by a dispute between E. D. Nixon, the effective organizer of the Montgomery bus boycott, and King and other leaders over the disposition of funds by the Montgomery Improvement Association. A long-time friend of Williams and active in interracial groups since the thirties, Nixon split with the other Montgomery leaders over the matter. Williams shared Nixon's distrust, and thought it "hopeless to try to work with people like [Benjamin] Mays, [Rufus] Clements," and others in the NAACP from whom, Williams alleged, King accepted advice. None of them, thought Williams, "have any place for SCEF in their work."[79] Williams thought more highly of the talents of Ella Baker, a YWCA worker and organizer for SCLC, whom he wished to have as a Fund staff member. As to meeting with King, he thought that it would be "a waste of time" to meet with his group since "the man who controls that is Benj[amin] May[s], and if a meeting is to [be] held for that purpose then we had better meet with Benj[amin]."[80]

Cooperation continued between the two groups, despite Williams' suspicions and hesitations based on past experience with Mays. SCLC leader Fred Shuttlesworth preferred to have news of Birmingham events reported by the Fund since its news services and releases were of professional caliber; and King continued to urge the Bradens and other Fund representatives to attend SCLC meetings. As part of this growing relationship Carl helped to put white ministers in the South in touch with black clergymen active in the King group.[81] A new bond also began to develop between the Fund and the student organizers of the sit-ins that had, since February, swept the South and captured the public imagination. The new threat that the sit-in movement posed to segregation did not go unnoticed by white supremacists. The Citizens Councils of America signalled the revival of efforts to reinstate state sedition laws by the Congress. In April the Councils' monthly newspaper declared that the "'sit-down' Negro demonstrators are engaged in a seditious conspiracy against the state and municipal governments of the Southern states." It urged state and local, as well as national authorities, to prosecute the leaders "to the fullest extent of the sedition laws and other applicable statutes."[82] Fund sources in Washington alerted Dombrowski that Senator Eastland was again leading efforts to revive state sedition laws, waiting for a propitious moment to bring the House-passed measure before the Senate.[83] The Bradens reported that Louisville's board of aldermen had not only refused to pass an anti-discrimination ordinance but threatened instead to adopt a no-trespass ordinance to stop sit-ins, a procedure that numerous Southern communities followed in the face of the student upsurge.[84]

In a related development, the House Un-American Activities Committee also moved against the students. Frank Wilkinson reported that the Committee had scheduled hearings for San Francisco for May 10-13, issuing subpoenas for 40 persons. Fourteen of the witnesses were teachers called to a previous hearing subsequently cancelled because of vigorous public protests. The re-scheduled hearing involved persons who had one interest in common, Wilkinson reported. They had all "been exceedingly active in picket lines, boycotts, or some form of activity supporting the Southern student protest movement." Chairman of the sub-committee conducting the hearings was Representative Edwin Willis of Louisiana, a selection which seemed to bear out Wilkinson's hypothesis that the main purpose of the hearing was to discredit the protest movement and its supporters.[85]

Primarily the work of Southern black college students, the Student Nonviolent Coordinating Committee (SNCC) also included several white students in its leadership. One of them, Jane Stembridge, sought the help of the Bradens in working out a program for the new student organization.[86] Students had also added new strength to the Florida legislative project in October. At a meeting of the Tallahassee group, "the more advanced students" from Florida A & M and Florida State University took part, one elected secretary and another financial secretary of the committee.[87]

The renewal of the civil rights movement manifested in the varied activities of the Fund, the rise of new black organizations in the South, and the dynamism of student protest demonstrations roused the segregationist and national security advocates to intense activity. New red-baiting attacks upon integrationists confirmed the need, in the Fund's view, of alerting the integrationists to the character of their opposition. The civil rights movement had now forced the issues of race relations off the sidelines and into the center of national debate.

Old Foes, New Friends: 1961-1963

A test of the new ties the Fund had built with the Southern Christian Leadership Conference and other groups new to the Southern integration scene came with the second conviction and imprisonment of Carl Braden in his running battle with segregationists and their allies. On February 27, 1961, the United States Supreme Court, again split on 5-4 lines as it had since 1957 in civil liberties cases. It upheld the Congressional contempt citation of Carl Braden and Frank Wilkinson.

Justice Potter Stewart, for the majority, rebutted Braden's counsel on all points. Upholding *Barenblatt*, Stewart held that the House Committee's questions regarding Braden's integration activities had been pertinent to the three "concrete areas of investigation" it had announced as its aim in going to Atlanta. These were: Communist infiltration in basic Southern industry; Communist propaganda in the South; and, foreign Communist propaganda in the South. Stewart also turned back Braden's challenge to Rule XI, the overall authority Congress had given HUAC to undertake investigations. He accepted this as a sound basis upon which to investigate Communist activity in general despite the absence of specific definition of the term "Communist activity." Moreover, if in *Barenblatt* the Committee had been within its authority to investigate Communist activity in the field of education, it most certainly also had such right to investigate it in other areas, such as Braden's signing a letter and petition in opposition to the House Committee itself and to Congressional legislation providing states the right to prosecute for sedition. Braden had argued that the Committee had invaded his First Amendment right to petition when it demanded to know if he was a Communist Party member when he had signed such a letter and petition. As to Braden's standing on *Watkins* in refusing to answer Committee questions and, therefore, that he had not been "willful" in doing so since the *Watkins* ruling had been in force at the time of the Atlanta hearing in 1958, Stewart disagreed. He accepted the argument of *Sinclair v. United States*:

> The gist of the offense is refusal to answer pertinent questions. No moral turpitude is involved.... There was no misapprehension as to what was called for.... He was bound rightly to construe the statute. His mistaken view of law is no defense.[1]

In two memorable dissents, Justices Black and Douglas assailed the majority position for fundamentally crippling the First Amendment. Douglas saw Braden's contempt citation to be a consequence of the *Nelson* and *Brown* decisions. The Justice "had supposed until today that one could agree or disagree with those decisions without being hounded for his belief and sent to jail for concluding that his belief was beyond the reach of government." In the six questions asked of Braden which he refused to answer, the House Un-American Activities Committee did not in any way tie him to a conspiracy to overthrow the government, nor did it link his activities "to communism, subversion, or illegal activity of any sort or kind." Neither did it show "where and how the Committee was ever granted the right to investigate those who petition Congress for redress of grievances." The only "evidence" of any of these "acts" was the bare word of the Committee, Douglas asserted. Black was even more trenchant in his dissent. Asserting that the majority opinion is "a decision which may well strip the Negro of the aid of many of the white people who have been willing to speak up in his behalf," he warned that if the Committee

> is to have the power to interrogate everyone who is called a Communist, there is one thing certain beyond the peradventure of a doubt--no legislative committee, state or federal, will have trouble finding cause to subpoena all persons anywhere who take a public stand for or against segregation.... The very foundation of a true democracy and the foundation upon which this nation was built is the fact that government is responsive to the views of its citizens, and no nation can continue to exist on such a foundation unless its citizens are wholly free to speak out fearlessly for or against their officials and their laws.
>
> When it begins to send its dissenters, such as Barenblatt, Uphaus, Wilkinson, and now Braden, to jail, the liberties indispensable to its existence must be fast disappearing. If self-preservation is to be the issue that decides these cases, I firmly believe they must be decided the other way....[2]

Braden and Wilkinson were to enter Federal prison for one year terms beginning on May 1.

Civil libertarians and civil rights activists began two related, though separate, moves to gain wide public support for freeing Braden and Wilkinson and to shift opinion against the House Un-American Activities Committee. The previous Fall a National Committee to Abolish the House Un-American Activities Committee took shape under the leadership of Alexander Meiklejohn, Clarence Pickett, Aubrey Williams and a roster of distinguished figures in many fields. Wilkinson had been serving as leg man for the committee and his effective work was the principal reason for the House Committee subpoenaing him in Atlanta. The new committee now began to devise a petition for clemency to President Kennedy for both Braden and Wilkinson. Both men composed it with the aid of Professor Stringfellow Barr, H. H. Wilson and Irving Brant. With a score of prominent sponsors, Williams hoped to gain as many as 10,000 signatures for the appeal.[3] In a telegram to President Kennedy, Williams took note of the President's recent appeal to Soviet Premier Khrushchev on behalf of anti-Castro Cubans and wrote to

> beg of you, put your eloquent praise of Cubans who defend their right to freedom into an act of your own and issue a ringing pardon for Wilkinson and Braden as similarly entitled to praise for their defense of the rights of American citizens as set forth in our Bill of Rights.[4]

Concurrent with the national clemency effort, Anne Braden spoke to Martin Luther King about sponsoring a clemency petition and delegation to the President in behalf of her husband, emphasizing his imprisonment as a direct retaliation for Braden's integration activities.[5] King thought the petition should be restricted to Braden so as to dramatize the integration struggle as central to his inquisition and conviction. Anne Braden agreed, noting that much of the analysis of the Braden-Wilkinson case stressed their part as critics of the Committee as reasons for the attack upon them, while Braden's integration activities as a causative factor was "lost in the shuffle."[6] They also agreed that the sponsors of the petition include King, Shuttlesworth, C. K. Steele of the SCLC, and Bishops Love and Tucker of the Fund, and that six Southern whites be asked to join them.[7]

In the course of the campaign for clemency, internal disputes in the SCLC compelled King to back off, although he became one of a number of initiators of the petition. Militants such as Shuttlesworth and Ralph

179

Abernathy wanted the organization to step out in front on behalf of "those who stand for freedom"; however there were others on the board of the SCLC who were more cautious and concerned about identifying it with the Southern Conference Educational Fund.[8] When Braden and Wilkinson surrendered to authorities in Atlanta, King issued a vigorous statement in their behalf, stating that he had "no doubt they are being punished, particularly Mr. Braden, for their integration activities." Affirming his support of Justice Black's dissenting opinion warning against the abuse that would follow if the committee had unlimited power to investigate, King professed to see in the imprisoning of Braden and the severity of the sentences "the rise of McCarthyism in the South again because all other weapons of the segregationists have failed." He also called for the abolition of the House Un-American Activities Committee.[9]

As the clemency campaign picked up, Anne Braden kept King informed of developments. She passed along information about the white supremacist ties of Richard Arens, former HUAC and Eastland Committee counsel, which had been published in the Washington *Post* and other journals. Apparently, Arens, along with Eastland and Congressman Francis Walter, chairman of the HUAC, was a consultant for a private "immigration committee" financed by textile heir Wycliffe Draper who had been quoted as saying that "the country would be better off without Negroes." Draper's committees, including a "genetics" committee with Eastland as a member, were attempting to give some scientific validity to the belief that blacks were a genetically inferior race. Following these disclosures, HUAC quietly dropped Arens, who also had been subsidized by Draper.[10] Anne Braden thought that the material would be useful to King to counter criticism of his support of clemency for Braden.

The Southern Christian Leadership Conference gave the lead to the petition campaign, its Fall conference officially endorsing it.[11] Besides King, who also worked behind the scenes, SCLC aide Wyatt Tee Walker played a leading role in pushing affiliate organizations to sign the clemency petition. Stressing the connection between Braden's prison term and his effort for integration, Walker declared to his associates that "we must be loyal to the courageous white friends who pay a terrific price to be companions in our struggle for full freedom....We need dedicated co-workers who absolutely refuse to compromise...."[12] Walker, together with Ralph D. Abernathy, also led a delegation to Washington which pleaded the case for clemency before

Harris Wofford, Kennedy's assistant for civil rights, and Dee White, assistant in charge of clemencies.[13]

A second, larger delegation appeared in Washington in November, appealing for clemency for both Braden and Wilkinson. The delegation refused to discuss pardon since both men had rejected that as an admission of guilt. Harris Wofford again conferred with the delegation, along with Reed Cozart of the Attorney-General's pardon office. Both were sympathetic; Wofford had even encountered stern objection from the President's personal staff Pardon Attorney who claimed jurisdiction and did not attend the conference. In addition to the broad ground of civil libertarian principles, the delegation "tied our internal kite chiefly to the integration movement" because of Braden and because of the Administration's purportedly "firm" stand upon civil rights. Bishop Love and Dr. C. Herbert Marshall, who helped organize the Fund's vote hearings in the capital, had the assistance of Attorney William Kunstler, fresh from defending the "Freedom Riders" in Jackson, Mississippi. They pressed the point that it would do the Administration little good politically "to talk in broad general terms of racial equality while one outstanding integrationist" like Braden "languished in jail." Despite the strong presentations of the group, it appeared that other considerations weighed more heavily upon the Administration.[14] By December Aubrey Williams had concluded that "the Kennedy brothers do not mean to do anything about Carl and Frank." He began to feel that it was even "dangerous to talk too much to them" about Braden and Wilkinson. "They want to please the Birchers, do nothing for liberals but everything to appease the Rightists, except in Race-problems."[15] Both Braden and Wilkinson served ten months and were released in February, 1962. Though the Braden-Wilkinson decision was the last major victory for the HUAC in the Supreme Court, the fact that the two men served almost a year in prison without executive clemency for nothing more heinous than asserting their rights of free speech and association cast doubts upon the depth of the Kennedy Administration's regard for civil liberties.[16]

The clemency effort offered the Fund the opportunity to enlighten the integration movement on the question of civil liberties. It held a series of workshops at Chapel Hill in October, 1961, for key people in the movement. Enlisting discussion leaders from civil liberties groups outside the South the workshops were a "great success." They attracted about 300 activists of both races--though only about 50 had been expected--and the discussions were "vigorous, the panelists excellent." Since the meeting had been arranged with only a few weeks' preparation, the results encouraged Anne Braden and the Fund to plan a larger conference for the following year.[17]

At the Chapel Hill conference, Anne Braden took issue with a speaker who declared that the American people had rejected McCarthy and his investigations of "subversives." While repudiating McCarthy the man and the excesses he had perpetrated, she believed that "the majority of the American people do approve of this sort of investigation at this time." As evidence of popular feeling, she pointed to the mere six votes against continuing the Un-American Activities Committee that opponents had been able to muster in the House of Representatives. While many more Congressmen privately opposed the Committee, the weight of public opinion forced them to vote with it. In her view, this was in accord with democratic theory. She did not approve of public officials voting contrary to their own constituents.

> In a democracy, if we want to bring about a change of any kind, we don't begin at the top, asking favors of people in high places. Rather, it is the essence of democracy that we begin at the bottom. We take our cause to the public and there we try to win adherents for it.

It was the function of the Fund, and other like-minded groups, to present a different set of attitudes and concepts to the masses of Americans "and spur them to rethink this issue." Public education, "not propagandizing people," nor imposing one's ideas upon them, was the best and only alternative to the current widespread ignorance of, and hence opposition to, the elements of the Bill of Rights. As the Fund labored among the masses of white Southerners on the problem of integration, it also sought to stimulate existing civil rights organizations to take a new and fresh look at the significance of civil liberties in their own movement.[18]

Buoyed by the support of the Southern Christian Leadership Conference and its agreement to cooperate with the Fund, Fund leaders worked diligently to convene a broad conference of Southern civil rights groups in Atlanta. Anne Braden had the cooperation and strong support of Mrs. Eliza Paschall of the Atlanta Council on Human Relations, Wyatt Walker, and some SNCC leaders. She spoke for it at a SNCC conference in April, 1962, outlining the connection between civil liberties and the civil rights struggle in the South. She also pointed out the paralyzing effects of the Cold War and domestic witch hunts upon white Southerners in the previous fifteen years; when the Supreme Court declared segregation unconstitutional in

1954, she noted, few whites were willing to take the risks of speaking out and acting to enforce the ruling.[19]

Plans for the conference were ambitious. In addition to including the NAACP, CORE, SCLC, SNCC, and a number of other national church groups and social action organizations, the sponsors proposed to invite as speakers and discussion leaders Supreme Court Justices Black and Douglas, Robert Hutchins of the Fund for the Republic, Congressman James Roosevelt, Federal Judges J. Skelly Wright and Elbert Tuttle, and Attorney General Robert Kennedy. Though some, such as James Farmer of CORE, favored participating in the conference, they soon declined because of pressure from their more cautious boards of directors. By September, 1962, it was clear that most of the larger, influential liberal organizations, still fearful of the Communist label, would have nothing to do with an affair sponsored, coordinated and in part financed by the Fund.[20] Most vigorously opposed was the Southern Regional Council which used its considerable influence to bar the Fund from membership in the Southern Inter-Agency Conference, a group that included most Southern civil rights organizations and operated primarily as an information exchange. Similar to the National Leadership Conference on Civil Rights, the Southern Agency also acted as a coordinating body setting the larger policy direction of the integration movement in the South.[21]

The pressure of these defections also began to affect Martin Luther King. SCLC received much of its financial support from individuals who were also constituents of groups such as the NAACP, the SRC and CORE. Because King was attempting to build "a unity of some kind" with these groups, their negative attitudes toward the Fund cooled SCLC enthusiasm for participation in the proposed affair.[22] By December, SCLC had decided not to co-sponsor the conference. Anne Braden sought an urgent meeting with King, for she believed that "SCLC's very soul was involved."[23] For his part, King was torn between his heavy dependence upon the larger liberal organizations and his personal loyalty to the Fund staff. By instinct a compromiser, King, apparently hoped to have both the Fund and the other groups cooperate. Anne Braden thought that the larger groups would never be swayed by rational arguments, since they were too fearful of smears from the same brush as the Fund, and she did not believe that King understood the depth of their convictions. Nor was she, in the last instance, confident where King would jump "if the push ever comes to the shove." She thought that, basically, King was unaware of his own strength, that he *could* cooperate with both the Fund and the larger organizations on his own terms for "these other people cannot do entirely without him." At this juncture, however, King pulled his group out of the conference, offering to enlist SCLC affiliates for workshops.[24]

This latest disappointment brought Anne Braden to the brink of despair over the future of the Fund itself. Tenacious and firm in the face of attacks upon it by segregationists and, more importantly, other civil rights groups, the Fund nevertheless was unable effectively to reach white Southerners and activate them in behalf of integration. She hated the thought of the Fund finally disbanding; it would be a tragedy, she believed, "but we are living in an age of tragedy in many ways."[25]

Her discouragement was brief, however, and on reflection she returned to the idea of a workshop on civil liberties on a smaller basis than the conference idea. A large conference seemed to be more of a public demonstration instead of a serious, intensive effort to stimulate key people in the South to oppose red-baiting and defend civil liberties in the movement.[26] Instead, the Fund organized another workshop on a more modest basis with the aid of groups and individuals within its own orbit. An important factor influencing Anne Braden's change of spirits was the excellent working relationship the Fund had developed with the Student Nonviolent Coordinating Committee.

Soon after the sit-ins had catapulted the Student Nonviolent Coordinating Committee to the forefront of public attention, the Fund made contact with student activists. Anne Braden developed close ties to a number of white women students in the organization, and this relationship, particularly with Jane Stembridge, encouraged Anne to devise a project among white students that the Fund would finance. Her idea was to stimulate white students in Southern colleges to take a public stand and join the predominantly black SNCC group with similar activities of their own. Realistic enough not to expect great numbers of Southern white students to involve themselves as yet, she hoped that a significant minority who were ready to step out ahead of their fellows could be assisted in doing so.

Anne Braden's proposal met with a receptive response from the Fund and also from SNCC leaders when she made it clear that she intended neither to set up a rival student organization nor to insert the Fund into the student scene in order to gain publicity. Her aim was to channel white students into the existing local and regional student organizations. The Fund would finance a white student, either a member of SNCC or one acceptable to that organization, on a full-time basis for a trial period subject to renewal if the results were satisfactory to SNCC and the Fund. The Fund would not publicize its part in the project, nor would it attempt to keep it *sub-rosa*. If the student organizer felt it necessary or useful, he could inform other students that the Fund was financing the project. The Fund, in turn, would only mention the project as part of its fundraising efforts. The essential aspect of the plan was to develop an action program for and by white Southern students rather than merely bringing white and black students together for discussions, which was already a feature of the work of other groups such as the National Student Association and the YWCA. A more distant objective was to develop a number of young people who would later return to Southern communities and help to integrate them. It was hoped that they would also become future contacts and members of the Fund itself.[27] Anne Braden's proposal, in structure and aim, was an extension to the student movement of the Fund's perennial philosophy. The hope of involving white Southerners in the integration struggle now lay with a new generation and the Fund sought to make early, close, and enduring contacts with it.

The SNCC people were enthusiastic about the project. Jane Stembridge had been thinking along similar lines. The project had been devised originally with her in mind as the white student organizer, although she declined eventually because of a desire to devote herself to writing.[28] Stembridge was akin to Anne Braden in her religious motivations. Stressing non-violence as the hope of the South, she urged the children of segregationists and "vague moderates" to enter the student movement whose ultimate goal "is the formation of real and vital community between persons." Not the movement of a particular class for its own ends, rather, it was "a quest for the freedom of all and the transformation of the South and America." Noting that black students were too involved in protest, too burdened with work, and often "too afraid, or timid still before the white Southerner," she was convinced that nonviolence aimed at "the salvation of these white students, at freeing them too from the damnation of segregation and hatred, sickness and fear." The movement needed them "because Negroes cannot integrate without white friends."[29] Moreover, she thought highly of the Fund as an organization "unique in its disregard for the usual...concerns of ORGANIZATIONS." What the Fund desired with this project was simply to get the job done, "Not in order to enlist membership into SCEF or to say look what we have done...but in order to move us closer to the New

South." Affirming to another SNCC member that she "cannot say enough about these two great people [Carl and Anne Braden]" she noted "their dedication and endless concern."[30] SNCC took up the project and reported on it favorably by December, and agreed to have several of its spokesmen look for a suitable candidate on their Southern trips.[31]

Anne Braden pushed hard for the Fund to come through on the project, taking pains at one point to protest sharply when Dombrowski revised her proposal by adding the student organizer to the Fund staff instead of insisting upon his independence from Fund direction or control. She informed Dombrowski that this would alienate the students, who were distrustful of all organizations, and would persuade them that "we are just another one of the dog-eat-dog organizations seeking to 'capture' the students for the glorification of our own organization." Recognizing their suspicions, and aware that students' own conceptions of what they sought to create were still vague, she insisted that the Fund respect their desires.[32] Though some in SNCC were skittish of the Fund because of its left-wing reputation, Wyatt Tee Walker, then influential among the student group, had worked hard to overcome objections to the Fund, acting as an observer at the Fall 1960 Atlanta Conference of SNCC. The student group never succumbed to red-baiting and, therefore, was even more to be encouraged.[33]

To insure its own non-interference, the Fund agreed to pay a sum of $5,000 in three installments to SNCC for the organizer, who would be on the SNCC staff.[34] The search for a suitable student organizer at length culminated in the selection of Robert Zellner, a white graduate of Huntingdon College in Montgomery. Zellner had achieved a certain notoriety in that all-white Methodist institution by attending, in the course of research for a sociology paper, the anniversary celebration of the Montgomery Improvement Association. As a result, two crosses were burned near his dormitory; the Klan distributed smear literature about him; the state attorney general summoned him and other students to his office to accuse them of Communist associations; and the college president asked for their withdrawal from the college. Zellner's father, a Mobile minister and alumnus of the extremely conservative Bob Jones University, had at one time been a member of the Alabama Ku Klux Klan. He had nevertheless undergone an inner transformation, becoming a social activist in the cause of interracial cooperation. He backed up his son vigorously.[35] After meeting the younger Zellner, Aubrey Williams recommended him highly for the project, noting his dedication, integrity and maturity. "It is my judgment that you have found something in the discovery of this boy," Williams wrote Anne Braden.[36]

Zellner went at his job with verve and enthusiasm. Beginning in September, 1961, he visited 28 Southern colleges, 15 of them white and he also contacted many students at conferences in the South and some in the North. He attended the National Associated Collegiate Press convention in Miami, buttonholing students from the University of Mississippi, Mississippi State, Louisiana State University, the University of South Carolina, Auburn, and others. He also attended the annual meeting of SCLC, a human relations seminar sponsored by the National Student Association in New Orleans, and a conference of the Students for a Democratic Society discussing a Southern political education project. Visiting black and white colleges, he was instrumental in arranging the regular association of students from Alabama State and Huntingdon Colleges in Montgomery, Birmingham Southern and Miles College in Birmingham and Stillman College and the University of Alabama in Tuscaloosa. In Talladega, Zellner assisted in the formation of the Talladega Improvement Association, comprising students and townspeople and modelled along the lines of the Montgomery Improvement Association which had so attracted him.[37]

Attempting to cut through "the cotton curtain" to the minds of Southern white students and inspire them to some personal commitment to the struggle for human dignity going on around them, Zellner found the primary obstacle to be repressive and sometimes "stark terror tactics" used by some Southern state and college administrations. At his *alma-mater*, Huntingdon College, he was arrested on the illegal orders of governor-elect George C. Wallace and an appointee-elect, Colonel Al Lingo of the state police. He had attempted to talk to fellow students about the reign of terror conducted by the White Citizens Councils against the black population of Selma, Alabama. At the University of Mississippi, Zellner found several white students who had dined with James Meredith, the first black student at the University, subjected to student-organized terror inspired by University authorities. Physically assaulted and their rooms ransacked by a self-styled "Rebel Underground," they eventually had to leave the University. Another white student acquaintance of Zellner's had been expelled from four Southern colleges for his interracial activities, his younger brother kidnapped and beaten by local police and his family investigated by a county grand jury, which never charged the family with a crime.[38]

Zellner soon realized that activating moderate white students was impossible unless he involved himself in the student movement directly. His own personality and psychological makeup drew him into action. In McComb, Mississippi, after joining a SNCC march, he went to jail for breach of the peace and contributing to the delinquency of a minor; in Albany, Georgia, he spent 12 days in prison for participating in an alleged "freedom ride" with several SNCC members after walking through the white waiting room of the train station; and in Baton Rouge, he went to jail with SNCC chairman Charles McDew on charges of criminal anarchy, merely for visiting another SNCC worker, Dion Diamond, who had been arrested previously. These incidents placed him in difficulty on white campuses. At his own Huntingdon College, the dean ordered him off campus and provoked a mob of white students to intimidate Zellner when he continued to meet with other students in their dormitories and the college cafeteria. In Birmingham, college authorities also ordered him off campus after he spoke at a meeting with the Reverend Fred Shuttlesworth. These incidents complicated Zellner's task and also contributed to a deepening sense of alienation from fellow white students. He soon faced the dilemma that other white integrationists had faced before him, relating to white Southern moderates who had no contact with blacks or the integration movement while working closely with the activist black students in SNCC. As a SNCC staff member, he was often in situations which compelled his direct participation with the black staff, and yet these very actions made for greater distance between himself and other young whites. He learned to shift between these two horns, firm in the knowledge that his active participation in the movement provided him with the insight which could help to broaden the horizons of more provincial Southern whites. This was, he soon understood, the very function for which the white student project had been devised.[39]

Zellner was, unusual for a white Southerner, well-liked by Southern black students. Jailed along with SNCC chairman Charles McDew and Zellner in McComb, SNCC field secretary Bob Moses wrote of the bitterness and hatred which many Southern blacks harbored toward whites. One black girl, who had declared that "we don't associate with pecker-woods," spoke of Zellner as her white brother; while, after Zellner left, another black youth talked about his laughter and good humor. These expressions moved Moses to sense "a new meaning...in the phrase 'Black and white together,'" the lyrics of the SNCC theme song.[40] The Fund raised $15,000 in bail money to release these three SNCC workers, along with ten others, from the McComb jail, after a stay of over a month without bond.[41] SNCC executive secretary James Forman expressed his appreciation for the Fund's support of the white student project and referred to its bail policy and publicity, for making "available to us certain channels of communication [that have] been vitally important to the movement in general."[42]

Besides putting up bail money and supporting the white student project, the Fund aided SNCC in a number of other practical ways. When calling upon the services of Zellner for Northern fund-raising appearances, the Fund took pains to split any proceeds with the student organization. Unlike other civil rights organizations, the Fund refused to use the students for its own purposes and gain.[43] W. Howard Melish, the New York fund-raiser, also assisted SNCC in setting up its own fund-raising activities in the North. James Forman had discussed with Carl Braden the need for this step so as to free the student organization from dependence upon CORE and other groups and to get away from the hit-and-miss operation the students had employed hitherto.[44] In the spring of 1962 SNCC leaders had appealed to the Fund for money to hold a conference in Atlanta to strengthen the student group's structure. There was a serious danger that the student group would dissolve, an eventuality the Fund looked upon with dread, for it regarded the student movement as "the hope and the heart of things." Whereas in 1960, the student group had the obvious support of "great masses of students in the South," by 1962 there was enough of a let-up in mass activity to enable the more established civil rights organization openly to oppose SNCC. Consequently, funds from these sources diminished to a trickle. Though faced with the burden of supporting the white student project and providing bond money for students who were filling Southern jails, the Fund agreed to raise money for the spring SNCC conference. Indeed, it may well have kept SNCC alive as a functioning organization.[45]

In addition, the Fund assisted SNCC to open up a new association with the Teamsters Union. The third annual SNCC conference at Atlanta in April, 1962, had proposed that Teamsters be asked to send experienced union organizers to a retreat to provide student field secretaries with a cram course in organizing such areas as Laurel, Mississippi. Any workers organized into a bargaining unit would then affiliate with the Teamsters, which had a positive integration record. The student organization also hoped to lay the basis for a future conference and cooperation on broader problems with the Teamsters. Carl Braden arranged a conference between SNCC aides and

Teamster attorney I. Philip Sipser, and he also succeeded in getting a contribution from the union for SNCC.[46]

Confronted by the students' bold tactics of civil disobedience, all civil rights organizations had to take their stand either in support or in competition, on pain of losing their credibility as tribunes of a new freedom in the South. As an interracial action group, the Southern Conference Educational Fund found the new climate especially congenial to its own tradition and style. The Bradens, in particular, increasingly inserted the Fund into the most troubled and conflict-laden sectors of the South. In September, 1961, Aubrey Williams, forced by serious illness to give up the presidency of the Fund and assuming a less active *emeritus* role, rested the mantle of leadership completely upon the shoulders of James Dombrowski and the Bradens.[47] As the field directors, the Bradens became "SCEF" in the eyes of other Southern activists.

Carl Braden journeyed to Talladega in April, 1962, to report on student sit-ins and marches in that tightly segregated small eastern Alabama college town. Robert Zellner, a participant in some of the demonstrations, had reported on the beatings administered to demonstrators by the town police, and Braden along with a reporter for the New York radical journal, *National Guardian*, sought to confirm these reports.[48] Shortly after their arrival, the reporters had an injunction served upon them by Circuit Judge William C. Sullivan barring them from the state of Alabama on penalty of prosecution for trespassing. Braden regarded the order as a violation of his rights as a citizen and as a journalist pursuing his profession. Moreover, he had been disgusted with the "craven way" and "backward tactics" by which NAACP and CORE had for six years "fought the injunction barring it from activity in the State of Alabama." In carrying the injunction into Federal Court, Braden had the support of Fund lawyer John M. Coe and several black attorneys. They saw the case as providing "a basis to kill off all these horse shit injunctions...and...also serve to destroy the practice of blanket injunctions to shut the mouths of bold persons and organizations...."[49] By legal maneuvers and his own violation of the injunction, Braden hoped to set an example for the students and the integration movement generally. "The Wobblies filled up the jails; it's about time the integration movement started doing it, and staying in jail," he wrote to Coe.[50] Pressure upon Alabama was intense by February, 1963. National publicity and legal moves revealed the untenable character both of the state court injunction and the Talladega ordinances which had imposed a state of near-martial law forestalling picketing and other demonstrations. This pressure forced the State of Alabama to drop charges against Braden, and the court then vacated the injunction.[51]

The Talladega affair was one of many conflicts between Southern segregationists and the civil rights movement in which Federal courts checked the wholesale use by segregationists of state courts to harass, obstruct, imprison and legitimate violations of constitutional rights of their opponents. The legal profession itself was split as integrationists found it almost impossible to get legal assistance from the Southern bar. During his trip through Mississippi on behalf of the SNCC white student project, Robert Zellner made a personal survey of white lawyers in the state in order to force them "to choose between their personal prejudices and their code of ethics as lawyers." He wrote to over 40 lawyers asking them to take his case in McComb. Among those he contacted were John Satterfield, the president of the American Bar Association who resided in Yazoo City, and Ross Barnett, Jr., son of the Governor of Mississippi. Both men refused to handle the case. Along with most of the others, they expressed hostility to Zellner personally and to his activities and beliefs. Refusing to take his case on such grounds, Zellner wrote, contradicted the legal code of ethics that lawyers pledged to uphold. Failing to get local counsel, Zellner decided to conduct his own defense as a protest against the refusal of legal representation to anyone involved in an unpopular cause in the South.[52]

The Bradens brought the matter of legal aid to the attention of friends in the National Lawyers Guild, hoping to interest that organization in assisting the Southern civil rights movement. Victor Rabinowitz, a Guild member and associate of Carl's counsel, Leonard Boudin, was sympathetic. In February, 1962, the Guild established a Special Committee to render assistance in the South.[53] At first, the Guild committee centered its activities on assisting Southern lawyers who requested their aid. A young black lawyer from Norfolk, Len Holt, active in CORE and sometime associate of the Fund, also called upon the Bradens for assistance with the Guild. After increasing repression of civil rights workers, black farmers and rural laborers, the need for direct aid to the victims became apparent. The Bradens urged the Guild to broaden its work in the South. They forwarded reports of numerous incidents requiring direct legal aid, particularly in Southwest Georgia counties around the city of Albany where black farmers had been defrauded of their land by white officials in connivance with white lawyers.[54] Fund lawyers Benjamin Smith of New Orleans and John M. Coe, a past president of the

Guild, henceforth worked at extending that association's involvement with the Southern integration movement.

Braden continued his travels to Southern hot-spots in July, 1962, when he accompanied SNCC's Bob Moses on a tour and set up civil liberties workshops in the Mississippi Delta.[55] Criss-crossing 925 miles over the state from July 13-19, Braden and Moses acquired an intimate picture of the atmosphere of terror and hope. While there appeared to be fewer reports of killings of blacks than on Braden's previous trip in 1959, beatings of prisoners by police were a routine affair. At Greenwood, the core of White Citizens Council activity in the state, where killings of black people were formerly "an every day affair," police regularly administered beatings "with a leather whip about four feet long." These continued incidents impelled integration leaders in the state to call for a constant stream of reports to the nation. Braden and Moses discussed setting up seminars on the news media to give movement people from all over the South an intensive two-week course on gathering, assembling and distributing news of police brutality. With proper publicity, Braden was certain that they could put a stop to it "within six months."[56]

The wisdom of the Fund's helping to keep Amzie Moore in Cleveland, Mississippi, was apparent when Braden found that Moore's home was a base of operations for a number of SNCC workers in the Delta; both SCLC and SNCC were making good use of Moore's facilities, contacts and resources in pushing the voter registration drive in the Delta. That operation also strained the resources of the students, many of whom were running out of money for food and gasoline. Braden found one field secretary who ate once a day "about 2 o'clock in the morning before going to bed for a few hours because he doesn't like to go to bed hungry." Despite the terrorism and lack of funds, those engaged in the projects were happy and enthusiastic. They were not only registering people to vote, but also laying plans for sit-in demonstrations, picketing, and parades. This was one of the main reasons for Moses requesting Braden to conduct workshops around the states to inform people of their First Amendment rights and to discuss the philosophy of nonviolent direct action. Braden urged the Fund to raise money for the students if they were unable to attain further aid from the Voter Education Project of the Southern Regional Council.[57]

Braden's activities in Mississippi inevitably aroused the frenzy of the segregationists. The Jackson *Daily News* on August 31, 1962, highlighted an "expose" of Braden's alleged "communistic" activities in July at the Mt.

Beulah Christian Center where he had conducted a civil liberties workshop. In the course of a more or less factual report on the workshop, the newspaper offered photostats of questionnaires allegedly circulated by Braden, which asked respondents whether "a transition to the communist system would better or worsen the lot of the Negro in Mississippi?" Together with a totally misleading headline alleging "reds" at work in the integration movement to subvert the established order of Mississippi, the articles thoroughly alarmed the more timid members of the movement in Mississippi. Others in the Southern civil rights movement used them to further isolate and render ineffective the Southern Conference Educational Fund.[58] On investigation, the photostats turned out to be doctored; one was a composite containing the top of a voter registration survey, along with the question referring to "a transition to the communist system" taken from an entirely different document circulated in a sociology course at Tougaloo College.[59] By coincidence Braden happened to have been at the Mt. Beulah Center a week before the voter project sponsoring the survey and had also held a workshop there. Though he had seen no such questionnaires, the Mississippi journal took the opportunity of tarring the entire project by connecting Braden to it.[60] In addition, the journal had somehow gotten its hands on a letter from Braden to Dombrowski with the notation "Confidential" which Dombrowski had circulated to Fund members, summarizing Braden's experiences in Mississippi. With this added element of mystery, the paper gave the impression of nefarious undercover work at large under the direction of the Fund.[61]

Ludicrous as the charges were, officials of the Southern Inter-Agency Conference took them seriously. They not only continued to bar the Fund from membership in their group, but they also spread the word that Braden was a "liability" to civil rights programs in the South.[62] The Jackson *Daily News* article had been discussed at the Inter-Agency meeting and the most negative interpretation attributed to Braden's activities, though the Fund had not been asked to send a representative to present its case. For the following six months, the Bradens sent long memos and letters to the officers of the Inter-Agency Conference explaining Carl's activities, the origins of the red-baiting of the Fund, and the need for all civil rights groups to say "no" to the witch hunt if they were to remain "a moral movement." There is no evidence that these entreaties had any effect upon the thinking of these organizations, for the Fund continued to be excluded from their proceedings despite the efforts of Wyatt Walker of SCLC and SNCC to gain entry for it into the larger conference.[63]

The sensitivity of Inter-Agency officials to the red-baiting tactics of Mississippi white supremacists in part arose from the fact that they were engaged in a broad voter registration campaign subsidized by northern white foundation money and backed by the Kennedy Administration. In early 1961, the President and his brother, the Attorney-General, called in leaders of the various civil rights organizations: Roy Wilkins of the NAACP, Whitney Young of the Urban League, Martin Luther King of SCLC, James Farmer of CORE, SNCC's Edward King, and Leslie Dunbar of the Southern Regional Council. He informed them of his desire to aid blacks to register and vote in great numbers in the South as a way of defeating Congressional opponents of Administration programs, foremost among them civil rights. If the civil rights groups would join together in a common effort which was to be financed by friendly liberal foundations, the Administration would vigorously prosecute and pressure state and local officials who insisted upon intimidating prospective black voters. In the late fall of 1961, the Taconic Foundation of New York granted a quarter of a million dollars to a new Voter Education Program. The program was to be under the supervision of the Southern Regional Council which brought black Arkansas lawyer, Wiley Branton, to head up the project. The Voter Education Program in turn endowed special offices in the various civil rights organizations specifically to carry on registration activities. Combatting Southern witch hunters was not part of the plan apparently. The Kennedy Administration, none too vigilant an upholder of the First Amendment, said little about civil liberties. Moreover, the Southern Conference Educational Fund was conspicuous for its absence from the groups invited to participate in the new undertaking.[64]

When attorney Lloyd K. Garrison, a member of the New York City Board of Education and legal counsel for the Taconic Foundation, later proposed to bring fund-raising activities of all the major civil rights organizations under one unit, Aubrey Williams strongly advised against it. He noted the deadening effect upon the field of social work when a few top-drawer business leaders and professional fund-raisers gained control of the money side of social work and subsequently dictated agency policy and the selection of professional staff. "Controversial organizations" such as the Consumers League and the Community Planning Commission disappeared, and independent-minded persons were likely to be ousted from social work. The whole field of social work had changed after the departure of Florence

Kelley, Julia Lathrop, Jane Addams, W. A. Devine, Paul Kellogg and Helen Hall. "You and I grew up in the times when these were the people we looked to for moral and civic leadership," Williams declared, but they had "no counterparts today." As for the United Fund, the contemporary money-raiser for social work

> will not condone it. Any of today's social workers who attempted to head a reform movement, acting independently and without fear of vested interests, would be considered 'controversial.' Any agency involved in reform would be considered detrimental to the United Fund drive for contributions, and would soon be deprived of money from the Fund.

Independent efforts to raise money were met by the opposition of the United Fund which carried on a well-financed publicity campaign to convince the public that it was *the* fund for social causes; the result was the extinction of "maverick" groups. It was similar pressure, Williams noted, that had resulted in the resignation of a black college president from the Southern Conference Educational Fund. The civil rights movement would be imperilled if it took this unnecessary and perilous course, Williams warned.[65]

The Southern Conference Educational Fund helped smaller, independent efforts to meet the growing needs of the integration movement. One such effort was that of Operation Freedom, a Cincinnati-based organization of pacifist clergy and laymen who took over much of the financing of the West Tennessee blacks in Fayette and Haywood counties, extending money for food, shelter, clothing and other needs to those who were under enormous pressure because of their desire to register and vote. In 1962, Operation Freedom extended its program to the Mississippi Delta, supplying needs left unattended by other foundations whose funds went into the registration effort alone. Carl Braden assisted by calling upon Mississippi blacks to inform him of their needs for relay to the Cincinnati group. The Bradens also assisted black newspapers in publicizing the Mississippi situation and the relief needs through the *Southern Patriot* news service.[66]

Operation Freedom also cooperated in a unique educational effort in the Delta. Two SNCC workers, James and Diane Bevel, in association with Amzie Moore, envisioned a school for poor blacks along the lines of the Highlander Folk School. Because of dire poverty, illiteracy, segregation and extreme oppression of blacks in Mississippi, the voter registration program had achieved few significant successes. Without a sense of human worth and dignity, the Bevels believed, Mississippi's blacks would be unable to develop

195

the motivation that alone could inspire them to alter their conditions. Hitherto, civil rights organizations had spent their energy and resources sending trained people into the area to do things *for* the masses of black people; what was needed was training people to do things themselves, inspiring in them "the vision of freedom and an inner sense of their worth." In the absence of such a program, the winning of the vote, the end of literacy tests and the abolition of the poll tax would be meaningless. Black people would not take advantage of the vote or they would be manipulated by segregationists because of continuing black dependence upon them. The results of current efforts, in fact, the Bevels thought, "could actually be dangerous." They looked upon the Federal government's compelling the entrance of black student James Meredith to the University of Mississippi the previous year as "tokenism" because of the failure to follow it up with efforts to integrate all Mississippi schools.[67]

Highlander Folk School was a model because many of its students were active participants in their integration struggle. Mrs. Rosa Parks, acknowledged as "the mother of the present nonviolent movement in the South" because she had initiated the Montgomery bus boycott, had been a student at Highlander. The school's residential setting provided individuals the opportunity to break loose from their background and restricted world of ideas and associations and enabled them to catch "a glimpse of the beloved community." SCLC's Dorchester Center in Georgia provided similar opportunities, but it was located too far away for poor Mississippi blacks. The Bevels envisioned the school training local leaders in the skills and encouraging the initiative required for citizenship: reading, writing, organizing to vote, gaining a knowledge of available Federal programs for localities, developing new industry in their areas, stimulating black youth to go North for study and then return to provide leadership in Mississippi. They also hoped to provide community services for the surrounding area: a summer camp for youngsters, a day nursery and kindergarten for working mothers, an orphanage, an old-age home, and a general community center for youth. Such services were totally lacking for Delta blacks. The Bevels volunteered their own full-time services with salaries and staff paid by other civil rights organizations. They also expected many black and white students to volunteer for the center.[68] Myles Horton of Highlander was in enthusiastic accord with the plan, and Operation Freedom offered to receive funds for it; the Delta school was to be a model for other centers in the South.[69]

The Mississippi activities illustrated the close cooperation among the Fund, the Student Nonviolent Coordinating Committee and the Highlander Folk School. The Fund was the only interracial action organization in the South of persons outside the student category; SNCC was the pacesetter and dynamo of the entire integration movement; and Highlander was an educational retreat and workshop organizer at critical moments. The three organizations formed the radical wing of the Southern integration movement, a vital force continually setting goals several steps in advance of the remainder of the loose civil rights coalition. They were a goad also to the Kennedy Administration, seeking to prevent it from yielding to increasing conservative pressure from Southern Democrats and anti-Communists in both major parties.[70] The Fund went to great lengths to safeguard this relationship with both SNCC and Highlander. In 1963, after spending much time and energy in its annual money-raising affair in New York and arranging for Martin Luther King to speak at the benefit, the Fund discovered at the last minute that the SNCC had booked a concert-benefit for similar purposes only a week prior to the Fund's long-planned affair. The breakdown in communications threatened financial disaster for both groups, but the Fund, anxious to keep the student organization alive, agreed to let SNCC use its mailing list instead. Regarding SNCC "as the youth movement of the integration struggle and in a way as the youth branch of SCEF," the Fund could not allow SNCC to fail.[71] Operating thus on what Carl Braden referred to as "a principle of tangency," the Fund joined with other groups in common cause for civil rights at critical junctures. On the whole, however, it continued on an independent path and thereby remained a vital part of the resurgent civil rights movement.[72]

ELEVEN

Vindication

In New Orleans, on the afternoon of Friday, October 4, 1963, a hundred police and jail trustees in five simultaneous strikes, raided the offices of the Southern Conference Educational Fund, the law offices of Fund attorney Benjamin Smith and his partner, Bruce Walzer, and the homes of Smith, Walzer and Dombrowski. Though "Operation Tip Top" allegedly had been in the making for eleven months, the raiders came to the wrong office and broke down the door of an empty room with sledge-hammers before locating the Fund's headquarters elsewhere. At the law office of Smith and Walzer they terrified a secretary, who was alone at the time, by brandishing revolvers and proceeding to ransack the premises.

The Louisiana Joint Legislative Committee on Un-American Activities had lodged a complaint authorizing the raid. Jack Rogers, Committee counsel, accompanied the raiders to the Smith home where, without a warrant and contrary to the law and legal ethics, he methodically went through Smith's legal files and took notes on their contents. Police confiscated the mailing list of a New Orleans peace group, the Committee for Peaceful Alternatives, at the residence of Bruce Walzer, though he was not a member of the Fund; and also photographed his private telephone lists. They arrested Smith and Walzer at an integrated joint meeting of the National Lawyers Guild and Louisiana Civil Liberties Union, and took them, along with Dombrowski, into custody for violating the state Subversive Activities and Communist Control Law and the Communist Propaganda Control Act. The raiders also seized several thousand of the Fund's documents and its entire file system, packed them in a moving van and carted them away to state police headquarters in Baton Rouge.[1]

At a press conference the following day, Joint Legislative Committee counsel Jack N. Rogers termed the Fund the equivalent of "a big holding company" in alleged Communist infiltration of racial movements in Louisiana. He complained that it had been "giving us trouble all over the state," and he linked it with mass racial demonstrations that had cropped up in various Louisiana cities. The Tuesday before the raids, over 10,000 blacks and 300 whites had staged a mass civil rights rally at the New Orleans city hall. Asked if the raids had been coordinated with the FBI, Rogers, while proclaiming his faith in J. Edgar Hoover's direction of the FBI, displayed a newspaper clipping quoting President John F. Kennedy to the effect that the Justice Department had no information that any top leader of major civil rights groups was Communist. "We know that if we told the FBI about this raid, they would have to tell Bobby Kennedy," Rogers asserted.[2] "We cannot trust him and we expected he would tell his friend, Martin Luther King." In the course of the press conference, Rogers declared that the raids and arrests had grown out of a television appearance by Governor George C. Wallace in which Wallace had blamed the Fund's officers for "racial agitation" in Alabama.

If there was a single act that most influenced national attitudes toward events in the South it was the dynamiting of a black church in Birmingham, Alabama, on September 15, 1963, which caused the death of four small children and injury to a number of others. The reverberations shifted national public opinion against the segregationists, forcing them on the defensive more effectively than at any time since the 1954 *Brown* decision. Attorney General Robert Kennedy and Martin Luther King, Jr. denounced the perpetrators of the deed before national television audiences. King placed responsibility upon Alabama Governor George C. Wallace for creating the climate encouraging the crime. In response, Wallace dragged in the "red menace." On the nationally televised *Today Show* on September 27, Wallace held up photographs of Carl and Anne Braden, James Dombrowski, and a number of others who had participated in a conference of civil rights organizations in Birmingham in the Spring of 1962, which had discussed strategy for the coming year. In his running commentary, Wallace, using the testimony of various informers at the Eastland and Un-American Activities Committee hearings, described them as "identified members of the Communist Party." He alleged that the Birmingham conference was a Communist-run affair plotting the demonstrations that had followed. Wallace declared defiantly

> I feel that the people of Alabama bear no blame for this, these murders, and they are murders, and I feel that the Supreme Court of the United States and the Administration in Washington and the agitators who have come into this state in my judgment are more to blame for this dastardly act than anyone else.[3]

Despite efforts to secure time from NBC to reply to Wallace, the Bradens were unable to secure a transcript of Wallace's remarks from the network, contrary to Federal Communications Commission policy. Protests to the FCC also received a cold shoulder. The Commission accepted the network's claim that the Bradens had not been slandered and that their activities had been cited merely as illustrations by Governor Wallace and thus required no response.[4] The Wallace interview thus set the stage for events that offered the Fund its best opportunity to strike back at its perennial antagonists.

Released on bond, Fund officials and Walzer applied for, and received, a preliminary hearing on the charges on October 25. They achieved a moral victory when Judge Bernard J. Cocke of the Louisiana Criminal District Court for the Parish of Orleans discharged and dismissed the conspiracy charges against them because of total lack of evidence and "no probable cause" for the issuance of the warrants. Asked for the release of the Fund's records, LUAC chairman State Representative Pfister declared he could not do so because they had been subpoenaed by Senate Internal Security Subcommittee chairman Senator James O. Eastland.

Eastland had telephoned Pfister on the night of the raids to inform him of the subpoena and, on the following day, October 5, J. G. Sourwine, counsel for the Eastland subcommittee, had personally delivered the subpoena to Pfister. On October 26, the three plaintiffs requested a temporary restraining order and permanent injunction in Federal District Court to prevent removal of the seized records from Baton Rouge. At the hearing granted on October 28 after a number of postponements, Federal Judge Robert A. Ainsworth declared the question of an injunction moot because the records were no longer in the state. Early that morning, Sourwine ordered the Fund's records transported to the chancery court in Woodville, Mississippi, and a portion of them sent on to Washington, D.C. There Eastland's aides photostated their contents.[5]

Dombrowski and the Fund then filed suit in Federal District Court in Washington to restrain Eastland from using the documents and also asking for $500,000 in damages against Eastland and Sourwine for illegal seizure of records and property. They also filed a $750,000 suit in New Orleans on similar grounds. They also charged Pfister and other state officials with false arrest. In response Louisiana officials moved fast. On November 8, Pfister called a hearing of the Joint Committee, open to the press but not to the public, in order "to keep out agitators" and Fund witnesses. Photostatic copies of Fund documents and mailing lists appeared as "evidence" in an attempt to label the organization a "Communist front." The Committee then passed a resolution that the Fund "is in fact a Communist front organization and is also...subversive...because it is aiding and abetting the Communist conspiracy." Besides laying the basis for state prosecution of the Fund and its officers, the hearing was part of Pfister's re-election campaign.[6] Both sides--the Louisiana authorities in the state and local courts and the Fund officials in Federal courts--proceeded with attempts to thwart each other through a series of maneuvers.

On November 12, the Fund entered a suit in Federal District Court attacking the constitutionality of the state Subversive Activities and Communist Control law and requested a three-judge court to issue a declaratory judgment that the state law violated the U.S. Constitution. The Fund also requested an injunction restraining State authorities from using photo copies of the seized documents. Concurrently, the Joint Legislative Committee transferred its remaining documents to the New Orleans District Attorney's office and, on November 14, Criminal District Judge Malcolm V. O'Hara charged the grand jury, then in session, with responsibility for investigating for possible violations of the State Communist Control law. After a three-judge Federal court was appointed on November 15, Judge John Minor Wisdom, one of its members, issued an order restraining state and city officials from taking any action against the arrested persons pending a ruling on the constitutionality of the Louisiana statutes. His order also restrained officials from presenting evidence to the Orleans Parish Grand Jury for the purpose of showing a violation of the statute under attack.[7]

Filing suit in the Federal courts for relief from state actions, Dombrowski and his lawyers not only pitted themselves against the full resources of the State of Louisiana, but also challenged the doctrine of "abstention." Under that doctrine, a citizen seeking protection for his constitutional rights had no recourse to Federal courts before completely exhausting all remedies in state trial and appellate courts. The years of proceedings and financial drain, together with the small percentage of such cases ultimately reviewed by Federal courts, meant that state authorities opposing integration largely frustrated the efforts of those attempting to uphold civil rights. Charging that the enforcement of the Louisiana statutes was an attempt to enforce the state's policy of racial segregation, Dombrowski, Smith and Walzer hoped to show that the doctrine of "abstention" would force the effective closing down of the only meaningful judicial tribunals in the Deep South available for the vindication of fundamental Federal constitutional rights.[8] In the context of the widening movement of black citizens for equality, the elimination of any effective judicial forum for the prompt, decisive protection of Federal rights would create a constitutional crisis of grave dimensions by undermining the commitment to a theory of government under law.[9]

The Fund received the support of the American Civil Liberties Union, which filed an *amicus* brief in its behalf. Writing to Dombrowski and enclosing the ACLU brief, Attorney Arthur Kinoy, associated with William Kunstler in arguing the case for the Fund, emphasized the importance of the case for the entire civil rights movement. He professed to see a three-state conspiracy of Louisiana, Mississippi, and Alabama against the Fund and the civil rights movement itself. The states used the "Communist conspiracy" charge as a last resort, since all previous techniques involving the doctrines of "interposition," "massive resistance," and "states rights" had been systematically rejected by the Federal courts. Attacks on CORE in Louisiana, SNCC in Georgia, SCLC in Virginia, and the NAACP in Mississippi, in an effort to label the "greatest social movement of our contemporary national history as a local adjunct of a broad, alien conspiracy to subvert our ideals and our institutions," were already under way. Should the Louisiana authorities be successful with this tactic against the Fund, the other groups would be left defenseless against similar charges. On the other hand, if the Fund were successful in having the Louisiana statute declared unconstitutional, it would have a profound effect on the direct action movement by providing a precedent for resisting the new segregationist counter-offensive. Moreover, Kinoy declared the Fund's suit signified the indivisibility of civil liberties and civil rights. The black movement for equality could not achieve its own objective without a persistent effort to protect First Amendment liberties against attacks from repressive laws or investigatory procedures. "The entire issue of the defense of the First Amendment has now become merged with the fight for racial equality," he asserted. "This is the deepest significance of the SCEF cases." The whole fabric of state "little McCarran Acts" and "Communist control laws" had to be swept away if the segregationist power structure was to be fought and defeated.[10] Dombrowski phrased it best when, in a Los Angeles speech, he declared that "what we call euphemistically 'the struggle for integration' is not that at all. It is more accurate to speak of the civil rights movement in the South today as a fight for the right to advocate integration." The simple right to advocate without being arrested, beaten, gassed, hosed, and bitten by police dogs; in fine, elemental civil liberties were the core of much of the Southern struggle.[11]

The *Dombrowski* suit alleged that the Louisiana Subversive Activities and Communist Control Law and the Communist Propaganda Control Law were, on their face, in violation of the First Amendment "because [their] overbreadth makes them susceptible of sweeping and improper application...."[12] It further alleged that the plaintiffs had affidavits and offered written proof that threats to enforce those laws had been made "not...with any expectation of securing valid convictions, but rather part of a plan to employ arrests, seizures, and threats of prosecution...to harass appellants and discourage them and their supporters from asserting and attempting to vindicate the constitutional rights of Negro citizens of Louisiana."[13]

At the hearing on December 9, Arthur Kinoy argued for the Fund that "the statutes were written as if the First and Fourteenth Amendments to the U.S. Constitution did not exist...."[14] Judge Wisdom agreed with Kinoy that prosecution of subversion as it concerned the "worldwide Communist conspiracy" was a national rather than a state concern, but the other two judges, E. Gordon West and Frank B. Ellis, upheld their constitutionality.[15] Reserving final decision to January 10, the three-judge panel at that time again split 2-1 upholding the Louisiana statutes as constitutional; refused to hear testimony to prove that even if constitutional, the laws had been applied illegally; and withdrew the restraining order of Judge Wisdom, thereby opening the way for the State to resume criminal proceedings against the three plaintiffs.[16] In an unprecedented move, the three judge panel, on February 4, reversed its previous ruling by invoking the doctrine of "abstention." It left the matter of constitutionality to be decided by the state courts, and dismissed the suit.[17]

Judge Wisdom dissented from all rulings, and in a stinging rebuke to the majority declared

> The main issue is whether the state is abusing its legislative power and criminal processes: whether the state, under the pretext of protecting itself against subversion, has harassed and humiliated the plaintiffs and is about to prosecute them solely because their activities in promoting civil rights for Negroes conflict with the state's steel-hard policy of segregation.... None of the decisions relied on in the majority opinion present the all-important issue raised here that the state was subverting its laws in order to maintain its segregation policy.[18]

Rejecting the majority's opinion remanding to the state courts the question of the constitutionality of the statutes, Wisdom concluded his lengthy dissent by stating

Under any rational concept of federalism the federal district court has the primary responsibility and the duty to determine whether a state court proceeding is or is not a disguised effort to maintain the State's unyielding policy of segregation at the expense of the individual citizen's federally guaranteed rights and freedoms. This Court should get on with its work.[19]

The majority made a plea of a different nature. It hoped

that the case would reach the Supreme Court so that the matter of State-Federal relations in the judicial field might be clarified. If the federal district judges are to act as a police force to ride herd over state and municipal courts then we had best be so instructed and the matter for once and for all laid to rest along with a vital part of the state judicial system already weakened by a constant federal encroachment in both the statutory and judicial fields....[20]

The way was clear for an appeal direct to the U.S. Supreme Court. The State also moved; on January 29, 1964, the Orleans Parish Grand Jury indicted Dombrowski on two counts for being a member and officer of the Fund, Smith on the same two counts as well as for membership in the National Lawyers Guild, and Walzer for membership in the Guild.[21] Defendants obtained agreement from New Orleans District Attorney James Garrison to delay trial until the Supreme Court could hear the case.[22]

On June 15, 1964, the U.S. Supreme Court consented to hear the appeal in *Dombrowski v. Pfister*. Shortly thereafter, the American Civil Liberties Union and other civil rights organizations filed supporting briefs. The NAACP Legal Defense Fund, in its plea for reversal of the lower court decision, declared that "if the files of our legal staff and our cooperating attorneys may be subjected to the same lawless invasion as is here alleged to have occurred, without relief being available in the federal courts, our activities and, indeed, the cause of civil rights will be most severely prejudiced."[23] The entire civil rights movement, on the eve of an intensive organizing effort in Mississippi in the summer of 1964, awaited the outcome of the case. The Court ultimately decided on April 26, 1965, in favor of Dombrowski and his associates.

One of the most important Supreme Court pronouncements in the years since the civil rights upsurge began, *Dombrowski v. Pfister* reversed the decision of the Federal District Court, prohibited further acts enforcing the Louisiana Subversive Activities and Communist Control Law, and ordered the immediate return of all papers and documents that had been seized. Justice William Brennan, in behalf of the 5-2 majority, found that the

Louisiana statutes were unconstitutionally overbroad and that they were being employed in bad faith for the purpose of harassing the plaintiffs and discouraging them from engaging in constitutionally protected activity. The State's allegations were "irreparable injury," Brennan declared, in which mere defense against criminal prosecution was inadequate because "the chilling effect upon the exercise of First Amendment rights may derive from the fact of the prosecution, unaffected by the prospects of its success or failure."[24]

Overly broad criminal statutes, the enforcement of which would adversely affect constitutional freedoms, now could be enjoined by Federal courts. In this case, the Court held that the statutory definition of a "subversive organization" was invalid. The registration requirements of the Louisiana statute provided that citation or identification by a subcommittee of the United States Congress as a "Communist front organization" should be considered presumptive evidence of the factual status of the organization. This was "an impermissible burden upon the appellants to show that the organizations are not communist fronts," the Court declared.

The Court created a precedent when it declared that Federal judges no longer need refrain from examining the constitutionality of state statutes pending the outcome of state judicial proceedings. It declared

> We hold the abstention doctrine is inappropriate for cases such as the present one, where...statutes are justifiably attacked on their face as abridging free expression, or as applied for the purpose of discouraging protected activities.[25]

In cases of prosecution under vague and overbroad statutes, the necessity for immediate injunctive relief precluded abstention because "to abstain is to subject those affected to the uncertainties and vagaries of criminal prosecution...."[26] Agreeing with Judge Wisdom, Justice Brennan wrote that the appellants'

> allegation and offers of proof outline the chilling effect on free expression of prosecution initiated and threatened in this case. So long as the statute remains available to the State, the threat of prosecutions of protected expressions is a real and substantial one.[27]

The *Dombrowski* decision boosted the morale of civil rights workers throughout the South, and, in the view of one observer, was the Fund's single "most significant contribution to the civil rights movement during the 1960's."[28] The legal ramifications of the ruling were significant in affording *affirmative* relief in the form of injunctions and declaratory judgments in

Federal courts against state prosecutions, rather than, as hitherto, the more costly and *defensive* action against criminal prosecutions. Politically and psychologically, suits along the lines of *Dombrowski* enabled the hunted to become the hunter. Rather than passively awaiting government action to respond, the targets of government action could, in effect, put the government on trial. Civil Rights activists no longer need be subject to "exposure" and to the delay, expense, and inconvenience of a criminal prosecution. They could now abort segregationist attacks in the form of state prosecutions through civil suits. The invalidation of an unconstitutional law effectively excised it from the books, and the existence of such a law with its implicit threat of prosecution no longer could serve as a deterrent to others. The removal of this weapon from the segregationists' arsenal thus promoted the opportunity for dissent and effective action for integration.[29]

In a later development, the Fund terminated the false arrest and civil suits against the state of Louisiana. The state, in 1969, made a full public apology to the Fund and its officers for the incident. It also declared that the imputation of "Communist front" activities to the Fund and its officers had been misleading and, in essence, false.[30]

TWELVE

Perspectives
for a New South

The Southern black community, Northern black and white integrationists, and the Federal government, though not always in tandem, were primarily responsible for the civil rights victories of the sixties. But for fundamental change in the South and, thereby, the nation, one decisive sector was absent. The white population of much of the South remained largely unmoved and often adamant in opposition to social change. Without its active participation and assent, the new civil rights gains would be limited, imperiled, and superficial. The very successes of the integration movement threw into sharper relief its failure to reach white Southerners.[1]

Movements of social protest and change had neglected, bypassed, and even scorned the white South since the demise of the populists. This was the case except for a brief, halting interval in the late thirties with the formation of tenant-farmers unions and the early organizing of the CIO. The Southern white man, in particular the poor white, threatened to become what Aubrey Williams had often dreaded, a mass base for a "racist, fascist movement." The Fund had been the lone voice in the civil rights movement that persistently directed attention to Southern white people and the importance of enlisting them in the cause. The Fund's efforts among students as early as 1960, created a stir among some white Southerners and seemed, by 1963, to mark the fruition of its efforts.

The bomb that blew up the Sixteenth Street Baptist Church in Birmingham in September, 1963, also shattered the complacency of a good number of white Southern students and precipitated their entry into the civil rights movement. Sam Shirah, a Georgia-born white student, member of SNCC and successor to Robert Zellner as SNCC's white student project organizer, was enthusiastic over the "upsurge" taking place among Southern white college students in the fall of 1963. No longer simply a handful here and there, he noted that "often there are hundreds" forming social action groups on various campuses.[2] Shirah, who had taken over from Zellner in

September, 1963, began his tour of Southern campuses just after the Birmingham bombing. He first worked with a group of students at Birmingham Southern College and Miles College. At the University of Louisville he assisted in the organization of the Students for Peace and Freedom, which sought to affiliate with SNCC. In Tallahassee, he participated with a Student Nonviolent Action Group in a direct action project that resulted in his arrest along with a number of other white students. At the University of Florida in Gainesville and at Tulane in New Orleans, he encountered strong organizations of white activists. These groups expressed a desire for some ties with the predominantly black Student Nonviolent Coordinating Committee.[3]

Shirah's work received a strong boost at the November SNCC conference in Washington, D.C., when Bayard Rustin, long-time civil rights activist and organizer of the March on Washington the previous August, called upon white youth to stop putting on blue jeans and going off to Mississippi. Rustin urged them instead to go into their own white communities and work among the unemployed, the organized and unorganized workers, and other white people to form an alliance with the civil rights movement so that the disinherited of both races might together create a good society for all. Shirah saw this as a challenge to whites in the civil rights movement to offer hope to "the benighted white people of the South" whose lot was as bad as that of the Negro or worse. Many of them were hungry, jobless, denied the vote in some places and hemmed into slums as blacks were into ghettoes. "For too long," Shirah commented

> we have attempted to bring white people into the freedom movement. I think we must reverse this process and take the movement into the white communities. We must help white people see that the Negro has gained strength by casting off fear and that the white man is still the slave to fear but he can cast it off too.

A new lease on life was as much necessary for the white students, professors, ministers, and other professionals as for the poor and economically downtrodden. "All these," Shirah asserted, "are enslaved in the South, denied their free speech and their opportunity for the good life." He realized that the dream of uniting black and white Southerners was not new, that it had been tried during the Reconstruction, the Populist movement, and again in the early CIO drive of the thirties. Although "when the chips were down the white Southerner fled back to the false glory of his white skin," Shirah dared to hope that it could be different in the sixties because of three factors not present before. First, the appearance and spread of automation in industry which threatened to make the white worker superfluous, might also serve to overcome his long-held racial prejudices and awaken him to a new sense of common distress and interest with the black laborer; second, the Southern freedom movement was a source of strength revealing the black man as no longer a slave or a servant but one from whom whites had a great deal to learn; third, there was a growing number of white students, initially inspired by the civil rights movement, eager to pour their lives, energy and talents into constructive social movements in the white South. The risks were great also, for in the face of declining numbers of jobs whites and blacks might very well fight each other for the remainder unless a joint effort could be devised. The need for an expanded program to reach white students, and through their efforts, the larger Southern white community, formed the core of Shirah's appeal to SNCC and to the Southern Conference Educational Fund to help finance a program.[4] As a start in this direction, Shirah proposed the establishment of a pilot project among the unemployed and under-employed miners in the Cumberland and Allegheny regions of Kentucky, West Virginia, and Tennessee. He had already received the support and pledges of a number of students for community service projects involving educational programs and political action in support of the economic needs of workers. Local people were to direct and lead the program with students as aides and resource persons.[5]

Shirah had the support of the Bradens. They believed that the Fund could justly take some of the over-all credit for this new development because of its sponsorship of the white student project. The "sparks lit by this project have in many ways been responsible...for the growing fire among white students," Anne Braden reported.[6] Robert Zellner, Shirah, and another white student, Edward Hamlett, had done the spadework in what had been an effort to involve white students in the civil rights movement. That movement seemed now to promise the mobilization of "great numbers of white people" to work on related problems of academic freedom, civil liberties, and unemployment among "the white disinherited."[7] Speaking before the annual New York banquet of the Southern Conference Educational Fund, Shirah appealed for additional financial support for the white student project as a vital effort to organize the white poor before the right-wing groups got to them first. Noting the popularity of books like John Howard Griffin's *Black Like Me*, Shirah considered writing one titled *White Like Me*. He commented

211

in passing that some of "my best friends are white." Further, he urged his listeners to take advantage of President Lyndon Johnson's recently declared "war on poverty" to move into the white communities of the North as well as the South and there reclaim the opportunity that had been missed when white Southerners did not respond favorably to the Supreme Court's desegregation decision in 1954.[8]

Implementing his ideas, Shirah helped to coordinate a meeting of Southern white students and adult activists in Atlanta in February, 1964. It had been called at the behest of white students at three Nashville campuses: Vanderbilt University, Scarritt, and George Peabody Colleges. These students had opened an integrated campus grill in Nashville in January. Pressing on, they set up a fund to sponsor a conference for the purpose of reaching white Southern students with a program tailored to their needs, not necessarily oriented toward racial problems alone. Participating in the preliminary meeting in Atlanta in February were Anne Braden, Myles Horton, Ella Baker, Jane Stembridge and Shirah, as well as a number of white students. Some thought that the white students should attempt to reemphasize the concern with man as a total personality, "the whole man," advanced in the early days of the Student Nonviolent Coordinating Committee. Jane Stembridge expressed this view when she declared that if they conceived of man only as a worker they "will fail to meet his other needs as an individual." She thought that in moving from the campus and into the black community "SNCC has moved from the deeper point of view to the more shallow."[9]

The loose structure of SNCC had made for constant internal disputes. Yet the Atlanta participants generally agreed that a new organization must allow local and campus groups to set their own methods and goals as a way of easing moderate students into activity. Anne Braden stressed the importance of the new group undertaking projects immediately so as to get some successful experience behind them. This experience would help to prevent what had often happened before in other crises, i.e. the phenomenon of "the white Southerner [who] has always fled back to his own skin."[10] Myles Horton agreed and also urged the students to formulate a program first and then seek funds to support it rather than compromise themselves in appeals for money. Horton also insisted on the need for white students realistically to face the black-white relationship and "not pretend the white-Negro feeling does not exist." He suggested deeper discussion and attention to a problem that would remain critical for some time: how best to "further freedom for all white people." Was the proper method to be "under a Negro movement with Negro leadership," or, under a white-led movement that might alienate SNCC? Could a white-led movement retain the interest of SNCC? If not at first, might SNCC eventually come to see the importance of a white-led organization. If peace, poverty and integration were interrelated problems, how could a new group best tackle them?[11] Such questions set the tone for a larger conference in Nashville in the first week of April, 1964.

The Nashville conference assembled from Southern campuses about 150 white Southerners, involved in civil rights, peace, and other contemporary causes. The overriding problem of the conference, one that was to continue to perplex white students, was their relationship with the Student Nonviolent Coordinating Committee and with the black freedom movement at large. If they were not to be simply tokens, much as blacks had been tokens in white organizations, how were they to play a significant role in the freedom movement? Edward Hamlett of the SNCC white student project sounded the major theme of the conference. He attempted to broaden the white students' involvement in a whole range of social and political problems beyond civil rights: academic freedom in what seemed to him the stultifying atmosphere of Southern white campuses; the quality and nature of educational programs; the redirection of war budgets to the larger needs of peace and the domestic improvement of American society; the whole question of civil liberties in the nation as well as the South; their own region's one-party system which he thought had been founded upon segregation, white supremacy and economic exploitation. Hamlett argued that the civil rights movement had, in a sense, also liberated the white Southerner. By shaking the hold of white supremacy it had "allowed him to get outside himself, and to think about new ideas," he asserted. Part of the discovery was that most of the white students in the movement were more moderate than the blacks though far more liberal than most other whites in the South. They had yet to carve a niche out for themselves both in the South and in the nation.[12]

There was, however, a twin danger in this rising white involvement in the South, that of "Negro isolation" and "moderate obfuscation." On the one hand, some blacks were already rejecting white participation, as in the Northern Student Movement, where the black leadership expelled whites who were in subordinate, but crucial, positions. There were also rumblings of despair among Southern blacks who, frustrated by the white authority structure, demanded "Freedom Now!" Many whites reacted in fright at the new militancy and the strident rhetoric of blacks in SNCC. A subtler obstacle to meaningful white activity was "moderate obfuscation," by which Hamlett meant the tendency of the more perceptive Southern white political and economic leaders to rid themselves of "racist sheriffs." A good number of such leaders, Hamlett asserted, were "having tea with the Human Relations Councils [and] endorsing marches." He saw the 1964 Civil Rights bill as part of an attempt to co-opt troubled whites and those blacks who wanted to "breathe a sigh of relief and sit back and wait for freedom to come their way."

Aroused whites, such as those at the Nashville conference, had to be prepared for these new tactics.[13] An effective response, Hamlett thought, would be a coalition of blacks who would not isolate themselves to their own detriment with whites who could see through new strategies to put off desegregation. Hopefully, the present conference might provide such a response. Rhetorically asking if they had the "courage and vision to make a revolution," he left the delegates with a thought from Norman Mailer

> We gave our freedom away a long time ago. We gave it away in jails we did not enter, the revolutions we did not make, all the acts of courage we found a way to avoid....[14]

Hamlett did propose concrete activities for white students. They included creating "counter-university institutions" such as off-campus classes and speakers, tutorials and newspapers, as well as confronting campus authorities with direct action opposing all forms of segregation and discrimination on the campus and in the community peripheral to it. He suggested they link up with other black and white colleges in the same and neighboring communities to conduct joint projects and discover community issues including desegregation of restaurants and public accommodations, unemployment, job and housing discrimination, school dropout and other youth problems. Other possible activities included forming political coalitions in the community to gain full participation in community decision-making; running independent political candidates and joining with black political groups and possibly unions to work on state and national as well as local issues; and pushing voter education and registration campaigns.[15] Others saw the role of the Southern Student Organizing Committee (SSOC),[16] the new organization that was to emerge from the conference, as similar to that of the Southern Conference Educational Fund: "to establish a *dynamic* working form of communication...among students of the South, ranging from the moderate to the militant, in their efforts to promote equality and justice."[17]

All of these proposals the participants left in the hands of a continuations committee to formulate a specific program and structure.

Midway through the conference word came from Mississippi that the SNCC gathering there had decided to orient that organization toward the black community and away from the campus activity of its origins. The new turn of SNCC helped to resolve the debates over the racial makeup and direction of the Southern Student Organizing Committee. Those who desired it to be an interracial group prevailed, and the conference voted unanimously to strike from all of its literature statements limiting its scope to "predominantly white campuses." Further organizational steps were put off to another meeting since over ninety per cent of the delegates at Nashville were white. There was an awareness that without increased black participation the interracial character of the group would be farcical, if not an indication of its lingering insensitivity to the needs and aims of blacks. The "Southern consciousness" of the white students manifested itself in the symbol of the organization: a black and white handclasp superimposed upon a Confederate flag. At first the white leaders accepted it without a thought that it might offend most blacks in the movement, though they soon dropped it from the organizations's literature. The same was true of the group's newsletter, *The New Rebel*, which eventually because the *New South Student*. These and other expressions of Southern pride and chauvinism continued to plague the organization and made the Student Nonviolent Coordinating Committee wary of developing close ties with it.[18]

Before adjourning, the Nashville students adopted as their credo a manifesto in conscious rebuttal to one issued thirty-five years before in the same city by a group of Southern intellectuals known as the Southern Agrarians. The new manifesto, entitled "We'll Take Our Stand," in contrast to the previous declaration of faith in an older agrarian South, expressed the students' "determination to build together a New South which brings democracy and justice for all its people." Noting Franklin Roosevelt's depiction of the South as the nation's "number one domestic problem," they saw the struggle for equal opportunity for all men as still incomplete. Though a Southerner was now in the White House

a majority of our nation is living in an affluence which makes the specters of poverty and racism tenfold more inexcusable [for] our Southland is still the leading sufferer and battleground of the war against racism, poverty, injustice and autocracy.

Though some observers thought the South was coming of age, the students expressed a hope and a fear for her new industries and cities

> for we also are aware of new slums, newly unemployed, new injustices, new political guile--and the Old as well....Only as we dare to create new movements, new politics, and new institutions can our hopes prevail.

They expressed their debt to the black freedom movement as an inspiration to them "for a *beginning* of a true democracy in the South for all people." And they pledged to take their stand "to work for a new order, a new South, a place which embodies our ideals for all the world to emulate, not ridicule...."[19]

On May 9-10, a second conference of forty students met in Atlanta to continue discussions and plans for the new organization and also to establish fraternal ties with the Student Nonviolent Coordinating Committee and a predominantly Northern group, the Students for a Democratic Society. The Atlanta group chose its first officers and Executive Committee, which included Sam Shirah and Edward Hamlett of the Fund-supported white student project of SNCC.[20] Asked for her ideas as to the future structure of the group, Anne Braden pressed them to develop an organizational tie to SNCC so as to prevent driving deeper wedges between the races and "leaving it to some other generation on another day to bring the groups together." She advised that they set up their organization, elect officers, work out a program directed to both campus and community work as they desired, and then affiliate with SNCC as an autonomous body directed mainly toward white students. This could be done either through inter-locking directors, or SSOC representation on the SNCC board; all of her suggestions were based on the assumption that the SNCC would approve such a tie. Affiliation with SNCC would remove the troublesome question of whether SSOC was a segregated group since whites predominated in it. As to qualms that moderate whites might have because of the SNCC tag, she felt it was not a problem worth solving. In her estimation, the Southern Student Organizing Committee was a challenge to the moderate, helping him to see that "history is camping on his doorstep." Its purpose was not to make things easy for the white moderate. Rather, its function was, by identifying itself with the militancy and radicalism of the Student Nonviolent Coordinating Committee, to force the white student to "honestly and completely face the crucial question of race in the South and his own conscience."[21]

216

While its relations with SNCC were tenuous, SSOC sought fraternal ties with the Students for a Democratic Society, a radical student organization with many chapters on Northern campuses. The Southern group hoped to interest SDS in subsidizing several "campus travelers" to come South and help establish SDS chapters there and to furnish SSOC with literature. Seeking to persuade the organization to hold a major national meeting on a Southern campus, the SSOC, as an umbrella group uniting moderates and liberals saw itself as uniquely equipped to be of service to the SDS. Since many Southern moderates were not ready to join the more radical national organization, the SSOC, by furnishing them educational materials, speakers, and other services, could bring them to the point of affiliating with SDS. Since the civil rights movement was moving more in the direction of broader political activity and away from direct-action demonstrations, the SSOC also sought to persuade SDS of the importance of developing "a massive parallel movement of the poverty-stricken whites." Such a movement would provide the social weight that the black freedom movement alone did not have to transform society in the South and elsewhere. Because the Southern Student Organizing Committee was only a coordinating agency, it was important to encourage SDS to set up chapters in the South. They would be membership organizations that could provide SSOC with the base for rendering its own work effective in the South. The SSOC was, in a sense, urging the Students for a Democratic Society to undertake the tasks that it as yet felt unable or unwilling to perform.[22]

With its organizational structure and political attitude still fluid, the Southern Student Organizing Committee endorsed plans for a project among white communities in Mississippi. It was to be conducted in the summer of 1964 under the aegis of the Committee of Federated Organizations (COFO). A coalition of all civil rights organizations in the South, COFO had come together specifically to coordinate their work in Mississippi in the areas of voter registration, freedom schools, and related activity. SNCC white student organizer and new member of the Fund's board, Edward Hamlett, was to supervise the project which included twenty white Southern students. Highlander Center, formerly Highlander Folk School, provided a number of workshops for the project members in June while Myles Horton enlisted as an educational consultant afterwards.[23] The Fund agreed to raise money in the form of fellowships.[24] They were for the support of four students, one of whom, John Strickland, was a scholarship student at Harvard University. From a lower middle-class background, Strickland still had friends in the Ku

Klux Klan. After attending a civil rights rally in Savannah he had broken away and gone on to become a civil rights activist. He was anxious to help other white Southerners take a similar path.[25]

The "white folks project," as the program came to be called, centered in two Mississippi cities: Jackson and Biloxi. While a group of five to seven people worked among white moderate groups, including churches and the Human Relations Council in Jackson, the larger group selected Biloxi for concentration because it had a higher proportion of whites than most other areas in the state. Here the group divided its work on class lines. One section undertook to interpret to white middle-class persons the program of the COFO and its offshoot, the Mississippi Freedom Democratic Party (MFDP). An almost entirely black grass-roots political organization, the MFDP sought to give black Mississippians the opportunity to formulate and act upon policies furthering their own social and economic needs which the regular white-dominated Democratic party of the state neglected. The other group made contact with working-class whites in hopes of persuading them to recognize their own self-interest in developing a political alliance with the black population of Mississippi.[26]

After a month, evaluation of the project revealed that conflicts had developed between the two task forces. They decided to split up and find separate accommodations in the respective class communities. Originally living together as a group, the students soon found themselves diverting their energies into working out rules of inter-personal relations and collective living. Unconventional dress styles were a detriment to making contact with other whites; the mere existence of a collective drew adverse attention to the group and forced it to divide up into smaller living units. The greatest weakness was many members' lack of experience in the black community. They did not have an intimate acquaintance with the dramatic changes occurring among black people in the South. This left them inadequately prepared to inform white people about the state of mind and intention of Mississippi's blacks. An important factor in white feelings against blacks was fear of competition for jobs, especially in view of the new trend toward political organization manifested in the Freedom Democratic Party, and the intense voter registration and education work of white and black volunteers in the state.[27]

There were some surprises too. The reception from white workers was not hostile at first. Primarily, this was because an independent shrimp boat workers union had been active in Biloxi and had been broken by an anti-trust price fixing suit reducing the income of the workers from a high of $125 a barrel to $35. When the local union members showed an interest in the young volunteers who offered to join, however, community pressure forced them to cut off contacts. The landlord evicted the students from a store when they ineptly plastered its windows with COFO signs and SNCC posters. Hostile whites informed the landlord that the students were "trying to bring Negroes down there to get jobs." The hostility soon forced the group to depart from the area, though not without convincing some of them that, with patience and the experience of how to approach working-class whites, further projects would bear fruit.[28]

Bruce Maxwell, one of the project members, thought that the blacks, despite their misery, had a "certain spirit that does not exist in the white." The black movement had developed an elan, a community spirit, which revived hope, and provided the spark necessary for any upward development. The poor whites, whom Maxwell thought were "once the most radical force in American politics," now seemed to be the support for "demagogues [such] as [George] Wallace and [Ross] Barnett." They had to be shown that they had little stake in keeping the *status quo*. "Maybe it is whites going to jail for whites," Maxwell thought. "It needs to be something big; something that whites can say was done for them."[29] Aside from several whites registering for the Freedom Democratic Party, one Mississippian offering to work full-time on the project, and a number of new contacts in Jackson and Biloxi, the white folks project had little tangible result. Nevertheless, it whetted the appetite of some of the volunteers for further work among poor whites. The project director, Edward Hamlett, suggested that future efforts be confined to reaching poor and working-class whites in Mississippi, since other organizations such as the National Council of Churches and the American Friends Service Committee intended to work among middle-class whites in the state. More importantly, SSOC and SNCC's "most important thrust must be toward the lower-class white community [for] only when this movement ceases to be racist in its overtones and in actuality can we hope for peaceful and meaningful change...."[30]

Prior to the Nashville conference which founded the Southern Student Organizing Committee, representatives of the Fund, SNCC, and several miners' organizations along with over 100 students from Eastern colleges met in Allais, Kentucky, a suburb of Hazard. From March 26-29, they exchanged ideas at a Student-Miners Conference on Poverty and Unemployment. It was part of the general ferment among young people and concerned adults who sought to create movements dealing with problems of employment, peace, civil rights and civil liberties. Many persons focused on the South because social problems appeared to be more intense in that region and offered opportunities not available in other parts of the country. Carl Braden attended and reported that the demands upon the Fund's resources and organizing skills were heavy. The Hazard conference, he noted, brought together young students, mainly in their twenties, and older miners and their families, all in the ages from 45-70. The older group predominated. The meeting was large on enthusiasm to do something about the deepening unemployment and poverty of the Appalachian miners, Braden reported. But its lack of organizing skill was partial evidence of the effect of the Cold War and the red scare upon movements for social change since the generation from 30-45 was absent.[31]

The Appalachian Committee for Full Employment, composed of unemployed miners in the region, the Committee for Miners, the Southern Conference Educational Fund and the Student Nonviolent Coordinating Committee, had called the conference on request of the miners. These organizations offered to provide social organizational, educational and financial assistance to the miners in compiling an inventory of grievances to be documented and presented to proper governmental authorities for redress. The inventory was to cover substandard housing and schools, unsafe mine conditions, corrupt government officials, state government inactivity, inadequate and mishandled relief programs, police brutality, land erosion, and other injustices. Braden offered the services of the Fund for the period up to September 1, and in a report to Dombrowski stressed the importance of the Fund's further involvement "because the ultimate objective is to tie the struggle of the white unemployed into the struggle for freedom by the Negro unemployed." The miners were agreeable, Braden noted, but the machinery for accomplishing this remained to be worked out.[32]

The Fund's interest in Appalachia antedated the Hazard meeting. With the success of the civil rights movement in undermining *de jure* segregation, Fund members turned to deeper economic problems. To a man with neither a job nor the money to buy hamburgers, the right to sit at a lunch counter was meaningless. A program for the area had been launched in 1963, but the raids on the Fund's New Orleans office and subsequent embroilment with the State of Louisiana and Senator Eastland postponed its commencement. Braden wrote Bruce Maxwell of the COFO White Folks Project about the Fund's plans and their similarity to the Mississippi project. He offered to direct appropriate people to Mississippi should they appear in Appalachia. He hoped that the two projects could eventually link up and launch a wide ranging and radical attack on problems of poverty, unemployment, and regional development in the South.[33]

The Appalachian project also drew support and interest from persons who were less concerned with the civil rights movement than they were with the impact of automation upon the labor market and the need for concrete plans for a peace economy geared to disarmament. A group of academic intellectuals, old-time labor activists, and independent radicals formed an organization called the Alliance for Jobs and Income Now (JOIN) in the fall of 1964 to formulate a program of activity and education. The group emphasized the interrelationship of a guaranteed income and work in the transition to a cybernated-automated economy, disarmament for survival in the nuclear age, and full opportunity for "educational development, for social dignity and for useful contribution to society, without regard to color, beliefs or national origins." It aimed to bring together the white and black unemployed, insecurely employed and organized workers in support of these principles. Carl and Anne Braden had been invited to join the group which included David Dellinger, editor of *Liberation* magazine, Todd Gitlin of Students for a Democratic Society, David Livingston, president of District 65 of the Retail, Wholesale and Distributive ,Workers Union, largely based in New York City, Linus Pauling, Nobel Prize chemist and peace activist, and, in a sponsoring role, philosopher Bertrand Russell. The Bradens expressed interest in the program. Though unable to take an active part, they kept open communication with the group, which they saw as a possible ally in their own Appalachian work.[34]

The JOIN group, together with SCEF, SCLC, SDS, SNCC, SSOC, the Tennessee NAACP and various miner committees, scheduled a larger conference at Highlander Center in Knoxville for November. It was to develop a strategy for work in the Appalachian region and to formalize the various programs and ideas seeking closer links between civil rights, anti-poverty, and peace organizations.[35] The real sparkplugs of this conference were Carl Braden and Hamish Sinclair of the Appalachian Committee for Full Employment based in Hazard, Kentucky. They met in Louisville on October 14 to set up plans for the meeting and to invite other groups as sponsors. Basic to their approach was organizing the area's poor whites and blacks into a political force with the object of getting Federal government support in the form of either a guaranteed annual income of

$3000 or $60 per week for the duration of unemployment. They envisaged the Appalachian people organizing themselves, with the aid of the Fund and the other participating organizations, into political action councils from the district up to the state level as a means of compelling existing political parties to favor their demands. Public relations and adult education schools on the lines of the Mississippi freedom schools were to be provided by the outside organizations. Braden and Sinclair thought that the projects should begin in the eastern parts of Kentucky and Tennessee because a number of groups were already active there. It was their hope that an integrated movement would develop in this region and then spread into Georgia, Alabama, the Carolinas and Virginia. They thought it would be easier to organize the races jointly in eastern Kentucky and Tennessee because white people there were supposed to be less hostile to blacks. Among the prime movers of the project was the Reverend Frank Gordon, a black minister and head of the Tennessee NAACP, who had enlisted the aid of a poor white man in the region. This man had organized the people in his county to oust the members of the school board for refusing to allow his daughter to enroll in a previously all-black school.[36]

Meeting in Knoxville on November 27, the various organizations set up the Appalachian Economic and Political Action Conference (AEPAC). Each group had representation on the board of directors. A smaller working executive committee established day-to-day policy. A full-time coordinator acted as a liaison between the new group and its sponsors. It enlisted volunteers among students for various projects in the region, channelled resources to them, and carried on organizational work. Highlander Center offered to serve as consultant and workshop center for the group and also joined the conference.[37] Since many Appalachian communities depended upon Federal programs, Highlander also proposed to instruct organizers and community leaders in the details of Federal programs. Such instruction would provide the wherewithal to make them serve the needs of people in the region rather than permitting the local power groups and Federal bureaucrats in control of such programs to continue to dominate the lives of local inhabitants.[38] Sponsors of the new group shared a general distrust of the newly instituted Federal "anti-poverty" program because of fears that the local establishment and the power and coal companies would gain control of it.[39]

Though hopes were high for its accomplishments, the Appalachian Economic and Political Action Conference (AEPAC) had hardly begun before internal disputes, inadequate support from the participating organizations, and the general inexperience of the students and local people who staffed the organization rendered it ineffective. Some supporters of Highlander Center, which was a key part of the project, feared becoming officially attached to it. Its overtly political character imperiled Highlander with loss of its tax-exempt status as an educational organization. Several of the AEPAC staff were also with the Southern Mountain Project, the Southern Conference Educational Fund's newly-devised project for the area. Highlander supporters feared that in the public mind AEPAC would be seen simply as "SCEF" with another set of initials...."[40]

Local authorities and segregationists in Knoxville also developed hostility towards the Conference. Police harassed its members, often arresting the student workers on vagrancy and other petty charges, and followed the cars of interracial teams. The Knoxville Housing Authority at one point evicted the Conference from its headquarters in an urban renewal section before its lease had expired.[41] The most serious incident occurred in November, 1965, when a Ku Klux Klan-type group, calling itself STENCH, "Society to Exterminate Neo-Communist Harbingers," broke into the building, smashed typewriters and an office machine, stole cameras, soiled beds, carted off all records and files for 1965 and part of 1964, and partially burned the building. Despite protests to city authorities and appeals to Robert Weaver, head of the Federal Housing Authority and Tennessee Senator Ross Bass, both of whom had in previous correspondence been sympathetic, city police did nothing to apprehend the perpetrators.[42] These attacks, and the incessant public criticism and sniping of the conservative Knoxville *Journal*, which served to keep community hostility at high pitch, disoriented the youthful staff. The Conference went into quiet eclipse in December, 1965. In its wake, the Appalachian prospectus developed the previous year devolved upon by the Fund's Southern Mountain Project.[43]

In contrast to the hostility manifested in Tennessee, Braden informed Dombrowski, many miners and other local people in Eastern Kentucky were up in arms over the ravages of strip miners and coal companies. They were determined to force Kentucky authorities to take action. Leaders of agitation in the region were Tom and Pat Gish, editors of the Whitesburg *Mountain Eagle*, and former state legislator Henry M. Caudill, author of *Night Comes to the Cumberlands*, an analysis of the plight of Appalachia and an eloquent plea for national measures of relief and rehabilitation. At the moment, these native Kentuckians were drumming up popular support for a severance tax on coal, oil, gas, iron, and other minerals being taken out of the mountains. They estimated that a tax of ten cents a ton on coal and ten cents a barrel on oil would raise $14 million in the first year and help to remedy some of the desperate conditions in the mountains. Automation was also taking its toll, throwing hundreds of miners out of work. Local people were in need of organizers and Braden and Frank Fletcher, head of the Fund's Southern Mountain Project, agreed to shift operations to Hazard.[44] The eastern Kentucky mountain region remained a focus of the Fund's operations. It was an irritant to local politicians, coal companies, and the Senate Government Operations Committee headed by Senator John L. McClellan of Arkansas.

As the 1964 Civil Rights Act had legitimized civil rights gains of the previous four years and had forced whites in the movement to direct their energies elsewhere, so the 1965 Voting Rights Act provided new opportunities and dilemmas for civil rights activists. Many, including Fund members, now sought to give new meaning and direction to political debates and election campaigns. Basic policies underlying the Cold War, in particular the anti-Communist rationale of American foreign policy which had involved the nation in a war in Vietnam, drew their attention. The Gulf of Tonkin resolution adopted by the United States Senate in August, 1965, and the subsequent dispatch of the first American ground combat troops to Southeast Asia catalyzed peace organizations, anti-poverty groups, and civil rights activists into coordinating their efforts.

In August, 1965, the first national gathering of those opposing the war took place in Washington, D.C., at the Assembly of Unrepresented People. The Bradens attended and reported that, while often meeting separately, those who came from the Southern civil rights movement and the mainly Northern anti-war groups, soon came to understand the vital connection between the two movements. In fact, the anti-war movement was, thought the Bradens, in many ways "a child of the Southern civil rights movement." Many anti-war activists had first worked in Mississippi; their songs were freedom songs put to new words. The very concept of the Assembly, and its non-violent demonstrations in the capital, which avoided petitions to Congress, constituted a "parallel institution" along the lines of the Mississippi Freedom Democratic Party. It now hoped to find a way of restoring peace through popular mass activity rather than through existing institutions which the Assembly participants believed did not respond to popular needs. A number of the Southern participants looked upon the young people present as an important new source of strength for the Southern movement in the new period. After the legal victories of the mid-sixties, the more difficult conditions of *de-facto* segregation still persisted in much of the South, as well as the rest of the nation. The new coalition also attracted familiar critics and opponents: the House Un-American Activities Committee and the spokesmen of leading civil rights organizations who refused to join the Assembly in its criticisms of American policy in Vietnam.[45]

Earlier in the year, before the Assembly convened, the Southern Conference Educational Fund had discussed plans for a series of workshops in the South to stimulate thought about the Vietnam war.[46] Anne Braden had suggested that the Fund hire a full-time field worker to travel the South stimulating debate and discussion on the war and foreign policy generally, and she revived the idea after returning from the Assembly.[47] Now that the civil rights movement had "cracked open the whole question of segregation," though much remained to be done to take advantage of that success, it had also "opened the doors for consideration of all of society's basic problems." Having struggled for the right to vote for all, the movement had to "move on to finding something meaningful to vote for." She therefore proposed a project, "Operation Open Debate," to begin the process of public discussion of the war in the South. The field worker was to travel the South, contact known friends of the Fund and others who could arrange forums, debates, teach-ins and other public events. Speakers of different views including supporters of the war were to be invited so as to encourage large audiences.[48] After some board discussion, two students took up for a six-month period the task of discussing the Vietnam war in Southern campuses and communities.

From a position of restraint on the merits of the war itself, the Fund moved into active opposition to American policy in April, 1966. Opposing the resort to violence in many parts of the world and the use of American resources by the Administration "in the strategic bombing, the napalming, the gassing, the defoliation, in short, the wholesale destruction of people and property in Vietnam," the Fund also condemned the American and South Vietnamese "pacification" program "with its intensive interrogation, suppression of criticism and dissent, and political indoctrination...the earmarks of a police state." It believed the civil rights movement could not remain indifferent to the cost of a war which threatened to drain Federal funds needed for enforcement of the civil rights laws and the "present far-from-adequate and long-delayed anti-poverty programs." The Fund also saw a close relationship between the use of violence and repression in Vietnam and the use of violence and repression in the United States "and particularly in the South to maintain things as they are." It seconded the Student Nonviolent Coordinating Committee and the Southern Christian Leadership Conference which condemned the war as an improper means of solving social problems and declared that "mass murder can never lead to a constructive and creative government or to the creation of a democratic society in Vietnam." The Fund concluded with a call for ending the war by negotiation with the National Liberation Front on the basis of self-determination along the lines of the Geneva Agreement of 1954.[49]

As part of the Southern Committee to End the War in Vietnam, the Fund participated in a regional conference in Nashville on April 23-24, bringing together various peace groups and activists in the South, and helping to plant there the seeds for further anti-war activity.[50] Though a disappointment to some Northerners present, the Nashville conference brought together over 100 people from nine Southern states, many of them activists in the civil rights movement as well. Recognizing that the meeting was predominantly a white affair, Anne Braden commented that it was part of a larger crisis: "the whole matter of the rise of Black Nationalist sentiment and organization in the South... [part of] a growing 'go it alone' movement among militant Southern Negroes." There was a danger of a predominantly white peace movement developing in the South as a result of deepening white-black tensions in the civil rights movement. The one encouraging note about the Nashville conference was that Southerners of both races were meeting to talk about war and peace, "a life-and-death issue that affects them all," and not about race relations *per se*, something that had not happened in the region for many a year. Though peace groups were still weak and unpopular, especially in the South where there was a tradition of militarism and where "there sometimes seems to be a military academy at every crossroads," Anne Braden was not discouraged. For, "our band...at least exists and is determined to reach others."[51]

Anne Braden's reference to the rise of black nationalism in the South had implications that went far beyond its impact upon the peace movement and the Anti-Vietnam war agitation. The appearance of the slogan "Black Power" among Southern blacks, particularly in the ranks of SNCC in early 1966, marked the end of the civil rights coalition that had achieved the remarkable break-throughs against legal segregation in the previous half-decade. A new realignment of its forces within the black community in the South and the nation, as well as among white supporters of the black cause, was one of the important consequences of the new stance among the militant segments of the old civil rights coalition. Though it appeared to be a sudden, sharp break with all the ideas and values centering around integration of black people into American society that had motivated civil rights forces for a decade or more, the new mood among blacks was not an overnight phenomenon.

As early as the Spring of 1963, the *Patriot* had noticed stirrings of black nationalism at the Atlanta SNCC conference. The interracial makeup of the conference, about one-third white, prodded some blacks privately to express fears of white domination of the movement. A black student who voiced this sentiment, declaring the need for white votes and money, but not white leadership, received considerable applause. Comedian Dick Gregory, subtly approached the theme. In the course of his satiric routine which attempted to explain something about black people to the whites present, he turned to SNCC chairman Charles McDew and asked, "What do you call them, these non-colored friendly people?" McDew, a bit startled, hesitated a moment, shrugged his shoulders, and replied, "Just part of the movement, I guess."[52]

In the fall of 1963, blacks discovered during the course of the Freedom Vote campaign in Mississippi that the presence of Northern whites in large numbers brought Federal government protection to them that had never been given to black workers. Accordingly, the civil rights organizations issued a call for 1000 Northern volunteers to open up Mississippi in the summer of 1964. But when the volunteers came, the local blacks and many from other Southern areas who had carried on the day-to-day work of their own organizations, the mimeographing, typing and leg work, discovered their new white colleagues were more "efficient" in almost every way, and their hosts soon began to have second thoughts. It was almost a year before local participation in daily organizational work revived; but the feeling persisted that for whites to remain in Southern black communities would be extremely detrimental to black self-determination.[53]

Another sign with more radical implications was the formation of a nationalist group in Nashville in the spring of 1964, the Afro-American Student Movement, with membership in both North and South. It was among the first organizational expressions of black nationalism in the South, as distinct from the North where a variety of such groups had long existed. The organization had three main points of agreement: a resolve to unite with current African, Asian and Latin American revolutionaries; the repudiation of non-violence as a philosophy; and the selection of Robert Williams, then in Cuban exile, as its leader. *Patriot* editor Anne Braden after the conference interviewed a member of the Revolutionary Action Movement (RAM), a Northern group. Max Stanford, elected spokesman for the new student organization, expressed total disinterest in, and opposition to, integration as something from which black people had nothing to gain and much to lose. While supporting SNCC plans to elect blacks to Congress, Stanford took a dim view of that route for blacks since a small white minority controlled the country regardless of Congress. All whites were "racists," he asserted, even those in the civil rights movement. Moreover, Stanford had no confidence whatever in the Federal government as a protector of the rights of black people. Looking to "revolutionary black internationalism," the international cooperation of people of African descent to liberate themselves from colonial oppression, he believed that a world-wide race war was inevitable. Anne Braden thought his views and the formation of the new organization significant because "the unspoken support for its philosophy is...greater than its organizational strength."[54]

"Black consciousness," the symbol of new directions in the civil rights movement, came into wider public awareness in 1966. Two hundred black activists from North and South met in New Orleans in May at an Afro-American Festival to debate its meaning and significance. Among the participants was Robert Parris, hitherto Robert Moses, former Harvard student who had opened the SNCC drive in Mississippi in 1960. Parris had symbolized the distrust for personal leadership in SNCC by voluntarily leaving Mississippi in 1964, renouncing any intention of building for himself a personal base of power in the organization. He then became active in the anti-war movement in 1964, and at the New Orleans conference voiced approval of the new "black consciousness" as the best hope for black Americans.[55] His personal odyssey was also that of many in the Student Nonviolent Coordinating Committee and the civil rights movement after the sit-ins of 1960.

The New Orleans conference had a number of thoughts it wished to communicate to both whites and blacks: "that we Afro-Americans are the most strategically placed people in the world at this moment in history"; a desire to reconnect our people with land, history, and culture"; and the need "to begin our decolonization."[56] The theme of the festival was a stress upon the radical difference in the historical experiences of black and white people in America, best expressed in the reference to blacks as "Africans in exile." Comparing the enslavement of Africans and their transfer to the New World with the concurrent carving up of Africa by Europeans, the conference insisted that African slavery be understood as a colonizing process, and the Afro-Americans as a colonized people. The participants expressed the view that the American Constitution was irrelevant and the English language itself inadequate for blacks because they failed to encompass the unique historical and cultural experiences of black people in America. There was intense debate over the question of integrated organizing in the black community which expressed a deeper split among the participants. Basically, the conference divided into two opposing camps, much as blacks elsewhere in the civil rights movement were also participating. In one camp were those adhering to the "black revolution" as part of an international movement tending toward some type of affiliation with revolutionary movements in the "Third World" of Africa, Asia and Latin America. In the other camp were all those who subscribed to some concept of the "Negro revolution" which was essentially limited to American society. This group sought black integration into a broad American consensus including white people, a consensus which was fundamentally opposed to revolutionary movements in other parts of the world.[57] Much as whites formerly allied in the civil rights movement were dividing into those seeking greater reforms within the basic confines of American society and radicals looking toward revolutionary transformation of all American institutions, so blacks separated into those who desired the completion of their integration into contemporary American society, and radicals questioning the validity of that society itself.

Radical blacks rejected black-white unity, which had held the civil rights coalition together. The clearest statement of that rejection came from the Student Nonviolent Coordinating Committee. Their experience with poor blacks in Mississippi and other parts of the Deep South taught SNCC members that whites neither could nor would undertake the fundamental social and economic readjustments which alone might alter the condition of the mass of poor black people. The inability of the Mississippi Freedom Democratic Party to unseat the white supremacist regular delegation to the 1964 Democratic national convention, rested with the Johnson Administration and Northern Democrats who refused to make a fight on the issue. This, combined with the nomination by the Republicans of Senator Barry Goldwater for the Presidency with a strategy of appealing to the worst enemies of Southern blacks, soured SNCC supporters on the two major parties. Consequently, in Lowndes County, Alabama, in the heart of the black-belt, the organization formed its own Black Panther Party as a first step in the creation of all-black organizations to fight for the social and economic needs of black people. In SNCC's perspective, black people could neither rely upon half-hearted white allies nor look to the Federal government for protection of their rights. As evidence SNCC pointed to the inadequate performance of the Administration in preventing or solving the numerous killings that had occurred in the previous years of civil rights activity in the South.[58]

In line with the new political outlook of SNCC came changes in its leadership, with advocates of "black consciousness" and "black power" moving into commanding positions. Stokely Carmichael, Cleveland Sellers, and Ruby Doris Robinson, all original SNCC members, became outspoken advocates of the new viewpoint. Moving away from the loose organization it had been since its founding, SNCC began to tighten up its discipline. It rejected what it termed the "freedom high" atmosphere of the past whereby many young people had flocked to it mainly to practice their own personal styles of living. This had interfered with the difficult work of effecting social changes outside the organization. Tactically, the organization explicitly repudiated the concept of non-violence in favor of self-defense and the need for protecting black communities against white retaliation and terror. Whites on the SNCC staff now were told they no longer could work in black communities, but had to direct their attention to the white community since "white racism" was the major problem facing blacks. Were this not sufficient to arouse fears and suspicions among white friends, not to mention foes, the new leaders rejected integration as a legitimate goal for black people. Stokely Carmichael asserted that "integration is irrelevant when initiated by black people in the present society. It does nothing to solve their basic problems." And James Forman declared that integration "means moving Negroes into the mainstream of American life and its accepted value system. I reject this."[59]

SNCC's new line provoked criticism from others in the civil rights movement who still looked to coalition politics with white liberals and labor unions as basic for any black advances. To those outside the movement it was confirmation of fears that the organization wished to foment violence and chaos to accomplish its basically irrational demands. Many saw in the terms "black consciousness" and "black power" a new form of racial chauvinism, this time of the black variety. While the Southern Conference Educational Fund did not join in the chorus of criticism, it too was affected. SNCC refused to co-sponsor the Southern Mountain Project with the Fund, and SNCC people in the project began to leave. Carl Braden reported that, although "our old friends in SNCC, Carmichael, Forman, Sellers, Robinson," and others, favored working with the Fund, "the new element in SNCC is intensely nationalistic and is able to wield veto power in this matter." Braden was confident, however, that a mellowing would eventually set in.[60] The immediate reaction of the *Patriot* to the change of outlook in SNCC was sympathetic.

At first, it took issue with the definition of integration advanced by Forman, declaring that the Fund had a different conception of the term. It upheld the

> literal meaning of the word integrate: 'to make whole,' that is, to make whole the human race. It meant integration of people not into the existing society but into a new society that the movement would build where different groups of people could enrich each other's lives, where all men could be free, and where it was possible for men to live as brothers.[61]

It agreed, however, that this conception pointed to a dream rather than an existing reality. It was incumbent upon whites who believed in this conception of integration to understand that until there was "equality in strength between different groups of people" men could not be made whole. The concept of white supremacy, the journal declared, "which we must realize has been the cornerstone of our society" made this equality impossible at present. Those who believed in the making whole of humanity need not, however, fear SNCC's talk of "black power" for, "unless black people create their own power there can never be a meeting ground." Rather than a rejection of white people *per se*, SNCC's new policy of directing whites into white communities, declared the *Patriot*, "may be providing this generation with the last chance white people may ever have to overcome the racism and white supremacy by which Western man has come close to destroying this planet."[62]

Anne Braden had an opportunity to elaborate upon these views when the Southern Student Organizing Committee, in its May-June 1966 newsletter, criticized the Fund's Southern Mountain Project. The project's interracial makeup seemed to the student group its "Achilles heel." Instead, the students asserted the need for "white consciousness" as a counterpart to the new awareness of blacks. Replying to this criticism, she declared that one of the beneficial effects of the SNCC call for "black power" was the awakening of whites to the need for organizing in white communities, especially among poor whites. Though admitting that the Fund's Appalachian project might fail, it had not as yet done so and whatever reasons for failure might exist, its interracial character would not be one of them. A judgment could not be made about interracial organizations anywhere since no such energy had been poured into it as had been poured into the black communities in past years. She herself, she confessed, had "never seen this concept of white people flooding into black communities and organizing them." In over twenty years of interracial activity she had come to the realization that "Negroes did not need me or want me to either lead them or organize them." Consequently she believed her main duty was to reach white people to "convince *them* of the evils of racism and of the meaning of real democracy." This was the purpose of the Southern Conference Educational Fund, and the reasoning behind its support of the white student project of SNCC, the Southern Mountain Project, and other projects in white communities in the South. Despite its meager results, mainly because of the "feeble handful" of participants, the Mississippi white folks project that the Southern Student Organizing Committee undertook in the summer of 1964 was a worthwhile venture and one to be repeated on a wider scale in Mississippi and elsewhere in the South.[63]

There were pitfalls, however, in mechanically transferring the experiences learned in black communities. Most important was the analogy the white students were making between "black consciousness" and "white consciousness." Whereas there was an historically valid basis for "black consciousness" as a means of asserting the human dignity and value of black people and their culture "the last thing in the world we need is 'white consciousness,'" she declared. In fact, there was already enough "'white consciousness' with all the evil and destructiveness that indicates." What was necessary was to uproot it, and the most effective way toward that end was to meet the matter of white racial beliefs and practices head-on, primarily by the method of interracial organizing. Referring to the experience of well-intentioned grass-roots organizers elsewhere who did not tackle this problem at the outset, Anne Braden referred to the Chicago experience of community organizer Saul Alinsky. In the forties, after some success among blacks in that city, Alinsky had worked with poor whites and helped them to form the Back-of-the-Yards movement which became a strong community organization. Its chief defect, however, was its all-white character and it soon became "the backbone of a movement to keep Negroes out of that part of Chicago." That experience made it imperative that white people be persuaded that their best interest lay in alliance with blacks. On the other hand, blacks, as an oppressed group, might very well see the prior importance of getting themselves together before joining with whites in common causes. The initiative, however, must be with white people. Whatever the degree of their exploitation at the hands of other white people, in relation to black people, whites were part of a privileged group. Hence, any effective black-white coalition must originate from the white side and at the outset be an interracial effort. She agreed with one of the white student leaders, Robb Burlage, that "white people don't organize as white except for a bad purpose."[64] Thus, the Fund would persist in keeping its Southern Mountain Project, and any other enterprise in which it engaged, interracial. She urged the Southern Student Organizing Committee to pursue a similar course lest it fall by the wayside as another white people's organization gone wrong.[65]

The Southern Conference Educational Fund issued a strong statement of support for "black power" in November, 1966. The Fund viewed it as a healthy corrective, forcing to the surface "long hidden racist feelings latent in the American consciousness" which were manifesting themselves under the rubric of "white backlash." Noting that nearly every white American and "not a few Negro people" accepted as a premise that "what is white is superior," the Fund saw that the real challenge before the nation was to change "the mind-set of white America." There were broad democratic implications, also, in SNCC's new policy of sponsoring all black grass-roots political parties. Were this attempt to prove successful it would fulfill the promise of American democracy, for the "simple truth is that the rank and file of Americans have never really controlled their government." The new policy of the Student Nonviolent Coordinating Committee had reaffirmed the need for radical social change and, in the Fund's opinion, this was "the social imperative of our day for black and white." It reaffirmed the validity of the Fund's course of several decades to develop an alliance of the less privileged whites of the South and the masses of poor blacks "in a joint struggle for a more democratic America."

Though the political forms of this common effort had still to be developed, the grass-roots approach toward both groups would continue to be "one of the basic requirements for healthy social change." The statement rejected the equating of "black power" with violence, which the media was inculcating in the public mind. Violence, it asserted, was the product of no civil rights organization but was "endemic in the American scene, part and parcel of United States history," and even now an essential element of the foreign policy of "the American power structure" engaged "in one of the most violent and terrible wars in our nation's history." The issue of violence belonged on the doorstep of the white community, and of both the local and Federal governments, it asserted. Claiming that there was "a calculated attempt to divide the civil rights movement" by distinguishing between "responsible and irresponsible" organizations within it, the Fund believed that "everyone genuinely concerned with an effective movement is a responsible person," and it called for the inclusion of all in "one parallel stream." Vital to the movement was the presence of those, such as the Student Nonviolent Coordinating Committee. They served "to sting the conscience of America with its racist heritage." By advocating profound social changes they sought to bring about genuine brotherhood.[66]

The Southern Conference Educational Fund had come to the end of the course entered upon in 1948, and it had made a new beginning. With legal segregation finally interred, the Fund felt free to return to the broader purposes of the Southern Conference for Human Welfare. Having played an important part in breaking the pall of silence that had hung over the white South, the Fund now turned to giving a clearer sense of direction to white Southerners no longer inhibited from working with black Southerners toward common political objectives.

It worked to deepen opposition to the Vietnam war through anti-draft agitation, and it publicized the inequities of the draft system which worked greatest hardships upon blacks and other minorities. Fund organizer Joe Mulloy and Alan McSurely, white Kentuckians from Appalachia, and Walter Collins, a young Louisiana black and former SNCC member, faced trial on alleged "draft dodging" charges. Collins received an unusually severe five-year sentence in 1970. He had been active in a number of Fund activities in New Orleans where he was a thorn in the side of hostile authorities. Besides anti-draft activities, McSurely and his wife, Margaret, and Mulloy joined the Fund's Southern Mountain Project. Their activities in Pike County, Kentucky, involved them and the Bradens in a number of prosecutions, once again on sedition charges under new state laws seemingly designed with the Fund particularly in mind. The Fund also kept alive efforts to forge coalitions between black and white workers in the deep South. In Laurel, Mississippi, it aided workers on strike at a Masonite Corporation plant. Though the strike failed after months of picketing and boycotts, the Fund achieved some limited success in keeping white and black workers from falling victim to attempts to divide them on racial grounds. Finally, the Fund continued its function of providing publicity, raising funds and enlisting other support for numerous black radical organizations, such as the Black Panther Party, in various parts of the South where they faced police and other official harassment.

Claiming to be a radical organization working toward a restructuring of American society, the Fund was part of a nationwide revival of the political left. Though sharing long-term objectives with others on the left, including Communists, Trotskyists, and the varied sections of the "new left," the Fund did not develop a distinct theoretical approach. It remained eclectic in its theory, borrowing freely from others. As such, it has long since departed from the older regional emphasis of its origins, as well as a belief in the efficacy of social reform alone for the ills of American society.

Conclusions

The depression of the thirties had a devastating effect upon the South. Plagued with lower living standards and generally poorer social services made worse by the economic downturn, many Southerners began to question accepted folkways. Since existing institutions provided few outlets for their discontent, reform-minded Southerners created the Southern Conference for Human Welfare to work for the changes they desired.

In its search for ways to transform the South from the nation's "number one economic problem" into a prosperous, viable region, the Conference soon faced the major social issue of race relations. Repelled by the barbarities of Nazism among which violent racist prejudices were prominent, the SCHW broke with Southern traditions and came out strongly in opposition to racial discrimination and segregation. It accepted as members all those who would work to further its aims of ending Jim Crow, furthering labor union organization in Southern industry, upgrading education and health and general social reforms. Communists and Socialists joined in its work, and the organization earned the suspicion and hostility of a variety of groups who thought its cooperation with Communists a sign of naivete at best and betrayal of American ideals at worst. Despite the inaccuracy and distortion of the appellation "Communist Front" applied to it, the SCHW suffered under this label up to its demise in 1948.

The Southern Conference Educational Fund, originally the educational arm of the SCHW, took up its work in 1947. The problems of the South seemed insoluble so long as segregation continued in force. Focusing its energies upon ending segregation, the Fund made its most significant historical contribution in its early years. Through special editions of its journal, the *Southern Patriot*, and opinion polls of Southern educators, physicians, and administrators it revealed the fraudulent nature of the "separate but equal" rationale for segregation. The Fund also played an important part in thwarting attempts to maintain segregation in Southern higher education. By exposing the regional education program of the Southern governors in 1949 as a device for keeping Southern colleges and universities a preserve for whites with inadequate provisions for blacks, the

Fund helped to deny segregationists an important prop for their system. Because of its Southern complexion, the Fund's strictures against segregation had greater impact than similar criticism from Northern integrationists. Its program was a model of political education and a lasting contribution to the effort to free the mind from the shackles of race prejudice.

Principal credit for the success of the Fund in its early years lay with its two most active officers: Aubrey Williams and James Dombrowski. Dombrowski, the scholar-activist and able administrator, was the architect of the organization's program and the tactics of presenting it to the Southern public. Williams was the public advocate outspoken in support of racial equality and, importantly, the wire-puller who retained the interest and support of influential Northerners. Such support kept the Fund alive in the difficult years when segregationist attacks bore heavily upon it.

Until the mid-fifties, the Fund was an effective voice for racial equality in the South. Despite segregationist pressure, it had the cooperation of prominent Southern blacks and whites who had joined it during World War II and the immediate post-war years. It was Mississippi Senator Eastland's attack on the Fund at the 1954 New Orleans hearing under cover of the anti-communist preoccupation of that period that, in the short run, undermined the Fund's effectiveness as an instrument for social change in the South. The "Communist-front" label frightened away many supporters, particularly those in the North. By accepting Eastland's allegations against the Fund and including it on their own list of proscribed organizations, important Northern liberal supporters internalized the anti-civil libertarian attitudes of their opponents and contributed, albeit unwittingly, to strengthening the hand of segregationists. Without the firm support of Northern integrationists, the Fund dwindled to a beleaguered band of militants. When vindication finally came, first in a 1965 Supreme Court decision undoing the work of Louisiana segregationists who had raided Fund offices, and then in 1969 when the state of Louisiana publicly acknowledged the falsity of the "Communist-front" label it also had pinned on the Fund, it was much too late. The organization could not capitalize upon these successes.

After 1954, the Fund continued to be useful to the civil rights movement. Its many conferences on issues of civil liberties, integration and voting denials in the South helped to lay some of the foundations for the dramatic civil rights gains of the sixties. Its tireless activity for desegregation redounded less to its benefit, however, than to the larger cause itself. The Fund's devotion to the integration cause owed a good deal of its strength to the social gospel and evangelical Protestant background of its leaders, particularly Dombrowski and Williams. This religious aspect of its social practice received further reinforcement from the participation of a number of black churchmen such as Baptist Reverend Fred Shuttlesworth, who became Fund president after Williams, and A.M.E. Zion Bishop C. Ewbank Tucker, among others. The church ties of Fund supporters enabled the organization to form close links with black organizations such as the Southern Christian Leadership Conference and various state branches of the NAACP which had a strong church-connected following in the South. More than any single group, the black community's assistance maintained the Fund in the fifties and sixties after many Southern whites had departed. Thus, in the South, at least in the Fund's case, white supporters of the black freedom movement developed a closer working relationship with the black community than was true elsewhere in the nation.

The Fund consistently emphasized the positive consequences for white people of the elimination of segregation and discrimination. It was often critical of overly negative arguments for civil rights which emphasized undoing long-practiced injustices to black people. If whites, particularly Southern whites, were to change these practices they had to be convinced of the positive benefits to themselves in such a transformation of behavior. The Fund therefore stressed the gains to the South in terms of economic invigoration, educational upgrading, and general social advances which would result from ending Jim Crow. The emphasis on the positive attracted new recruits, mainly former students once active in other organizations such as the Student Nonviolent Coordinating Committee (SNCC) and the Southern Student Organizing Committee (SSOC). This infusion of new blood kept the Fund in motion after other organizations such as the Congress of Racial Equality (CORE) and even SNCC had lapsed into a state of torpor.

The positive approach to Southern whites also permitted the organization to revamp its program and take a more radical direction after 1966. When black radicals demanded "black power" rather than integration, thereby disrupting the civil rights movement, many whites withdrew fearing that a new racial chauvinism had seized control of the movement. Others, such as those in the Fund, perceived in black radicalism a challenge to whites to develop a black-white alliance through a sweeping reconstruction of American society. Carl Braden in particular, as a convinced socialist, proposed that the Fund work among poor whites in the deep South and white miners in

Appalachia as a beginning for a future interracial alliance. The Fund, largely an organization of white professionals of middle-class origins, rethought its role and program.

With the emergence of a new political left after 1965, the Bradens, who had become Fund directors upon the retirement of James Dombrowski, linked up with the broader left movement. Opposition to the Vietnam war, initiation of anti-draft agitation in the South, support for grass-roots organization on problems of poverty and unemployment as an alternative to Federal anti-poverty programs, and active cooperation with black and white labor union drives in the South became the core of the Fund's program. In place of the earlier emphasis upon blacks as a deprived minority, the Fund adopted the concept that blacks were a colonial people within America. Their liberation would require the rebuilding of social institutions in a far more drastic way than integrationists, including those in the Fund, had previously imagined.

Yet, its newly radical perspective did not result in a new expansion of the Fund. It remained a relatively small group of activists in the South. Partly this was because the radical left in America was itself a quite limited phenomenon, and also because the radical left had never established itself as a significant or continuous social force in the South. Thus the Fund, despite its programmatic shift to the left, remained a marginal group in the South. Its principal significance lay not in its political or social analysis, for its theory was largely handmaiden to its practice. Rather, it was in its quality of persistence, an example for those who would attempt serious social change.

Notes

INTRODUCTION

1.Thomas A. Krueger, *And Promises to Keep* (Nashville: Vanderbilt University Press, 1967).

2.Howard Zinn, *The Southern Mystique* (New York: Alfred A. Knopf, 1964).

CHAPTER ONE

1. Frank Freidel, *FDR and the South* (Baton Rouge: Louisiana State University Press, 1965), 35.

2. George B. Tindall, *The Emergence of the New South, 1913-1945* (Baton Rouge: Louusiana State University Press, 1967), 618-19.

3. Freidel, *op. cit.*, 36.

4. Tindall, *op. cit.*, 549. The best short account of New Deal policies in relation to blacks, and the basis for the previous discussion is Leslie Fishel, "The Negro in the New Deal Era," *Wisconsin Magazine of History*, Vol. 48, No. 2 (Winter, 1964-1965), 111-126.

5. See Leonard Dinnerstein, "The Senate's Rejection of Aubrey Williams as Rural Electrification Administrator," *The Alabama Review*, XXI, No. 2 (April, 1968),133-143. That Southern Democrats were the main instrument in his defeat for the REA post can be seen by comparing the votes on Williams' nomination to that of Henry A. Wallace to be Secretary of Commerce in the same session. Both were attacked by conservative Republicans and Southern Democrats. However, in the final Senate count, Wallace was approved with only 5 Democrats opposed; Williams lost, with 19 Democrats opposed, 15 from the South.

6. Thomas A. Krueger, *And Promises to Keep* (Nashville: Vanderbilt University Press, 1967, 3-19.

7. Gunnar Myrdal, *An American Dilemma* (New York and Evanston: Harper & Row Publishers, 1962, Twentieth Anniversary Edition), 466.

8. Anne Braden, "History of the Southern Conference Educational Fund, Inc.," typescript outline, October 9, 1963, Box 36, Carl and Anne Braden Collection. Wisconsin State Historical Society (hereafter cited as Braden Mss.).

9. See Krueger, *op. cit.*, 43. He accepts V. O. Key's estimates in the latter's *Southern Politics in State and Nation* (New York: Alfred A. Knopf, 1949), 617.

10. Krueger, *op. cit.*, 47.

11. *Ibid.*, 58.

12. Howard Odum, *Race and Rumors of Race* (Chapel Hill: The University of North Carolina Press, 1943), 171.

13. Quoted in Fishel, *op. cit.*, 122.

14. Virginius Dabney, "Nearer and Nearer the Precipice," *Atlantic Monthly*, 171 (January, 1943) 94-100, and "Press and Morale," *Saturday Review of Literature*, XXV (July 4, 1942) 5-6, 24-25, quoted in Richmond M. Dalfiume, "The Forgotten Years' of the Negro Revolution," *Journal of American History*, LV, Number I (June, 1968), 97.

15. OWI, Bureau of Intelligence, August 5, 1942, "Intelligence Report: White Attitudes Toward Negroes," and Hazel Gaudet Erskine, "The Polls: Race Relations," *Public Opinion Quarterly*, XXVI (Spring, 1962), 137-148, quoted in *ibid.*, 103.

16. Francis Butler Simkins, *The South Old and New: A History 1820-1947* (New York: Alfred A. Knopf, 1947), 464, 476.

17. The following discussion is based on Krueger, *op. cit.*, particularly chapters 3-6, which is the only full-length history of the Southern Conference for Human Welfare.

18. *Ibid.*, 134 ff.

19. Quoted in *ibid.*, 140.

20. *Ibid.*

21. *Ibid.*, 142. Highlander Folk School, Monteagle, Tennessee, an educational center for labor union organizers since the thirties, also suffered from the change in the CIO attitude, which disrupted the unionization of the South. Aubrey Williams noted that the "real cause of failure of unionization drives down here is distruction (sic) of education program by Van Bittner and Jim Carey when they pulled the rug out from under Highlander Folk School they threw the organizing of the south on its face. It has never recovered--you have got to change workers ideas and attitudes before you will ever be able to build a membership...."Aubrey Williams to Ralph Scoop White, editor, *Labor's Daily*, Bettendorf, Iowa, Jan. 3, 1957, Box 32. Aubrey Williams Papers, Franklin D. Roosevelt Library, Hyde Park, New York (hereafter cited as AW/FDR).

22. See Foreman to Dombrowski, Dec. 4, 1946; (Foreman?) to Paul Christopher, Dec. 4, 1946; Lewis Jones to Dombrowski, Dec. 5, 1946; Dombrowski to Jones, Dec. 7, 1946; Lucy R. Mason to Dombrowski, Dec. 6, 1946; Lucy Mason to Foreman, Dec. 8, 1946; Lucy Mason to Dombrowski, Dec. 11, 1946; Roscoe Dunjee to Lucy Mason, Dec. 11, 1946; Dombrowski to Foreman, Dec. 12, 1946; Lewis Jones to Dombrowski, Dec. 1946; Lucy Mason to Dombrowski, Dec. 19, 1946, all in Box 42, Braden Mss. See also Clark Foreman

to Freda Kirchwey, editor of *Nation*, Jan. 24, 1947, denying any political or ideological split within the Southern Conference for Human Welfare.

23. Aubrey Williams to Dombrowski, Dec. 26, 1946, Box 42, Braden, Mss.

24. Palmer Weber to Dombrowski, no date, but probably December, 1946, or January, 1947, Box 42, Braden Mss. George Mitchell, former member of the Southern Conference for Human Welfare Board, was then director of the Southern Regional Council.

25. *Minutes of Administrative Committee*, Southern Conference for Human Welfare, Washington D.C., June 21, 1947, Box 43, Braden Mss.

26. Foreman to Josephine Wilkins, Jan. 9, 1947, Box 43, Braden Mss.

27. See *Minutes of SCEF Board Meeting*, July 13, 1947, Richmond, Virginia, Box 34, Braden Mss.

28. Virginia Durr to Dombrowski, 1947, Box 36, Braden Mss.

29. See *Memorandum to Board of Directors of the SCHW*, April 19, 1947, Box 43, Braden Mss. The minutes do not indicate what response, if any, there was to the report.

30. The most complete account of the Wallace campaign is Curtis B. MacDougall, *Gideon's Army* (New York: Marzani and Munsell, 1965, 3 volumes. See Volume I, 37-137, 147-171, 209-247.

31. *Minutes of Southern Conference for Human Welfare*, April 19, 1947, Box 43, Braden Mss.

32. See James A. Dombrowski to C. B. Baldwin, April 23, 1947, Box 35, Braden Mss.

33. William Mitch to Dombrowski, March 31, 1948, Box 35, Braden Mss.

34. Luther P. Jackson to Virginia Durr, March 12, 1948, Box 35, Braden Mss.

35. *Ibid.*

36. *Final Resolution of the Southern Conference for Human Welfare, Minutes*, Nov. 21, 1948, Box 43, Braden Mss.

37. *Final Resolution of the Southern Conference for Human Welfare, Minutes*, Nov. 21, 1948, Box 43, Braden Mss.

CHAPTER TWO

1. Anne Braden, "History of the Southern Conference Educational Fund, Inc.," Box 36, Braden Mss.; see also Clark Foreman, "Decade of Hope," *Phylon*, XII, No. 2 (June, 1950).

2. Tindall, *The Emergence of the New South, 1913-1945*, 175.

3. M. Ashby Jones, quoted in *ibid.*, 181.

4. *Ibid.*, 182-3.

5. Quoted in *ibid.*, 280.

6. Myrdal, *An American Dilemma*, 847.

7. See Krueger, *And Promises to Keep*, 24-5.

8. Lillian Smith, "Southern Defensive-II," *Common Ground*, LV (Spring, 1944), 43.

9. Odum to Graves, July 17, 1944, quoted in Tindall,*op. cit.*, 720.

10. Foreman to Dombrowski, June 22, 1944, quoted in Krueger, *op. cit.*, 122. In contrast to the Southern Conference for Human Welfare, the Southern Regional Council did not publicly commit itself against segregation until 1951. See Tindall, *op. cit.*, 119-121. Aubrey Williams recalled some of his experiences with the council, contrasting it with the Fund. "Under Jim Dombrowski's leadership," he noted, "the SCEF developed an unequivocal across-the-board position in behalf of the rights of Negroes. This, I think, was the first such position involving white people that was taken in the South. The Will Alexander [illegible] Southern Regional Conference until George Mitchell took it over some time in the 50's had been much like the South American bird which wades out into the water until it touches its bottom, and then runs for the shore. I had been on the Board of Southern Regional Council until the Board refused to send a congratulatory telegram to North Carolina Baptist (white) convention, which had invited the Negro North Carolina Baptists Convention to join with it in one convention. Johnson, its Executive Secretary and Chairman Dabney, Editor of the Richmond newspaper opposed the motion on the grounds that 'It would hurt our influence.' I resigned saying 'I had been mistaken in accepting a place on the Board where I had thought they were engaged in working for integration, but this proved rather conclusively that this was not true." See Williams' unpublished manuscript in possession of Prof. Sheldon Hackney, Princeton University (hereafter cited as AW/Hackney) courtesy of Professor Hackney.

11. See *SCEF Minutes*, January 28, 1947, Box 34, Braden Mss.

12. *Southern Patriot*, August, 1947.

13. See *To Secure These Rights: The Report of the President's Committee on Civil Rights* (New York: Simon & Schuster, 1947), 139 ff.

14. Richmond *Times-Dispatch*, October 31, 1948; *Birmingham News*, November 2, 1948, quoted in William C. Berman, "The Politics of Civil Rights in the Truman Administration," unpublished Ph.D. dissertation, Ohio State University, 1963, microfilm copy, 62.

15. Quoted in *ibid.*, 62-3.

16. *Memo to the Board of Directors SCEF*, October, 1947, Box 43, Braden Mss.

17. Foreman to Dombrowski, November 3, 1947, Box 43, Braden Mss.

18. Rep. John Bell Williams, quoted in Berman, *op. cit.*, 76.

19. See Dombrowski to Foreman, November 6, 1947, Box 43, Braden Mss.

20. *Ibid.*, also Dombrowski to Mary Price, October 19, 1947, Box 43, Braden Mss.

21. Since these were years of depression and war, the statistics reflect the diminished sums available for public domestic needs. They do not, however, account for the disparities in sums spent for blacks and whites.

22. The statistical data and quotes in previous paragraphs are from the *Southern Patriot*, October, 1947.

23. See *Minutes of SCEF Board of Directors*, May 22, 1948, Box 34, Braden Mss.

24. Program for the Southern Conference Educational Fund, 1947, Box 34, Braden Mss.

25. *Ibid.*

26. See *Report of the Director, SCEF*, July 15-October 15, 1947. Dombrowski to the Adele R. Levy Fund, Inc. October 9, 1947. which includes a copy of Bernay's proposal Box 34, Braden Mss.

27. *Ibid.*

28. *Ibid.*, also Dombrowski to Ann Whitman, October 9, 1947. Dombrowski to Foreman, October 20, 1947, Box 43, Braden Mss.

29. See *Southern Patriot*, May, 1948.

30. See *Report of the Director SCEF*, November 21, 1948, Box 34, Braden Mss., and *Southern Patriot*, November, 1948.

31. See *Report of the Director SCEF*, November 21, 1948, Box 34, Braden Mss. Dombrowski had suggested to Aubrey Williams that the site be Durham, North Carolina. "Durham, as you know," he wrote, "was where the SRC [Southern Regional Council] had its inception in a Jim Crow conference of Negroes who drafted a statement on 'what the Negro wants' or some such title which was later replied to by a group of whites; then the two got together, a strategy devised of course in advance. It might he fitting to hold this meeting with the 'new and modern look' in the same place as a kind of historical reference...." Dombrowski to Williams, July 16, 1948, Box 39, AW/FDR.

32. Dombrowski to Editor of Richmond *News-Leader*, December 9, 1947, Box 39, AW/FDR.

33. Box 39, AW/FDR.

CHAPTER THREE

1. See Josephine Wilkins to Dombrowski, August 9, 1948, Box 39, AW/FDR.

2. See *New York Times*, November 21, 1948, Richmond *Times Dispatch*, November 20, 1948, and Charlottesville *Daily Progress*, November 20, 1948, clippings in Box 34, Braden Mss.

3. Declaration of Civil Rights, Box 35, Braden Mss.

4. Statistical and other data in the following paragraphs are from the *Southern Patriot*, March, 1948.

5. There was little, if any, difference between secular and church hospitals in regard to segregation and discrimination.

6. *Southern Patriot*, October, 1951.

7. *Ibid.*, March, 1948.

8. *Ibid.*, September, 1948.

9. Dombrowski to Dr. Chenault, August 30, 1948. Also Dombrowski to Dr. Samuel Proger, Pratt Diagnostic Hospital, Boston, Mass., September 9, 1948, asking his advice and requesting Proger to speak to Chester Barnard, new head of the Rockefeller Foundation. Box 39, AW/FDR.

10. Dombrowski to Marshall Field, December 3, 1948, Box 39, AW/FDR.

11. *Southern Patriot*, April, 1951.

12. *Ibid.*, December, 1951.

13. *Ibid.*, October, 1952.

14. *Ibid.*, March, 1952.

15. See *Minutes, Board of Directors*, February 23, 1952, Box 39, AW/FDR.
16. See *Ibid.*, April, 1953.
17. *Ibid.*, December, 1953.
18. *Southern Patriot*, March, 1952.

CHAPTER FOUR

1. The Southern Conference Educational Fund was instrumental in arranging for eighteen Southern lawyers, black and white and from each of the Southern states, to file an *amicus curiae* brief in behalf of Herman Sweatt before the U.S. Supreme Court. Dombrowski wrote to Aubrey Williams. "'We came out very well at the end--with at least 1 person signing from each Southern state. This is the first time a group of Southern lawyers has taken a stand against segregation, and has some historic significance.' January 6, 1950, Box 39, AW/FDR. See also *Southern Patriot*, January, 1950 .

2. Tindall, *op. cit.*, 562.

3. See Redding S. Sugg, Jr., and George Hilton Jones, *The Southern Regional Education Board. Ten Years of Regional Cooperation in Higher Education* (Baton Rouge: Louisiana State University Press, 1960.

4. *Ibid.*, 7 ff.

5. The *Southern Patriot* noted that a report on regional education at the Southern Governors Conference in New Orleans in 1945, according to a report in the New Orleans *Times-Picaynee*, "resulted primarily from a Supreme Court decision requiring equal and nondiscriminatory opportunities for all applicants for higher education in publicly maintained schools." See *Southern Patriot*, September, 1949.

6. Sugg and Jones, *op. cit.*, 11.

7. According to the Nashville *Banner*, at the Nashville meeting of the governors in October, 1947, Governor Jim McCord of Tennessee declared that the Southern States faced a dilemma, "Of either abandoning the fields of higher education and closing their present institutions, or permitting Negro students to attend such institutions on an equal basis with white students." Faced with this situation, Governor McCord suggested a regional plan as the solution, with Meharry as the first regional center....An important factor in stimulating the Governor's action was the fear of what would happen if Meharry closed, as a result of its $350,000 annual deficit. Mr. Cecil Simms, legal adviser to Governor McCord, speaking at a meeting of Southern governors in Washington, February, 1948, said "If Meharry closes, Negro students half way through would be going back to their states and demanding open doors." Reported in the *Southern Patriot*, September, 1949.

8. Quoted in Sugg and Jones, *op. cit.*, 13-14.

9. *Ibid.*

10. *Ibid.*, 14. The "observer's" comments tend to contradict the authors. They play down the importance of segregation to the whole regional scheme formulated by the governors. From the "observer's" comments it seems that "the larger possibilities' of regional cooperation were an afterthought.

11. Quoted in John N. Popham, "Medical College Offered to South," *New York Times*, January 19, 1948, 121.

12. In 1956, by amendment, another member was to be appointed by the governors, he to be a legislator. See Sugg and Jones, *op. cit.*, 16.

13. *Ibid.*, 18-19.

14. *Southern Patriot*, September, 1949.

15. See editorial, "Regional Education for Whites and Negroes, Richmond *Times-Dispatch*, January 23, 1948.

16. See editorial, "Evading the Costs of Segregation," *Pittsburgh Courier*, January 31, 1948.

17. *Southern Patriot*, September, 1949.

18. Sugg and Jones, *op. cit.*, 19-20.

19. Attempts were made to get white speakers at a Fund-sponsored Conference on Higher Education in Atlanta in 1950 to discuss "Why I support the Regional Plan." However, "the entire Board of the Regional Plan have declined for one reason or another, except Hollis Price [a Negro college official] ...." Dombrowski to Aubrey Williams, no date, Box 39, AW/FDR.

20. Dombrowski also noted that the program's director, George V. Denny, had scheduled a discussion on racial segregation and had invited two segregationists to participate. He chided Denny for not including a Southerner favoring integration. "To fail to do so tends to confirm the mistaken impression throughout the country," he informed Denny, "that there are no Southerners opposed to segregation." Dombrowski to George V. Denny, November 5, 1948, Box 39, AW/FDR.

21. Aubrey Williams to John R. Steelman, December 14, 1948, Box 39, AW/FDR.

22. John E. Ivey, Jr., to Williams, March 1, 1950, Box 39, AW/FDR.

23. Aubrey Williams to Ivey, March 6, 1950, Box 39, AW/FDR.

24. However, Ivey failed to mention the important qualification that the Kentucky legislature added to its ratification: "in its participation in the regional compact...the Commonwealth of Kentucky shall not erect, acquire, develop or maintain in any manner any education institution within its borders to which Negroes shall not be admitted on an equal basis with other races, nor shall any Negro citizen of Kentucky be forced to attend if there is in operation within the Commonwealth at the time an institution that offers the same course of study to students of other races. Quoted in the *Southern Patriot*, May, 1950.

25. Ivey, to Williams, March 8, 1950. Williams noted to Dombrowski, attached to same, "This is very sad." Box 39, AW/FDR.

26. See *Southern Patriot*, March, 1950.

27. Clipping, in Box 39, AW/FDR.

28. Aubrey Williams to Thomas Johnson, attorney, Macon, Georgia, A. D. Beitel, James Rankin, attorney, Atlanta, Lucy Mason, Dr. Glen Rainey, Atlanta, and Harry Gershon, Atlanta, March 9, 1950, Box 39, AW/FDR.

29. Quoted in *Southern Patriot*, April, 1950.

30. *Ibid.*

31. See opinion, filed April 14, 1950, by Judge Markell in the case of *Esther McCready v. Harry Byrd, el. al.*, quoted in Sugg and Jones, *op. cit.*, 46.

32. See Minutes, *Meeting of the Executive Committee SREB* October 4, 1949, quoted in Sugg and Jones, *op. cit.*, 45.

33. *Ibid.*

34. See unpublished statement by James Mackay, the Board's attorney, "Recent Legal Developments Concerning Segregation in Higher Education," October 2, 1950 quoted in ibid., 46.

35. *Southern Patriot*, May, 1950.

36. See also letters from James Dombrowski to Rep Howard Elliott, State Capitol, Missouri, April 4, 1949, Rep. Bernard S. Melnicove, Maryland House of Delegates, April 4, 1949, congratulating them on sponsoring legislation in their respective statehouses to eliminate segregation at state colleges and universities. Also Dombrowski to Harold W. Stoke, President of Louisiana State University, April 7, 1949, suggesting he open graduate and professional schools of LSU to all qualified persons, black and white, and to follow the example of the University of Arkansas voluntarily rather than wait for a Supreme Court order. Box 39, AW/FDR.

37. Simkins, *op. cit.*, 529.

38. *Southern Patriot*, May, 1953.

39. See memo on Fund activities for Mrs. Franklin D. Roosevelt, Madame Pandit and Mrs. Mary McLeod Bethune, *Minutes of the SCEF Board of Directors*, 1950, Box 34, Braden, Mss.

40. Paul Gaston has brilliantly analyzed this mythology in a work which appeared while the author was writing this chapter. His analysis of the "New South Creed," developed in the eighteen eighties and accepted by most of Southern white, and a good deal of black opinion, until the contemporary civil rights upsurge, parallels the views presented here. See Paul M. Gaston, *The New South Creed* (New York: Alfred A. Knopf, 1970).

41. Title of editorial, *Southern Patriot*, January, 1954.

CHAPTER FIVE

1. See *Memoirs*, unnumbered pages, Box 44, AW/FDR.

2. Quoted in Robert G. Sherrill, *Gothic Politics in the Deep South* (New York: Grossman Publishers, 1968), 204.

3. *Ibid.*, 205.

4. This is from the subcommittee proceedings as quoted in *ibid.*, 205.

5. This was James Dombrowski's conviction, writing to Fund attorney, Leonard Boudin, September 6, 1960, concerning the SCHW and Black. "...As a matter of fact, much of the early animus against the Conference [SCHW] was a desire to smear and discredit the New Deal and FDR....Black, as you know, received the first Thomas Jefferson award in 1938....Senator Eastland's attack upon the SCEF in 1954 involving Cliff & Va. Durr, was motivated without doubt by a desire to smear Justice Black through his sister-in-law...." Box 35, Braden Mss.

6. Williams noted in his unpublished memoirs: "'After the debate I had heard that Young Gene Talmadge had told a group in Atlanta that wanted to start a sort of State of Georgia 'Un American Committee' that there was no need to spend the money of the Georgia taxpayers, that he had arranged for all the witch hunting committees to come South, Eastland, McCarran and McCarthy as well as Woods." *Memoirs*, 3-4, Box 44, AW/FDR. In a letter to Senator Hubert H. Humphrey, February 4, 1954, he also stated: "...First, Jenner gave it out in his recent report that his Committee was investigating the 'Communistic activities of the Southern Conference Educational Fund, Inc.' Then all of the Dixiecrat newspapers gave it the works. There was very evident collusion and they had been tipped off that it was coming. I only cite this to show the indubitable connection between what Jenner is doing and the Tories, and worst political elements down here...You will not be wrong if you say the Jenner group went to Atlanta and there conferred with Gov. Herman Talmadge, and other Southern reactionaries, and afterwards announced that 'they were coming South.' And Talmadge announced the abandonment of plans to have a Georgia investigation, saying that it would be handled by Congressional committees...." Box 41, AW/FDR.

7. See text of telegram to Sen. William E. Jenner, Jan. 31, 1954, Box 38, AW/FDR.

8. Williams to Cannon, Roosevelt, Jr., and McCormack, February 5, 1954; and to Humphrey, February 4, 1954, Box 38, AW/FDR.

9. Williams to Humphrey, February 4, 1954, Box 38, AW/FDR.

10. Myles Horton to Sen. Kefauver, February 9, 1954, Box 41, AW/FDR.

11. Sen. Murray to Williams, February 22, 1954, Box 41, AW/FDR.

12. Martin Agronsky to Williams, March 15, 1954. Kenneth Roberts, Congressman from Alabama, called Williams from Washington to tell him that "nothing was in the mill on either the Conference or myself," which may indicate the secretive manner in which these investigations were handled, away from the eyes even of other members of Congress. Williams to Dombrowski, February 23, 1954, Box 41, AW/FDR.

13. Williams to Clarence Mitchell, February 8, 1954; Jonathan Daniels to Williams, February 27, 1954, Box 41, AW/FDR.

14. Williams to Mrs. Bethune, March 7, 1954, Box 41, AW/FDR.

15. Williams to Dombrowski, March 7, 1954, Box 41, AW/FDR; Williams to Marshall Field, March 10, 1954, Box 36, AW/FDR.

16. See *Memoirs*, 10-11, Box 44, AW/FDR.

17. Williams to Benjamin Mays, March 5, 1954, Box 38, AW/FDR.

18. Williams later remarked on Mays' resignation: "...This is something that has troubled me, that Negroes who are so courageous and clear sighted in the matter of Civil Rights have not always been so clear sighted in the matter of Civil Liberties and have not realized that when the constitutional guarantees are broken down to get at any group, who may be unpopular or even considered to be dangerous, that their own safety is endangered and that they must protect the rights of all people to obtain their own rights, but this has not been the case and many of the leading Negroes have again and again joined in the witch hunt against the Communists, the Socialists, the Trotskyists or who have you, and do not seem to realize they are

preparing their own grave...." In following years, these differences were to plague the Fund's relations with other civil rights organizations, white and black, in the South. See *Memoirs*, 11, Box 44, AW/FDR.

19. Williams later expressed his misgivings: "I may been wrong but my reasoning was that few of those associated with it [SCEF] would stick...I felt that anything less than a wholly frank and full statement of my beliefs, and position would be a great disservice to whatever work was underway to secure a greater measure of justice and equality for the Negro in the South. I was right and I was wrong. I was wrong to cooperate with the subcommittee, for in so doing I participated in what should never have been allowed to happen. That is invasion of a man's private beliefs by any government....But I was right too. For whatever it was worth the SCEF was the lone small voice of white men and women in the South which had been raised against the brutality of the segregation and jimcrowism which constitutes so-called Southern culture. Nothing would have served the Dixiecrats, and the White-Supremacists more at that time than to have been able to parade the leaders of this group as 'Fifth Amendment Communists.' I figured the only way to lick these people was to cut the ground from under them by answering all questions. Looking back upon the decision I now think I made the wrong decision. I think I did the country a disservice by cooperating with the subcommittee and succeeded in saving the SCEF from very little of the smear which was the real purpose of the so-called 'hearings.' There is a lesson in this...and that is when ever any person allows consideration for the well-being or strength of a particular institution or a concern for one's own influence to override adherence to principle and right the outcome is most always that neither the object sought to be protected nor the larger institution nor the person involved escape harm...." *Memoirs*, 5-6, Box 44, AW/FDR.

20. Press release, quoted in *Memoirs*, 8, Box 44, AW/FDR.

21. *Memoirs*, Chapter one, 4, Box 44, AW/FDR.

22. *Ibid.*, 4a-1.

23. *Memoirs*, 16-19, Box 44, AW/FDR.

24. See transcript of *Hearings*, Subcommittee to Investigate the Administration of the Internal Security Act and Other Internal Security Laws, Committee on the Judiciary, United States Senate, New Orleans, Louisiana, March 18, 19, 1954, Vol. I, 2-3, Box 38, Braden Mss; hereafter cited as *Hearings*.

25. See Walter Gellhorn, "Report on a Report of the House Committee on Un-American Activities," *Harvard Law Review*, LX, Number 8 (October, 1947), 1193-1234.

26. Walter Goodman, *The Committee* (Baltimore, Maryland: Penguin Books, Inc., 1969 edition), 200. See also Krueger, *And Promises to Keep*, 167 ff.

27. See *Ibid.*, Vol. I, 81-2, 90 ff.

28. *Ibid.*, 105 ff.

29. *Hearings.*, Vol. 2, 218. This was Crouch's testimony. Williams preferred to believe that Crouch was a "traitor" convicted for organizing "mutiny, sabotage and rebellion" in the Army and sentenced to Alcatraz for forty years until pardoned by President Coolidge in 1925. Williams apparently relied on the following statement by counsel for the Broyles Committee of the Illinois legislature, in the spring of

1944: "...In 1921, Mr. Paul Crouch was a member of the armed forces of the United States, stationed in Hawaii. He was arrested, tried and convicted for Communist propaganda among the troops urging them towards treason. As a result of his treason he was sentenced to a forty year term, later reduced by President Coolidge. When he came out of prison, he became and remained for years a Communist Party organizer in the South." Box 34, Braden Mss. Williams' comments are in his *Memoirs*, 7, Box 44, AW/FDR.

30. *Hearings*, 1, 113 ff.

31. *Ibid.*, 1, 120.

32. *Ibid.*, 123.

33. *Ibid.*, 126.

34. *Ibid.*, 2, 200-201.

35. *Ibid.*, 203-239.

36. See also *Memoirs*, 34-5, Box 44, AW/FDR.

37. *Hearings*, 2, 223-4.

38. Crouch's testimony so enraged Clifford Durr, seated in a side jury-box, that he lunged at Crouch, shouting "Talk about my wife that way, I'll kill the son-of-a-bitch!" Carried into the hallway, Durr suffered a mild heart attack after this incident. *Memoirs*, 48, Box 44, AW/FDR.

39. See *Hearings*, 2, 260-4; *Memoirs*, 46-7, Box 44, AW/FDR.

40. *Hearings*, 2, 284-5; *Memoirs*, 35-41, Box 44, AW/FDR.

41. *Memoirs*, Chapter One, 8, Box 44, AW/FDR.

42. *Ibid.*

43. *Ibid.*, 1; see also St. Petersburg, Florida, *Times*, March 25, 1954, editorial "Eastland Follows McCarthy."

44. See Montgomery *Advertiser*, March 5, 10, 1954.

45. New York *Times*, July 9, 1954.

46. *Memoirs*, 53-55, Box 44, AW/FDR.

47. See New York *Times*, July 9, 1954, clipping in Box 34, Braden, Mss. The Crouch affair did not end there Williams recollected that after being sent to Hawaii, "the poor mentally sick wretch died of cancer, his wife writing many of his victims, myself among them, asking for money, saying that the American Legion which had put him up to telling the untruths he did had turned on him and he was dying for want of medical care...." *Memoirs*, 7, Box 44, AW/FDR.

48. *Memoirs*, 56, Box 44, AW/FDR.

49. *Ibid.*, 64-5.

50. *Ibid.*, 65.

51. See Williams to Mrs. Roosevelt, March 26, 1954: "...I am afraid that this first Hearing is but the first of a series of such which the reactionaries intend to hold in various parts of the South. Eastland announced at New Orleans that a hearing would be held in Birmingham some time in June. I could be wrong but I have the feeling that by putting all persons who make any effort to fight for the Negro in a bad light that they hope to destroy them and whatever influence they may have. It is all tied up in my mind with their determination to keep segregation in every possible segment...." Box 41, AW/FDR.

52. See Williams' unpublished manuscript, unnumbered page, AW/Hackney.

53. *Ibid.*

54. *Ibid.*

55. *Ibid.*

56. *Ibid.*

57. *Ibid.*

58. The author learned this in an interview with Myles Horton in Madison, Wisconsin, November 30, 1970.

59. Unpublished manuscript, AW/Hackney.

60. *Ibid.*

61. Alfred Maund, "Aubrey Williams: Symbol of a New South," *The Nation*, October 10, 1953.

62. See Williams to Mrs. William Korn, no date but probably 1947, AW/Hackney; also Alfred Maund, *op. cit.*

63. See clipping in Box 38, Braden Mss.

64. See Jack Peebles, "Subversion and the Southern Conference Educational Fund," unpublished master's thesis, Louisiana State University-New Orleans, 1970, 8-11; courtesy Mr. Peebles.

65. *Ibid.*

66. See Williams to Mrs. Roosevelt, May 12, 1954, Box 38, AW/FDR; *Memoirs*, 5-6, Box 44, AW/FDR.

67. See Petition in Box 34, Braden Mss.

68. *Memoirs*, 66, Box 44, AW/FDR.

69. See SCEF *Minutes, Board of Directors*, June 12, 1954, in Box 39, Braden Mss. Dombrowski reported to the Board, on May 12, 1954: "It is now apparent that the attack of the Jenner-Eastland Committee has strengthened rather than weakened the Fund. At least one or two of our new board members would not have agreed to serve had it not been for this attack upon us. The letters of acceptance from our new members were notable and encouraging." He noted also that a visit by Mrs. Bethune to the Board meeting on May 8 contributed "much to the inspiration of the meeting." Twenty-two new members were elected and all agreed to serve, which "is the best answer I can think of to Senators Eastland and Jenner, and others who seek to harass the Fund and to impede our efforts.

70. See Lister Hill to Williams, March 25, 1954; Hubert Humphrey to Williams, March 31, 1954; Paul Douglas, to Williams, April 13, 1954, Box 41, AW/FDR.

71. Williams to L. B. Johnson, April 5, and to Robert S. Allen, April 20, 1954. Box 41, AW/FDR.

72. See Williams to Editor, *Firing Line*, May 28, 1955; also to Louis Johnson, former Secretary of Defense under Truman and a power in the Legion, whom Aubrey knew. He urged Johnson to use his influence with the paper to get it to print Aubrey's scathing reply. Williams to Johnson, August 2, 1955, *ibid.*, Box 41, AW/FDR.

73. *Memoirs*, 52-3, Box 44, AW/FDR.

74. Quoted in Krueger, *And Promises to Keep* , 68.

75. See *ibid.*, 60-93.

76. Williams to Ralph McGill, December 9, 1953, Box 39, AW/FDR.

77. See *Southern Patriot*, October, 1950, which editorially criticized McGill's opposition to a suit against the Atlanta public school board by Negro parents who charged discrimination in its expenditures for Negroes. Governor Talmadge bitterly opposed the suit and used state resources to prevent registration of Negro students in white schools.

78. Williams to McGill, December 19, 30, 1957, Box 38, Braden Mss.

79. For an account of the McGill, *Atlanta Constitution* and *Atlanta Journal* relationship with Talmadge, et al., see Robert G. Sherrill, *Gothic Politics in the Deep South*, 49-53.

80. See *Minutes, Board of Directors*, June 3, 1956, Box 38, AW/FDR.

81. Williams to Dombrowski, July 31, 1956. Also Williams to Mrs. Roosevelt, July 26, 1956. Mrs. Roosevelt was "shocked by the things which come out in your letter to Mr. Randolph. Strangely enough, I mentioned both the Durrs and you in making a speech at an NAACP Board Meeting, saying they should give you every possible support; nobody spoke up to tell me that they were not doing so...." Mrs. Roosevelt to Williams, July 19, 1956, Box 38, AW/FDR.

82. Dombrowski to Barnett, October 5, 1956, Box 35, Braden Mss.

83. Barnett to Wilkins, December 4, 1956, *ibid.*

84. Barnett to Wilkins, December 24, 1956, *ibid.*

85. Wilkins to Barnett, February 4, 1957, *ibid.*

86. Barnett to Wilkins, February 11, 1957, *ibid.*

87. Barnett to Wilkins, February 18, 1957, *ibid.*

88. John A. Morsell to Barnett, April 3, 1957, *ibid.*

89. Barnett to Morsell, April 9, 1957, *ibid.*

90. Apparently Barnett had discovered this in the course of his correspondence, for Williams replied to him on August 1, 1957, in response to a letter of July 31 from Barnett, not in the records, "What you tell us undoubtedly explains some other things, namely why SCEF can't get recognition in the Civil Rights Coordinating Com. etc. But I am shocked that they use such a strong category--subversive--that is a strong term. I don't know whether Phillip Randolph can do anything or not but I intend writing him...." Box 37, Braden Mss.

91. Myles Horton interview, November 30, 1970.

92. Williams to Dombrowski, February 18, 1957, Box 38, AW/FDR.

93. See Al Maund to Dombrowski and Williams, July 31, 1957, and Dombrowski to Maund, August 2, 1957, Exhibits 14, 15, 16 in The Joint Legislative Committee on Un-American Activities, State of Louisiana, *Report No. 6 Part 3*, "Activities of the Southern Conference Educational Fund, Inc. in Louisiana," January 19, 1965 42-44 (hereafter cited as LUAC Reports).

94. Williams to Robert Hutchins, August 13, 1957, Box 37, Braden Mss.

CHAPTER SIX

1. *Brown v. Board of Education* in *Race Relations Law Reporter*, I (February, 1956), 9.

2. *Ibid.*, 9.

3. *Southern Patriot*, January, 1954.

4. *Ibid.*, June, 1954.

5. Issue of October 23, 1953, quoted in *ibid.*

6. *Ibid.*, and September, 1954.

7. See SCEF *Board Minutes*, June 12, 1954, Box 39, AW/FDR.

8. See *Policy Statement*, adopted at Board of Directors meeting, Atlanta, Georgia, June 12, 1954, Box 39, AW/FDR.

9. Dombrowski to Aubrey Williams, August 10, 1954; August 26, 1954, Box 39, AW/FDR; see also Numan V. Bartley, *The Rise of Massive Resistance* (Baton Rouge: Louisiana State University Press, 1969), 76-7.

10. See Bartley, *op. cit.*, 67, 85 ff. Also, on the White Citizens Councils, see Dan Wakefield, *Revolt in the South* (New York: Grove Press, 1960), 44 ff.

11. *Southern Patriot*, October, 1954.

12. Dombrowski to Williams, August 24, 1954, enclosing a form letter and editorial from Dr. Hewitt B. Vinnedge, August 24, 1954, Box 39, AW/FDR.

13. Dombrowski to "Tina," (Mrs. Eldridge Bruce), October 1, 1954, Box 39, AW/FDR.

14. *Southern Patriot*, January, 1955.

15. Dombrowski to Williams, August 10, 1954, Box 39, AW/FDR.

16. *Southern Patriot*, December, 1954; see "Proposal for holding compliance conference on *Brown*, 1954," Box 39, AW/FDR.

17. *Southern Patriot*, May, 1955.

18. *Ibid.*

19. *Brown v. Board of Education*, in *Race Relations Law Reporter*, I (February, 1956), 11-12.

20. Both papers quoted in *Southern Patriot*, June, 1955.

21. *Ibid.*

22. Bartley, *The Rise of Massive Resistance*, 82-4.

23. Quoted in *ibid.*, 86.

24. *Ibid.*, 88-92.

25. *Ibid.*

26. The term "neo-Bourbon" refers in this essay to those politicians and political activists who led the segregationist opposition to the *Brown* decision and to other desegregation policies in the South. They were similar to the older Bourbons of the late 19th century in opposing any attempts to upset the traditional economic, political and social patterns of the South which would favor racial equality, political democracy and a more diversified, industrialized economy. The core of support for the neo-Bourbon politicians was in the black-belt counties with relatively rich farm land and high black populations. While their strength was primarily here, neo-Bourbons also had strong support and control in cities with an Old South heritage, such as Charleston, New Orleans, Montgomery and Jackson, and others with special corporate interests and old business-plantation ties, such as Birmingham and Shreveport. Politically, through the county-unit system and general weighing of representation in favor of rural areas, they dominated much of the South up to the 1960's. Generally, neo-Bourbons were suspicious of "progress," denounced "creeping socialism" and the Federal bureaucracy; lamented the passing of Southern

civilization based on cotton and caste; and bemoaned the impotence of the South in national politics. This is similar to Numan V. Bartley's characterization in *The Rise of Massive Resistance*. He distinguishes the neo-Bourbons from the "business conservatives" representing largely urban and suburban business and professional groups, and "neo-populists" who carried on the tradition of rural democracy from the Populists and the scalawags of the Reconstruction period.

27. Bartley, 106.

28. *Ibid.*, 117-118.

29. *Ibid.*, 119.

30. Quoted in *ibid.*, 121.

31. *Ibid.*, particularly Chapters 6 and 7. Bartley's account is the most detailed history of the Citizens Councils in print.

32. *Southern Patriot*, October, 1955; Bartley, *op. cit.*, 82; also Buford Posey, "Where Do We Stand on Integration?," *American Socialist*, Vol. 3, No. 11 (November, 1956), 14.

33. See Posey, *op. cit.*, 14-15.

34. *Southern Patriot*, February, 1956; Bartley, *op. cit.*, Chapter 11.

35. *Southern Patriot*, February, 1956.

36. *Ibid.*

37. Dombrowski to Mr. and Mrs. Marshall Field, September 15, 1955, Box 38, AW/FDR.

38. *Ibid.*

39. Dombrowski to Mrs. Roosevelt, September 15, 1955, Box 38, AW/FDR.

40. *Southern Patriot*, October, December, 1955.

41. *Ibid.*, March, 1956.

42. *Ibid.*

43. *Ibid.*

44. *Ibid.*, April, 1956.

CHAPTER SEVEN

1. See *Congressional Record*, 84th Congress, 2nd Session, March 12, 1956, 3948, 4004.

2. Bartley, *The Rise of Massive Resistance*, 115-116.

3. *Southern Patriot*, April, 1956.

4. Williams to Hill, March 13, 1956, Box 38, AW/FDR.

5. *Ibid.*

6. See *Statement by W. F. Riggs, Jr., Executive Vice President of Chamber of Commerce, New Orleans Area in the Robert Barnes Case*, Box 37, Braden Mss; Williams to President Robert W. Elasser, and Board of Directors, Chamber of Commerce, New Orleans, March 30, 1956, Box 38, AW/FDR.

7. Williams to J. David Stern, February 27, 1957, Box 38, AW/FDR.

8. See articles and letters between Juliette H. Morgan and James Dombrowski, Box 26, Braden Mss.

9. Williams to Dombrowski, July 18, 1957, Box 37; Virginia Durr to Anne Braden, April 20, 22, 1959, Box 26, Braden Mss.

10. Williams to Dombrowski, October 24, 1957; Williams to Marshall Johnson, May 27, 1957, Box 37, Braden Mss.

11. Dombrowski to Williams, May 29, 1958, Box 37, Braden Mss.

12. Dombrowski to Williams, May 28, 1958, Box 37, Braden Mss.

13. See Donald R. Mathews and James W. Prothro, "Political Factors and Negro Voter Registration in the South," *American Political Science Review*, LVII (1963), 365.

14. *Southern Patriot*, October, 1956.

15. Williams to Dr. H. E. Finger, Jr., March 25, 1958, Box 37, Braden Mss.

16. Dombrowski to Williams, November 27, 1957, Box 38, AW/FDR.

17. Williams to Winthrop Rockefeller, March 25, 1958; Williams to Governor Leroy Collins, November 7, 1958, Box 37; also *Memo 1957 SCEF Activities*, Box 67, Braden Mss.

18. Dombrowski to Williams, May 3, 1956, Box 38, AW/FDR.

19. *Southern Patriot*, June, 1956.

20. See Margaret Price, *The Negro and the Ballot in the South* (Atlanta: Southern Regional Council, 1959), 15-16.

21. *Southern Patriot*, June, 1956.

22. *Ibid.*, November, 1956; see also Margaret Price, *op. cit.*, 16-21, and *The Negro Voter in the South* (Atlanta: Southern Regional Council, 1957), 4. In 1956, black registration in the South was 24.9 per cent of the number over 21 eligible to vote, while white registration came to 52.5 per cent." Florence B. Irving, "The Future of the Negro Voter in the South," *Journal of Negro Education*, XXVI, No. 3 (Summer, 1957), 390-1. Mathews and Prothro found that political intimidation and other political factors doubled the explanatory power of socio-economic variables such as illiteracy and poverty in accounting for low black registration in the South. *Op. cit.*, 367.

23. M. Price, *op. cit.* (1959), 9.

24. *Ibid.*, 15.

25. See *New Republic*, February 20, 1956, 5-6; *Christian Century*, February 22, 1956, 228 and February 29, 1956, 280+.

26. Wilma Dykeman and James Stokely, "In Clinton, Tennessee," *Nation*, December 22, 1956, 531-33; *New Republic*, December 17, 1956, 7-8.

27. *Southern Patriot*, September, 1956.

28. *Ibid.*, October, 1956.

29. *Ibid.*, and September, 1956.

30. *New Republic*, December 17, 1956.

31. See special issue of the *Journal of Negro Education*, XXVI, No. 3 (Summer, 1957).

32. *Southern Patriot*, September, 1957.

33. See Oscar Handlin, "Civil Rights After Little Rock: The Failure of Moderation," *Commentary* (November, 1957), 392-6.

34. Lyndon B. Johnson to Williams, July 23, 1957, in *Southern Patriot*, September, 1957.

35. Williams to Johnson, August 1, 1957, Box 37, Braden Mss.

36. See Bartley, *The Rise of Massive Resistance*, 60-1; James M. Nabrit, Jr., "Future of the Negro Voter in the South," *Journal of Negro Education*, XXVI, No. 3 (Summer, 1957), 422; Donald S. Strong, *Negroes, Ballots, and Judges* (University of Alabama Press, 1968), 1-9.

37. Dombrowski to Williams, August 2, 1957, Box 37, Braden Mss.

38. See announcement in *Southern Patriot*, September, 1957.

39. See Harry S. Ashmore, "The Untold Story Behind Little Rock, *Harper's*, June 1958, 10+; also Handlin, *op. cit.*

40. See Williams to Eisenhower, quoted in *Southern Patriot*, November, 1957.

41. Albert S. Cartwright, "Lesson from Little Rock," *Christian Century*, LXXIV, No. 40 (October 2, 1957), 1193-4.

42. *Southern Patriot*, December, 1957.

43. See *Report of SCEF Board Meeting*, February 3, 1957, Box 38, AW/FDR; and Memo from Dombrowski, October 7, 1958, Box 1, Braden Mss.

44. *Southern Patriot*, December, 1957, and January, 1958.

45. See *Memo to all SCEF Board and Advisory Committee Members*, March 9, 1958, Box 65, Braden Mss.

46. See *Minutes of Conference on Local Arrangements*, January 21, 1958, Box 65, Braden Mss.

47. Dombrowski to Bishop Edgar Love, January 27, 1958, Box 65, Braden Mss.

48. Anne Braden to Dombrowski, March 18, 1958, Box 65, Braden Mss.

49. Anne to Carl Braden, March 20, 1958, Box 65, Braden Mss.

50. *Ibid.*

51. Dombrowski to Anne Braden, March 31, 1958, Box 65, Braden Mss.

52. Dr. Francis Gregory to Mrs. Muriel M. Alexander and Dr. Charles H. Thompson, dean of Howard University, co-chairmen, Subcommittee on Attendance, February 21, 1958; Gregory to C. Herbert Marshall, II, February 25, 1958, Box 65, Braden Mss.

53. Carl Braden to Justice Wise Polier, May 7, 1958, Box 65, Braden Mss.

54. *Southern Patriot*, April, 1958.

55. *Ibid.*

56. Anne to Carl Braden and Dombrowski, March 28, 1958, Box 65, Braden Mss.

57. Anne Braden to Williams, March 31, 1958, Box 65, Braden Mss.

58. *Ibid.*

59. Box 65, Braden Mss.

60. Dombrowski to Anne Braden, April 16, 1958, Box 65, Braden Mss.

61. Aubrey Williams, "Report from the South," April 27, 1958, Box 43, AW/FDR.

62. *Ibid.*

63. See *Reports on Voting Restrictions in Southern States*, April 27, 1958, Box 65, Braden Mss.

64. See *Summary of Reports on Voting Restrictions in Southern States*, by James M. Nabrit, Jr., Esq., April 27, 1958, Box 65, Braden Mss.

65. Anne Braden to Alice Hunter, May 7, 1958, Box 65; Braden Mss.; also *Southern Patriot*, May, 1958.

66. Williams to Civil Rights Commission, April 28, 1958, Box 65, Braden Mss

CHAPTER EIGHT

1. Washington *Post and Times-Herald*, July 29, 1958; New York *Times*, July 30, 31, 1958.

2. Williams to Celler, July 1, 1958, Box 32, AW/FDR.

3. Williams to Johnson, July 2, 1958, Box 36; Williams to Sam Rayburn, July 2, 1958, Box 32, AW/FDR.

4. Carl Braden to Don (Stephens?), July 8, 1958, Box 13, Braden Mss.

5. Williams to Roosevelt, July 9, 1958, Box 17, Braden Mss.

6. See text of "Open Letter to the U.S. Congress," Washington *Post and Times Herald*, July 31, 1958, in *Southern Patriot*, September, 1958.

7. See memo from Dombrowski, August 9, 1958, Box 17, Braden Mss.

8. Clipping from Los Angeles *Tribune*, July 11, 1958, Box 17, Braden Mss.

9. See comments reprinted in *Southern Patriot*, September, 1958.

10. *Southern Patriot*, September, 1958; also Walter Goodman, *The Committee* (Baltimore, Maryland: Penguin Books, 1969 edition) 420.

11. See Statement of Carl and Anne Braden to the press, July 27, 1958, Box 14, Braden Mss.

12. See bill of particulars, December 2, 1958, Box 13; also Braden's memo to press and wire services, December 29, 1958, correcting their emphasis on his "alleged Communist affiliations," as an unfair "oversimplification" which "overlooks the fact that the alleged Communist Party affiliations constituted only one of the six counts of the indictment." Box 14, Braden Mss.

13. See accounts of the hearing in the New York *Times*, July 31, and Washington *Post and Times Herald*, July 31, 1958; also Carl and Anne Braden to Williams and Dombrowski, August 16, 1958, Box 35, Braden Mss.

14. Clark Foreman to Anne Braden, August 19, 1958, Box 13, Braden Mss.

15. Williams to Walter, August 9; Walter to Williams, August 14, 1958, Box 17, Braden Mss.

16. Anne and Carl Braden to Williams and Dombrowski, August 16, 1958, Box 35, Braden Mss.

17. Wilkinson to Anne and Carl Braden, August 18, 1958, Box 13, Braden Mss.

18. Dombrowski to Bradens, August 22, 1958, Box 13, Braden Mss.

19. Braden to Dombrowski; Dombrowski to Braden, September 22, 1958; Boudin to Coe, October 1, and Coe to Boudin, October 4, 1958; Carl Braden to Boudin, October 7, 1958, Box 13, Braden Mss.

20. Carl Braden to Boudin, December 1, 1958, Box 13, Braden Mss.

21. Barnett to Bradens, December 7, 1958, Box 13, Braden Mss.

22. See Samuel Newman to Dombrowski, July 31, 1958; Dombrowski to Newman, August 4, 1958; also Franklin W. Thomas to Senator Mike Monroney (undated); Monroney to Thomas, September 23, 1958, Box 13, Braden Mss.

23. Anne Braden to Barnett, December 29, 1958, Box 13, Braden Mss.

24. *Ibid.*

25. Anne Braden to Frank Wilkinson, December 29, 1958. Williams to Anne Braden (undated): "You make me feel very bad. You were more right than I was, so please don't say any more." Box 13, Braden Mss.

26. C. Herman Pritchett, *Congress Versus the Supreme Court: 1957-1960* (Minneapolis: University of Minnesota Press, 1961), 20 ff.

27. *Ibid.*

28. *Ibid.*

29. Javits to John M. Pickering, August 14, 1958, Box 13, Braden Mss.

30. Williams to Johnson, August 20 1958 Box 17, Braden Mss.

31. Johnson to Williams, August 21, 1958, Box 17, Braden Mss.

32. Dombrowski to Mrs. Roosevelt, June 4, 1959, Box 38, Braden Mss.

33. Don (Stephens?) to Williams and Dombrowski, June 15, 1959, Box 37, Braden Mss.

34. Williams to Dombrowski and Frank Bancroft, June 6, 1959, Box 37, Braden Mss.

35. *Ibid.*

36. Williams to Senator Joseph C. O'Mahoney, June 6, 1959, Box 32, AW/FDR.

37. *SCEF News*, June 12, 1959, Box 14, Braden Mss.

38. Quoted in Pritchett, *Congress Versus the Supreme Court: 1957-1960*, 83.

39. *Ibid.*, 13-14.

40. *Ibid.*, 50 ff.

41. *Ibid.*, 56; also SCEF memos and evaluations Box 13, Braden Mss.

42. News release from Committee of First Amendment Defendants, December 10, 1959, Box 13, Braden Mss.

43. John M. Coe to Leonard B. Boudin, September 12, 1959, Box 35, Braden Mss.

44. Leonard Boudin to Carl Braden, November 10, 1960, Box 13, Braden Mss.

45. Anne Braden to Melish, August 8, 1958, Box 3, Braden Mss.

46. See Anne Braden, *The Wall Between* (New York: Monthly Review Press, 1958), esp. Chapters 1-4.

47. Anne Braden to Harvey O'Connor, April 2; Dombrowski to Bradens, June 7, 1957, Box 5, Braden Mss.

48. Anne Braden to Melish, August 8, 1958, Box 3, Series 2, Braden Mss.

49. See *Memo to SCEF Board and Advisory Committee on Conclusion of Southwide Trip*, May-July, 1958, unprocessed boxes, Braden Mss.

50. *Ibid.*, 10-11.

51. Carl Braden to Harry Golden, June 9, 1958, Box 41, Braden Mss.

52. See *Report on Trip to Mississippi, Memphis and Montgomery*, August 23-31, 1958, Box 23, Braden Mss.

53. *Ibid.*; see also *Minutes of Board of Directors SCEF*, Nashville, October 4, 1958, noting a report by Nixon on disposition of $700 to the Alabama State Coordinating Association for Registration and Voting to set up an office and other expenses. Nixon stated that he had received money from other sources and thus had more than half of the grant remaining and offered to return it to the Fund. He noted that, in twelve trips to various Alabama communities, he had estimated there

were nearly 500 new voters as a result of the project. Unprocessed boxes, Braden Mss.

54. See Mrs. Roosevelt's column in Chicago *Sun-Times*, March 8, 1958, Box 68, Braden Mss.

55. Williams to Anne Braden, March 31, 1958, Box 37, Braden Mss.

56. Carl Braden to Dombrowski, March 21, 1958, Box 37, Series 2, Braden Mss.

57. Carl Braden to Williams, April 1, 1958, Box 3, Series 2, Braden Mss.

58. Williams to George Pratt, October 29, 1958; Box 37, Braden Mss.

59. Carl to Anne Braden, and Dombrowski, November 12, 1958, Box 35, Braden Mss.

60. See Melish resume, unprocessed boxes, Braden Mss.

61. Dombrowski to Williams, December 19, 1958, Box 37, Braden Mss.

62. Dombrowski to Mrs. Roosevelt, February 25, 1959, Box 38, Braden Mss.

63. Mrs. Roosevelt to Dombrowski, February 27, 1959, Box 38, Braden Mss.

64. Dombrowski to Mrs. Roosevelt, March 11, 1959, Box 38, Braden Mss.

65. *Ibid.*, marginal note.

66. Frank Wilkinson, discussing fund-raising on the West Coast, criticized Fund practices there. "...Tho' I know the need is really genuine, I'm troubled by the knowledge of your SCEF RESERVES (capitalization accidental or Freudian); and, by the tendency in Jim's operation to appeal to wealthy, older women. I don't like our occasional tendency to appeal to persons of means either; that's why I'm so thankful that essentially we're supported by average monthly $3 sustainers. Money out here that goes to Jim...is really white conscience money; it is filled with the hypocrasy [sic] of failure to integrate their own block!..." Wilkinson to Anne Braden, November 11, 1959, Box 7, Braden Mss.

67. Maurice H. Mogulescu, chairman of the New York Committee, to Dombrowski, March 31, 1959, Box 35, Braden Mss.

68. Melish to Anne Braden, May 30, 1959, unprocessed box, Braden Mss.

CHAPTER TEN

1. Carl Braden to Boudin, October 2, 1958; Taylor & Mitchell, Raleigh attorneys, to Rabinowitz & Boudin, December 19, 1958; See fact sheet on Lassiter case, all in Box 21, Braden Mss.

2. Taylor & Mitchell to Rabinowitz & Boudin, December 19, 1958; Braden to Samuel Mitchell, June 5; Mitchell to Braden, June 10, 1959, Box 21, Braden Mss.

3. See file on Committee to Combat Racial Injustice, Box 7, Braden Mss.

4. Dombrowski to North Carolina SCEF Board Members, April 23, 1959, Box 40, Braden Mss.

5. Carl Braden to A. Moseley, September 12, 1959, Box 40, Braden Mss.

6. Bradens to Melish, March 6, 1959, Box 40, Braden Mss.

7. See clippings from North Carolina papers, September 30, 1959, Box 40, Braden Mss.

8. George Weissman to Braden, January 21, 1959, January 28, February 8, 11, 19, 1959, in Committee to Combat Racial Injustice Mss.

9. Braden to Weissman, February 22, 1959, Box 7, Braden Mss.

10. Braden to Weissman, October 30, 1959, Box 7 , Braden Mss.

11. See Oklahoma City Black *Dispatch*, June 19, 1959, clipping in Box 26, Braden Mss.

12. Braden to Weissman, October 30, 1959, Box 7, Braden Mss.

13. Barbara Gordon to Dombrowski, April 12; Shirley Zoloth to Dombrowski, April 13, 1959, unprocessed boxes, Braden Mss.

14. *Ibid.*

15. *Ibid.*

16. Dombrowski to Barbara Y. Gordon, April 28, 1959, unprocessed boxes, Braden Mss.

17. Carl Braden to Barbara Gordon, Reverend Albert J. Kissling, Jacksonville, and Dr. Hal G. Lewis, Gainesville, September 26, 1959; Lewis to Carl and Anne Braden, September 29, 1959, Box 10, Braden Mss.

18. Shirley Zoloth to Dombrowski, September 30, 1959, Box 10, Braden Mss.

19. Carl Braden to Shirley Zoloth and Barbara Gordon, October 4, 1959, Box 10, Braden Mss.

20. Anne Braden to Shirley Zoloth and Barbara Gordon, October 4, 1959, Box 10, Braden Mss.

21. Dombrowski to Melish, October 5, 1959, Box 10, Braden Mss.

22. See William H. Melish, "3,725 Miles Through the Deep South with Carl Braden," November 6-25, 1959, 9-10, 16-17, unprocessed boxes, Braden Mss.

23. *Ibid.*, 13-14.

24. *Ibid.*, 19.

25. *Ibid.*, 9-10.

26. *Ibid.*, 24-5.

27. Dombrowski to Carl Braden, December 28, 1959, Box 10, Braden Mss.

28. Dombrowski to Shirley Zoloth and Barbara Gordon, January 5, 1960, Box 10, Braden Mss.

29. Quoted in Foster Rhea Dulles, *The Civil Rights Commission 1957-1965* (Michigan State University Press, 1968), 33.

30. *Ibid.*, 41.

31. SCEF Memo, unprocessed boxes, Braden Mss.

32. William P. Mitchell, Chairman, Voter Franchise Committee, Tuskegee Civic Association, to Carl Braden, September 10, 1959; Bradens to Mitchell and Charles V. Hamilton, of TCA Political Education Committee, September 12, 1959, Box 12, Braden Mss.

33. Bradens to Dombrowski, September 12, 1959, Box 12, Braden Mss.

34. Braden to Gomillion, January 19, 1960, Box 12, Braden Mss.

35. Carl Braden to Dombrowski, January 20, 1960, Box 35, Braden Mss.

36. SCEF Board of Directors, *Minutes*, January 30, 1960, Washington, D.C., unprocessed boxes, Braden Mss.

37. Excerpt from letter to Anne Braden from King, October 7, 1959, in LUAC, *Report No. 5, Part 2*, April 13, 1964, Exhibit 33, 83.

38. See King to Carl Braden, October 22, 1959, Box 20, Braden Mss.

39. Dombrowski to Anne Braden, October 33, 1959, Box 8, Braden Mss.

40. Anne Braden to Selma Samols, and C. Herbert Marshall II, November 4, 1959, Box 66, Braden Mss.; Anne Braden to M.L. King, November 23, 1959, Box 66, Braden Mss.

41. Dombrowski to Brooks, November 24, 1959, Box 66, Braden Mss. John M. Brooks was NAACP Southern Director, as well as head of a Virginia group, the Crusade for Voters.

42. Anne Braden to King, November 23, 1959, Box 66, Braden Mss.

43. Dombrowski to Mrs. Roosevelt, November 27, 1959; Mrs. Roosevelt to Dombrowski, December 2, 1959, Box 66, Braden. Mss.

44. Dombrowski to Representative William H. Meyer, Vermont, December 16, 1959; Russ Nixon, United Electrical Workers Union Washington lobbyist, to Dombrowski, January 4, 1960. Dombrowski to Bishop Love, December 2, 1959 Box 66, Braden Mss.

45. Nixon to Dombrowski, January 4, 1960, and January 12, 1960, Box 66, Braden Mss.

46. See Dombrowski to Mrs. Roosevelt, January 26, 1960, Box 38; Carl Braden to Dombrowski, January 24, Box 66, Braden Mss.

47. See Braden to Dombrowski, January 10, 1960; and clipping from Baltimore *Afro-American*, February 13, 1960, Box 66, Braden Mss.

48. See statements of S. T. Nero, Holly Springs, Mississippi; Dr. Daniel W. Wynn, Professor of Philosophy, Tuskegee, Alabama; John McFerren, Fayette County, Tennessee; and Dombrowski to Mr. M. M. Coleman, Minden, Louisiana, January 12, 1960, Box 66, Braden Mss.

49. From the Baltimore *Afro-American*, February 2, 1960, Box 66, Braden Mss.

50. Carl Braden to Dombrowski, February 16, 1960, Box 66, Braden Mss.

51. See. Dulles, *The Civil Rights Commission*, 96-98.

52. Clipping from Louisville *Times*, January 18, 1960, Box 66, Braden Mss.

53. Carl Braden to Dombrowski, January 24, 1960, Box 66, Braden Mss. Bartley, in *The Rise of Massive Resistance*, notes that the 1957 and 1960 civil rights laws "were most significant perhaps as heralds of important future legislation...[but] had little effect on race relations in the South." 60-61.

54. Dombrowski to A. Williams, July 19, 1960, unprocessed boxes, Braden Mss.

55. See Board *Minutes*, January 30, 1960, unprocessed boxes, Braden Mss.

56. See memo in *ibid*.

57. Dombrowski to Albert Barnett, April 26, 1960, Box 38, Braden Mss.

58. Carl Braden to Dombrowski, December 11, 1959, Box 48, Braden Mss.

59. See *Tentative Proposal for a Project in South Carolina*, 1960, unprocessed boxes, Braden Mss.

60. *Ibid*.; see also Dombrowski to Joan Miller, Wellesley College Service Organization, August 22, 1960, unprocessed boxes, Braden Mss.

61. See Memo "History of Fayette Count Struggle," published by Fayette County Civic and Welfare League, June 1, 1962, Box 22; also Dombrowski to Mr. John B. Pell, New York, September 1, 1962; Dombrowski to Mr. and Mrs. McFerren, September 14, 1960, unprocessed boxes, Braden Mss.; Dombrowski to Mrs. Roosevelt, September 20, 1960, thanking her for writing in her column "one of the

first pieces of national publicity" after he sent her information about the Fayette-Haywood situation. Box 38, Braden Mss.

62. See Ben Wyland to Bradens, February 16, 1960; *Report on Orlando Meeting*, March 12, 1960, Box 10, Braden Mss.

63. Carl Braden to Gordons and Zoloths, May 26, 1960, Box 10, Braden Mss.

64. Memo to Dombrowski on Florida Legislative Project, July 1, 1960, Box 10, Braden Mss.

65. Mrs. Roosevelt to Dombrowski, January 22, 1960, Box 38, Braden Mss.

66. See Mrs. Roosevelt to Aubrey Williams, April 5, 1960, Box 38, Braden Mss.

67. See Williams to Dombrowski, April 13, 1960, LUAC, *Report No. 4*, Exhibit 53, 115.

68. See Williams to Dombrowski, April 6, 1960, LUAC, *Report No. 4*, Exhibit 52, 114.

69. Williams to Justine Wise Polier, May 4, 1960 LUAC, *Report No. 4*, Exhibit 54, 116-117.

70. Anne and Carl Braden to Melish, April 7, 1960, unprocessed boxes, Braden Mss.

71. See Braden to Dombrowski, December 5, 1958, LUAC, *Report No. 6*, Exhibit 13, 41.

72. Melish to Anne Braden, April 14, 1960; Anne Braden to Dombrowski, April 17, 1960, unprocessed boxes, Braden Mss.

73. This was Melish's opinion expressed in a letter to Anne Braden, April 14, 1960, unprocessed boxes, Braden Mss.

74. See Aubrey Williams to Justine Wise Polier, May 4, 1960, LUAC, *Report No. 4*; Dombrowski to Mrs. Roosevelt, April 11, 1960, Box 38, Braden Mss.

75. Melish to Anne Braden, April 14, 1960, unprocessed boxes, Braden Mss.

76. Anne Braden to Dombrowski, April 17, 1960, unprocessed boxes, Braden Mss.

77. Anne Braden to Aubrey Williams, June 21, 1960, Box 35, Braden Mss.

78. Aubrey Williams to Dombrowski, February 26, 1960, LUAC, *Report No. 4*, Exhibit 42, 98.

79. Aubrey Williams to Dombrowski, June 24, 1960, LUAC, *Report No. 5*, Exhibit 32, 82.

80. See Carl Braden to Dombrowski, September 21, 1960; September 28, 1960, LUAC, *Report No. 5*, Exhibits 34, 35, pp. 86-87.

81. Quoted in *SCEF News*, April 11, 1960, Box 14, Braden Mss.

82. Carl Braden to Dombrowski, April 7, 1960, Box 35, Braden Mss., reporting on information from Russ Nixon of the United Electrical Workers Union.

83. Anne Braden to Melish, April 28, 1960, unprocessed boxes, Braden Mss.

84. Anne Braden to Aubrey Williams, May 4, 1960, Box 35, Braden Mss.

85. See Carl Braden to Dombrowski, September 28, 1960, LUAC, *Report No. 5*, Exhibit 35, 87; also Anne Braden to Melish, September 5, 1960, unprocessed boxes, Braden Mss. She wrote of her wish to attend the second Southwide student conference in Atlanta in October since "SCEF has established very good relations with the southwide student committee, and I feel it's important for one of us to attend this fall conference...."

86. Carl Braden to Dombrowski, October 1, 1960, Box 10, Braden Mss.

CHAPTER TEN

1. See *Braden v. United States* (1961), quoted in Jared Joseph Spaeth, *Braden v. United States: A Constitutional Case History* unpublished master's thesis, Butler University, 1968, 76.

2. Both Black and Douglas decisions quoted in *SCEF News*, March 1, 1961, Box 14, Braden Mss.

3. A. Williams to Alexander Meiklejohn, April 18 1961, Box 38, Braden Mss.

4. A. Williams to President Kennedy, April 19, 1961, Box 38, Braden Mss.

5. Carl Braden to Irving Dilliard, March 2, 1961, Box 14, Braden Mss., thanking him for his letter of support and noting developments in anti-HUAC campaign.

6. Anne Braden to King, March 14, 1961, Box 14, Braden Mss. W. Goodman, *op. cit.*, stresses Braden's arranging for 200 blacks to protest HUAC's Atlanta hearing as the reason for his subpoena.

7. Anne Braden to King, March 14, 1961, Box 14, Braden Mss.

8. See Memo from Anne Braden to Dombrowski and A. Williams re clemency petition, not dated, Box 14 and also Anne Braden to Dombrowski, April 20, 1961, Box 14, Braden Mss.

9. Quoted in Atlanta *Journal*, May 2, 1961, clipping in Box 13, Braden Mss.

10. See leaflet from ECLC on Draper's committees as culled from Washington *Post*, March 13, 1960, Box 13; also *SCEF News* June 21, 1960, Box 5; Anne Braden to King, May 7, 1961, Box 13, Braden Mss.

11. Memo from Anne Braden to Dick Criley, Otto Nathan, Russ Nixon, Dorothy Marshall of NCA-HUAC, no date, but probably October, 1961, Box 16, Braden Mss.

12. Walker to SCLC affiliates, November 6, 1961, Box 13, Braden Mss.

13. Anne Braden to Sylvia Crane, July 30, 1961, Box 16; Statement by Ralph D. Abernathy, spokesman for Carl Braden Clemency Appeal Committee, August 17, 1961, Box 13, Braden Mss.

14. See long letter discussing the delegation and conference, Sylvia Crane, Member of New York Committee to Abolish HUAC, to Carl Braden, November 13, 1961; including letter from Grenville Clark to Wofford. Clark saw the "rigid 5-4 split in the Supreme Court...in civil rights cases as a clear result of the suspicion, fears and pressures engendered by the arms race and the Cold War. No such split existed in any such rigid and persistent way until very recent years...." Box 16, Braden Mss.

15. A. Williams to Dombrowski, December 14, 1961, Box 38, Braden Mss.

16. See W. Goodman, *The Committee*, 421.

17. See Anne Braden to Jean Wilkinson, November 6, 1961, Box 16, Braden Mss.

18. See Anne Braden, "Education of the Public as a Weapon Against Fear," paper delivered at the Chapel Hill conference on civil liberties, Box 4, Braden Mss.

19. See her paper, "Civil Liberties and Free Speech as Essential Weapons in the Struggle for Civil Rights, " Atlanta, April 27-29, 1962, Box 5, Braden Mss. The Fund and SCLC held a joint conference in November, 1960, at which broad cooperation between them was agreed upon.

20. See B. Tart Bell, Executive Secretary of American Friends Service Committee, to Dorothy Miller of SNCC, September 18, 1962, Box 35; D. Miller to Anne Braden September 18, 1962, Box 2, Braden Mss.

21. See letters from Eliza Paschall to Anne Braden, July-December, 1962, Box 2; also Anne Braden to Dombrowski, December 13, 1962, Box 2; Bradens to Inter-Agency Conference, March 11, 1963, Box 5, Braden Mss.

22. See Anne Braden to Dorothy Miller, November 21, 1962; Anne Braden to Dombrowski, November 27, 1962, Box 2, Braden Mss.

23. Anne Braden to King, December 1, 1962, Box 2 Braden Mss.

24. See Anne Braden to Dombrowski, December 13, 1962, Box 2, Braden Mss.

25. *Ibid.*

26. *Ibid.*

27. See "Memo on Proposed Student Project of SCEF," October 22, 1960; also Anne Braden to Marion S. Barry, Jr., chairman of SNCC, November 22, 1960, Box 47, Braden Mss.

28. Jane Stembridge to Anne Braden, October 31, 1960; Anne Braden to Ella Baker, November 22, 1960, Box 47, Braden Mss.

29. Jane Stembridge to Anne Braden, October 25, 1960, Box 47, Braden Mss.

30. Jane Stembridge to Sandra Cason, November 17, 1960, Box 47, Braden Mss.

31. Charles Jones, Student Secretary, SNCC, to Anne Braden, December 5, 1960, Box 47, Braden Mss.

32. Anne Braden to Dombrowski, March 9, 1961, Box 47, Braden Mss.

33. *Ibid.*; also Anne Braden to Dotty Miller, a SNCC staff member, April 24, 1963, Box 2, Braden Mss.

34. Dombrowski to R. Zellner, June 13, 1961, LUAC, *Report No. 5, Part 2,* Exhibit 46, 102. Anne Braden to Charles McDew, chairman SNCC, August 8, 1961, Box 47, Braden Mss.

35. See Edgar A. Love, "Claiming the Right to Choose: A Profile," *Motive,* November, 1962, in Box 68; also Bonnie Day, "An Integrationist from the South," the Providence, Rhode Island, *Journal,* October 11, 1964, in Box 63, Braden Mss.

36. Anne Braden to Dombrowski, May 8, 1961; Aubrey Williams to Anne Braden, May 14, 1961, Box 47, Braden Mss.

37. See "Report of John Robert Zellner on White Student Project (School Year 1961-62)," May 19, 1962, Box 47, Braden Mss.

38. See rough draft of an unpublished article by Robert Zellner, no date, Box 68, Braden Mss.

39. See "Report of John Robert Zellner on White Student Project (School Year 1961-62)," May 19, 1962, Box 47, Braden Mss.

40. Bob Moses to Dombrowski, November 1961, Box 47, Braden Mss.

41. *SCEF News* December 8, 1961, Box 47, Braden Mss.

42. Forman to Dombrowski, February 28, 1962, Box 35, Braden Mss.

43. Anne Braden to Melish, January 16, 1962, unprocessed boxes, Braden Mss.

44. Carl Braden to Melish, April 9, 1962, unprocessed boxes, Braden Mss.

45. See Anne Braden to Dombrowski, March 22, 1962, LUAC *Report No. 5*, Exhibit 50, 106; James Forman to Dombrowski, June 16, 1962, Box 35, Braden Mss, expressing appreciation for $1,000 donation. Forman noted that "This conference was vitally necessary to the development of the Southern Protest Movement. Communications and coordination between the protest groups was at low ebb--despite the fact that our staff was performing miracles. As you may know when the Student Nonviolent Coordinating Committee was founded, very little attention was paid to fund raising for the projection of long-term plans. Consequently, many people and several organizations capitalized on the efforts of the student movement. These groups have not reinvested in the program of the southern student, proportionate to value they have obtained...."

46. Len Holt to I. Philip Sipser, May 13, 1962, Box 47; Carl Braden to Dombrowski, September 23, 1962, Box 35, Braden Mss.

47. See A. Williams to Dombrowski, September 26, 1961; SCEF Board to Aubrey Williams, October 29, 1961, Box 38, Braden Mss.

48. Anne Braden to Dombrowski, May 17, 1962; Dombrowski to Bradens, May 15; *SCEF News* release April 27, 1962, Box 48, Braden Mss.

49. Carl Braden to Coe, May 31, Coe to Carl Braden and Ben Smith, June 4, 1962, Box 48, Braden Mss.

50. Braden to Coe, June 25, 1962, Box 48, Braden Mss.

51. See telegram to Dombrowski from Braden, Coe and Bishop Tucker, February 7, 1963, Box 48, Braden Mss.

52. See Zellner, *op. cit.*, 1962, Box 47, Braden Mss.

53. See V. Rabinowitz to Anne Braden, January 8, 1962; Anne Braden to V. Rabinowitz, January 16, 1962; Len Holt to the Bradens, September 27, 1962, Box 35, Braden Mss.

54. See Len Holt to Bradens, September 27, 1962; Anne Braden to Dombrowski, October 11, 1962; Anne Braden to Ernest Goodman, Detroit, Guild Officer, December 12, 1962, Box 35, Braden Mss.

55. Carl Braden to Melish, July 12, 1962, unprocessed boxes, Braden Mss.

56. Braden to Dombrowski, July 23, 1962, Box 36, Braden Mss.

57. *Ibid.*

58. See A. Williams to editor, Jackson *Daily News*, September 3, 1962; Carl Braden to Dombrowski and Coe, September 2, 1962, Box 23, Braden Mss.

59. See Anne Braden to A. Williams, October 3, 1962, Box 35, Braden Mss.

60. *Ibid.*

61. Bradens to Southern Inter-Agency Conference, March 11, 1963, Box 5, Braden Mss.

62. See Wiley A. Branton, Project Director, Voter Education Project of Southern Regional Council, to Carl Braden, September 21, 1962, Box 19; B. Tart Bell, Executive Secretary, American Service Committee, to Dorothy Miller, SNCC, September 18, 1962, Box 35, Braden Mss.

63. See Carl Braden to Branton, October 29, 1962; Branton to Anne Braden, October 24, 1962; Anne Braden to Reverend Cornelius Tarplee, chairman of Southern Inter-Agency Group, October 12, 1962; Tarplee to Anne Braden, December 12; Anne Braden to Dombrowski and Tarplee, December 24; Anne Braden to Herman Long, December 31, 1962; Long to Anne Braden, January 4, 1963; Anne Braden to Dombrowski, March 5, 1963; Box 19, Bradens to Southern Inter-Agency Conference, March 11, 1963, Box 5, Braden Mss.

64. See details in Louis Lomax, *The Negro Revolt* (New York: New American Library, 1963) 247-256.

65. Williams to Lloyd K. Garrison, July 7, 1963, Box 38, Braden Mss.

66. Anne Braden to Frank Stanley, Jr., publisher of the Louisville *Defender*, January 4, 1963, Box 23, Braden Mss.

67. Proposal from Reverend James Bevel and Mrs. Diane Bevel, no date, Box 8, Braden Mss.

68. *Ibid*.

69. See Myles Horton to Anne Braden, January 29, 1963; Anne Braden to Horton, February 11; Anne Braden to Dombrowski, February 20, 1963; Anne Braden to Bevels March 6, 1963; Myles Horton to Bevels, March 18, 1963; Jack McKart, Operation Freedom, to Bevels, April 12, 1963; Box 8, Braden Mss.

70. See Report on "SCEF's Relations with SNCC and Highlander," May 25, 1963, Box 5, Braden Mss.

71. See Melish to Dombrowski, January 10, 1963; Dombrowski to Melish, January 15; Dombrowski to SCEF Friends, January 15, 1963, unprocessed boxes, Braden Mss.

72. See "SCEF Relations with SNCC and Highlander," Box 5, Braden Mss.

CHAPTER ELEVEN

1. See fact sheets and articles on the raid in Box 37, Braden Mss; also Jack Pebbles, "Subversion and the Southern Conference Educational Fund," 45-50.

2. See *SCEF* Fact Sheets, Box 37; Pebbles, *op. cit.*, 58-9; and Student Civil Liberties Coordinating Committee, "The Attack on the Southern Conference Educational Fund, A Report," Box 37, Braden Mss.

3. See Transcript of Today Show, NBC, New York, WNBC-TV and NBC-TV Network, September 27, 1963, in Box 27, Braden Mss.

4. See Carl Braden to William R. McAndrew, NBC, October 10; McAndrew to Carl Braden, October 11; Carl Braden to Complaint Division, FCC, October 12; Carl Braden to McAndrew, October 14; McAndrew to Carl Braden, October 18; Carl Braden to McAndrew, October 23; Ben F. Waple, Secretary, FCC, to Carl Braden, October 21; Carl Braden to Waple, December 20, 1963; Waple to Carl Braden January 21, 1964. Carl Braden to Waple, February 21, 1964, Box 27, Braden Mss.

5. *Ibid*.

6. See Marjory Collins, "Witchunt Southern Style," *The Minority of One*, May 1964, 18-19, in Box 37, Braden Mss. It did Pfister little good, however, for he was defeated by a 2-1 margin.

7. *SCEF News* and Fact Sheets, Box 37, Braden Mss.

8. See Peebles, *op. cit.*, 69.

9. *Ibid.*, 70-71.

10. Kinoy to Dombrowski, December 24, 1963, Box 37, Braden Mss.

11. See James Dombrowski, "Civil Rights and Civil Liberties in the South--1964," delivered at Unitarian-Universalist Fellowship, Los Angeles, 1964, Box 37, Braden Mss.

12. *380 U.S. at 482*, quoted in Robert Allen Sedler, "The *Dombrowski*-Type Suit as an Effective Weapon for Social Change: Reflections from Without and Within," Part I, *Kansas Law Review*, Vol. 18, No. 2 (January, 1970), 241.

13. *Ibid.*

14. Quoted in M. Collins, *op. cit.*, 19.

15. See Sedler, *op. cit.*, 241.

16. *Ibid.*; see also SCEF Fact Sheets, Box 37, Braden Mss.

17. *Ibid.*; also Collins, *op. cit.*, 19.

18. Quoted in *SCEF News*, Box 37, Braden Mss.

19. *227 F. Supp. at 583*, quoted in Sedler *op. cit.*, 241.

20. *227 F. Supp. at 564*, quoted in *Ibid.* 241-2.

21. Sedler, *op. cit.*, 242.

22. See Peebles, *op. cit.*, 74.

23. Quoted in William M. Kunstler, *Deep in My Heart* (New York: William Morrow and Company, 1966), 243; see Jack Greenberg, NAACP Legal Defense and Educational Fund, to Arthur Kinoy, July 23, 1964, Box 37, Braden Mss; Peebles; *op. cit.*, 74.

24. *380 U.S. at 486-87*, cited in Sedler, *op. cit.*, 243.

25. *380 U.S. at 489-90*, cited in Sedler, *ibid.*, 248.

26. *380 U.S. at 492*, cited in *ibid.*, 248; see Kunstler, *op. cit.*, 244-5; and Peebles, *op. cit.*, 78-9.

27. Quoted in Kunstler, *op. cit.*, 244.

28. Peebles, *op. cit.*, 80.

29. See Sedler, *op. cit.*, 353-7. Sedler stresses the political significance and uses of *Dombrowski*-type suit in later years, particularly in the anti-draft agitation and other aspects of opposition to the Vietnam war.

30. Carl Braden informed the author, in February, 1970, of this conclusion to the affair.

CHAPTER TWELVE

1. See Anne Braden, "The Southern Freedom Movement," *Monthly Review* (July/August, 1965).

2. See "A Proposal for Expanded Work among Southern White Students and an Appalachian Project," no date but probably late 1963 or early 1964, Box 45, Braden Mss.

3. *Ibid.*

4. *Ibid.*

5. *Ibid.*

6. Memo to Dombrowski and the Board of the Fund, no date, but probably spring 1964, Box 5, Braden Mss.

7. *Ibid.*

8. See Typescript of proceedings at annual Fund banquet, Hotel Roosevelt, New York, February 3, 1964, Box 5, Braden Mss.

9. See Minutes of evening session, February 21, 1964, Box 44, Braden Mss.

10. *Ibid.*

11. *Ibid.*

12. See text of speech by Edward Hamlett, Nashville, April 3, 1964, Box 26, Braden Mss.

13. *Ibid.*

14. *Ibid.* Citation not given.

15. *Ibid.*

16. Carl Braden wrote: "The name Southern Student *Organizing Committee* was suggested deliberately. It shows that the group's purpose is to organize now and decide later where its permanent berth will be. It follows the pattern of the labor upsurge of a generation ago, when we had such groups as the Steel Workers *Organizing Committee*, which later became the United Steelworkers of America. During and after the organizing drive it was a part of the Committee for Industrial Organization, which became the Congress of Industrial Organizations, first as an organizing committee and later as an integral part of the CIO. Such can be the relationship of SSOC and SNCC, now and later. This leaves great flexibility in dealing with those you seek to organize." The Fund also paid the way of some students to attend the Conference. See C. Braden, "Memo to Dombrowski on Hazard, Kentucky and Nashville Conferences." April 15, 1964, Box 44, Braden Mss.

17. Papers on the role, organization, structure and goals of the Southern Student Organizing Committee, their emphasis, Box 44, Braden Mss.

18. See Anne Braden's comments on the Nashville conference in a draft for an article in the *National Guardian*, Box 45; see also Harlon E. Joye, "Dixie's New Left," *Trans-Action*, Vol. 7, No. 11 (September, 1970), 50-56, 62.

19. "WE'LL TAKE OUR STAND," Nashville, April 4, 1964, Box 45, Braden Mss.

20. See SSOC Papers, Box 44, Braden Mss.

21. See Anne Braden, Memo to SSOC Continuations Committee, no date, Box 45, Braden Mss.

22. See analysis of SSOC resolution on SDS role in the South and relations between the SDS and SSOC, by SSOC Executive Committee, Box 45, Braden Mss.

23. Myles Horton to Anne Braden, June 30, 1964, Box 45, Braden Mss.

24. Dombrowski to SCEF friends, May, 1964, Box 45, Braden Mss.

25. *Ibid.*

26. See "Report to SNCC-COFO on White Folks Project" by Edward Hamlett, White Community Project director, July 26, August 27, 1964, Box 44, Braden Mss.

27. *Ibid.*; see also Bruce Maxwell, "Memo on White Folks Project," undated, Box 24, Braden Mss.

28. *Ibid.*

29. *Ibid.*

30. Hamlett, *op. cit.*

31. Memo to Dombrowski, April 15, 1964, Box 44, Braden Mss.

32. *Ibid.*; the Committee for Miners was a New York group composed primarily of students.

33. See Carl Braden to Brace Maxwell, September 22, 1964, Box 44, Braden Mss.

34. See Marjory Collins and Francis Witlin to Bradens, September 15, 1964; Carl to Collins and Witlin, September 18, 1964; Collins and Witlin to Bradens, October 25, 1964, Box 44, Braden Mss.

35. See "Proposal for a joint project in Appalachia...," Braden to James Forman, SNCC Executive Secretary, November 1, 1964, Box 44, Braden Mss.

36. Carl Braden to Clark Kissinger, National Secretary, SDS, November 5, 1964, Box 44, Braden Mss.

37. See AEPAC File, Box 44, Braden Mss.

38. See Memo from Myles Horton to Appalachian Provisional Organizing Committee, no date, but probably late fall, 1964, Box 44, Braden Mss.

39. See Don West to Anne Braden, December 7, 1964, Box 44. Carl Braden to Stuart M. Rich, Whitewater, Wisconsin, March 1, 1965, Box 46, Braden Mss. Rich had noted that Professor Robert Lampman of the University of Wisconsin, "one of the chief architects of the Anti-Poverty bill (Economic Opportunities Act of 1964)" had spoken at the state university there on Appalachian problems and Carl replied that "the Economic Opportunities Act of 1964, which Professor Lampman helped to draft,...does nothing to get at the basic causes of poverty and unemployment in Appalachia. The same goes for the Appalachian Recovery Act which we are about to get...."

40. See Myles Horton to Carl Braden, May 12, 1965; Hamish Sinclair to Bradens, April 6, 1965; Carl Braden to Horton, June 1, 1965; Carl Braden to Dombrowski, June 26, 1965; Dombrowski to Carl Braden, May 28; Washington Butler, SCLC, to Ivanhoe Donaldson, SNCC, May 25, Box 44, Braden Mss.

41. See Carl Braden to William Kunstler, October 19, 1965, James Dombrowski Papers, WSHS.

42. Carol Stevens, secretary of AEPAC, to Carl Braden, October 27; SCEF memo, November 21, 1965, to SCEF Friends, Box 44, Braden Mss.

43. See "Report on AEPAC and Southern Mountain Project," December 24, 1965, Carl Braden to Dombrowski, Box 45, Braden Mss.

44. *Ibid.*, see also "Anti-Poverty Effort in Appalachian Region Has Trouble with Bureaucrats, Politicians," York, Pennsylvania, *Gazette and Daily*, June 30, 1965, in Box 44, Braden Mss.

45. See *Southern Patriot*, October, 1965.

46. See Minutes of SCEF Board Meeting, Americus, Georgia, no date, 1965, Box 5, Braden Mss.

47. See Anne Braden to Dombrowski, November 4, 1965, Box 5, Braden Mss.

48. See prospects, "For a Project to Open Channels of Debate on Foreign Policy in the South," no date, but probably late 1965, Box 28, Braden Mss.

49. See SCEF resolution on Vietnam, April 18, 1966, Box 40, Braden Mss.

50. See program and report, Box 28, Braden Mss.

51. See Anne Braden to Dr. Herbert Schwartz, Connecticut, May 26, 1966, Box 29, Braden Mss.

52. *Southern Patriot*, May, 1963.

53. *Ibid.*, May, 1966.

54. *Ibid.*, May, 1964.

55. *Ibid.*, May, 1966.

56. *Ibid.*

57. *Ibid.*

58. *Ibid.*

59. Quoted in *Ibid.*

60. Carl Braden to Melish, September 14, 1966, unprocessed boxes, Braden Mss.

61. *Southern Patriot*, May, 1966.

62. *Ibid.*

63. Memo to Southern Student Organizing Committee, December, 1966, unprocessed boxes, Braden Mss.

64. *Ibid.*

65. *Ibid.*

66. See excerpts from SCEF Board statement, *Southern Patriot*, November, 1966.

Bibliographical Sources

I. MANUSCRIPT COLLECTIONS

Wisconsin State Historical Society

1. The Carl and Ann Braden Papers furnished the primary source material. This is an unusually large collection which includes the records and correspondence of the Southern Conference Educational Fund, as well as a portion of the minutes and records of the Southern Conference for Human Welfare. The papers also include a wealth of material on other organizations and social movements in which the Bradens were active. They thus provide an important source of information on the people, history and philosophy of a number of movements, including labor unions, church organizations, civil liberties and civil rights organizations, and various political organizations. The personal papers of the Bradens and correspondence of Aubrey Williams and James Dombrowski are important parts of the collection. Included also are tapes, films, and other documentary recordings.

2. Committee to Combat Racial Injustice Papers.
3. James Dombrowski Papers.

Franklin Delano Roosevelt Library, Hyde Park, New York

Aubrey Williams Papers.

Princeton University

Aubrey Williams Memoirs. Unpublished manuscript in the possession of Professor Sheldon Hackey, Department of History.

II. PERSONAL INTERVIEWS

1. Carl Braden, February, 1969, February, 1970, Madison, Wisconsin
2. John Salter. November, 1969, Chicago, Illinois.
3. Myles Horton. November, 1970, Madison, Wisconsin.
4. Laurel and Henry Hawkins. 1970, Madison, Wisconsin.

III. PUBLIC DOCUMENTS

Congressional Record. 84th Congress, 2nd Session. Washington, D.C.: United States Government Printing Office, 1956.

Hearings. Subcommittee to Investigate the Administration of the Internal Security Act and Other Internal Security Laws, Committee on the Judiciary, United States Senate. New Orleans, Louisiana, March 18, 19, 1954. 3 volumes.

Reports, Numbers 4, 5, 6. "Activities of the Southern Conference Educational Fund, Inc., in Louisiana." Joint Legislative Committee on Un-American Activities, State of Louisiana. Baton Rouge, Louisiana, 1965.

To Secure These Rights: The Report of the President's Committee on Civil Rights. New York. Simon and Schuster, 1947.

IV. SECONDARY SOURCES

A. Newspapers and Magazines

1. Birmingham *News*
2. Christian *Century*
3. *Commonweal*
4. Montgomery *Advertiser*
5. *Nation*
6. *New Republic*
7. New York *Times*

8. Pittsburgh *Courier*
9. Richmond *Times-Dispatch*
10. *Southern Patriot*
11. St. Petersburg *Times*
12. Washington *Post and Times-Herald*

B. *Dissertations and Theses*

Berman, William C. "The Politics of Civil Rights in the Truman Administration." Unpublished dissertation, Ohio State University, 1963.

Peebles, Jack. "Subversion and the Southern Conference Educational Fund." Unpublished master's thesis, Louisiana State University, New Orleans, 1970.

Spaeth, Jared Joseph. *"Braden v. United States*: A Constitutional Case History." Unpublished master's thesis, Butler University, 1968.

Articles:

1. Ashmore, Harry S. "The Untold Story Behind Little Rock." Harpers, June, 1958, 216:10+.
2. Braden, Anne. "The Southern Freedom Movement." *Monthly Review*, July/August, 1965.
3. Cartwright, Colbert S. "Lesson from Little Rock." *Christian Century*, LXXIV, No. 40 (October 9, 1957), 74:1193-4.
4. Collins, Marjory. "Witchunt Southern Style." *The Minority of One*, May, 1964, 18-20.
5. Dalfiume, Richard M. "The 'Forgotten Years' of the Negro Revolution." *Journal of American History*, LV, Number 1 (June, 1968), 90-106.
6. Dinnerstein, Leonard. "The Senate's Rejection of Aubrey Williams as Rural Electrification Administrator." *The Alabama Review*, XXI, Number 2 (April, 1968), 133-143.
7. Dykeman, Wilma and Stokeley, James. "Courage in Action in Clinton, Tennessee." *Nation*, December 22, 1956, 183: 531-3.
8. Fishel, Leslie. "The Negro in the New Deal Era." *Wisconsin Magazine of History*, Vol. 48, Number 2 (Winter 1964-1965), 111-126.

9. Foreman, Clark. "Decade of Hope." *Phylon*, XII, Number 2 (June, 1950), 137-150.

10. Gellhorn, Walter. "Report on a Report of the House Committee on Un-American Activities." *Harvard Law Review*, LX, Number 8 (October, 1947), 1193-1234.

11. Handlin, Oscar. "Civil Rights After Little Rock: The Failure of Moderation." *Commentary*, November, 1957, 24:392-6.

12. Irving, Florence B. "The Future of the Negro Voter in the South." *Journal of Negro Education*, XXVI, Number 3 (Summer 1957), 390-9.

13. Joye, Haron E. "Dixie's New Left " *Trans-Action*, Vol. 7, Number 11 (September, 1970), 50-56, 62.

14. Love, Edgar A. "Claiming the Right to Choose. A Profile." *Motive*, November, 1962, 5-7.

15. Mathews, Donald R. and Prothro, James W. "Political Factors and Negro Voter Registration in the South." *American Political Science Review*, LVII (June, 1963), 355-367.

16. Maund, Alfred. "Aubrey Williams: Symbol of a New South." *Nation*, October 10, 1953, 177:289-90.

17. Nabrit, James M. Jr. "Future of the Negro Voter in the South." *Journal of Negro Education*, XXVI, Number 3 (Summer, 1957), 418-23.

18. Posey, Buford. "Where Do We Stand on Integration?." *American Socialist*, Vol. 3, Number 11 (November, 1956), 12-15.

18. Sedler, Robert Allen. "The *Dombrowski*-Type Suit as an Effective Weapon for Social Change: Reflections from Without and Within." Part I, *Kansas Law Review*, Vol. 18, Number 2 (January, 1970), 237-276.

19. Smith, Lillian. "Southern Defensive--II." Common Ground, LV (Spring, 1944), 43-5.

Books and Pamphlets

1. Bartley, Numan V. *The Rise of Massive Resistance*. Baton Rouge: Louisiana State University Press, 1969.

2. Braden, Anne. *The Wall Between*. New York: Monthly Review Press, 1958.

3. Dulles, Foster Rhea. *The Civil Rights Commission, 1957-1965*. Lansing: Michigan State University Press, 1968.

4. Freidel, Frank. *FDR and the South*. Baton Rouge: Louisiana State University Press, 1965.

5. Gaston, Paul M. *The New South Creed.* New York: Alfred A. Knopf, 1970.
6. Goodman, Walter. *The Committee.* Baltimore: Penguin Books, Inc., 1969 edition.
7. Key, V. O. *Southern Politics in State and Nation.* New York: Alfred A. Knopf, 1949.
8. Krueger, Thomas A. *And Promises to Keep.* Nashville: Vanderbilt University Press, 1967.
9. Kunstler, William M. *Deep in my Heart.* New York: William Morrow and Company, 1966.
10. Lomax, Louis *The Negro Revolt.* New York: New American Library, 1963.
11. MacDougall, Curtis B. *Gideon's Army.* New York: Marzani and Munsell, 1965, 3 volumes.
12. Myrdal, Gunnar B. *An American Dilemma.* Twentieth Anniversary Edition; New York and Evanston: Harper & Row, Publishers, 1962.
13. Odum, Howard. *Race and Rumors of Race.* Chapel Hill: The University of North Carolina Press, 1943.
14. Price, Margaret. *The Negro Voter in the South.* Atlanta: Southern Regional Council, 1957.
15. — *The Negro and the Ballot in the South.* Atlanta: Southern Regional Council, 1959.
16. Pritchett, C. Herman. *Congress Versus the Supreme Court: 1957-1960.* Minneapolis: University of Minnesota Press, 1961.
17. Sherrill, Robert G. *Gothic Politics in the Deep South.* New York: Grossman Publishers, 1968.
18. Simkins, Francis Butler. *The South Old and New: A History 1820-1947.* New York: Alfred A. Knopf, 1947.
19. Strong, Donald S. *Negroes, Ballots, and Judges.* University: University of Alabama Press, 1968.
20. Sugg, Redding S., Jr. and Jones, George Hilton. *The Southern Regional Education Board: Ten Years of Regional cooperation in Higher Education.* Baton Rouge: Louisiana State University Press, 1960.
21. Tindall, George B. *The Emergence of the New South, 1913-1945.* Baton Rouge: Louisiana State University Press, 1967.
22. Wakefield, Dan. *Revolt in the South.* New York: Grove Press, 1960.
23. Zinn, Howard. *The Southern Mystique.* New.York: Alfred A. Knopf, 1964.

Index

Abernathy, Ralph
support of Carl Braden clemency petition, 179-180
Adams, Sherman, 128
AEPAC (Appalachian Economic and Political Action Conference), 221-223
AFL-CIO, 172-173
Afro-American Student Movement, 227
Agnes Scott College, 60
Agricultural Adjustment Administration
and blacks, 7
Agronsky, Martin, 75-76
Alabama, University of, 61
enrollment of Autherine Lucy, 122
Alabama Polytechnic Institute
program in veterinary medicine, 61, 62
and the Committee of Southern Regional Studies and Education, 61
Alexander, Will W., 16, 30-31, 88
Alinsky, Saul, 232
Alliance for Jobs and Income Now (Join), 221
American Civil Liberties Union, 10
and *Dombrowski v. Pfister*, 203, 205
American Communist Party
and popular front, 94-95
American Council on Education, 61
American Federation of Labor, 10
American Jewish Congress
in Florida, 161, 162, 164
American Medical Association
discrimination by, 52
poll of members on segregation, 55-56
American Newspaper Guild, 10
Americans for Democratic Action, 128, 172-173
lack of support for SCEF's 1958 hearings, 129-130
American Teachers Association
opposition to Southern Regional Education Board, 65

Anderson, Fred, 84
Appalachian Committee for Full Employment
and Student-Miners Conference on Poverty and Employment (3/64), 219-220
Appalachian Economic and Political Action Conference (AEPAC), 221-223
Arens, Richard, 84, 138
counsel to Senate Internal Security Subcommittee, 79-82
HUAC counsel, 135-138
and Wycliffe Draper association, 179-180
Arkansas, Medical School
admission of black student, 54
Arkansas, University of
and the Committee of Southern Regional Studies and Education, 61
Arnall, Ellis, 16
Assembly of Unrepresented People, 224-225
Atlanta *Constitution*
attack on Conference on Discrimination in Higher Education (1950), 68-69
Atlanta University, 60
Atlanta University System, 60
Avery, Maltheus R.
death of, 54-55

Baker, Ella
Aubrey William's opinion of, 174-175
and conference on reaching white Southern students (2/64), 212
Bankhead, Senator, 86
Barenblatt v. United States, 145-146
effect on Carl Braden case, 146-147
Barkley, Alben, 36
Barnes, Robert, 118-119
Barnett, Albert D., 140
and rejection of SCEF by Leadership Conference on Civil Rights, 96-97